VIOLENCE AS WORSHIP

VIOLENCE AS WORSHIP

Religious Wars in the Age of Globalization

Hans G. Kippenberg

Translated by Brian McNeil

STANFORD UNIVERSITY PRESS

STANFORD, CALIFORNIA

Stanford University Press
Stanford, California

Violence as Worship was originally published in German under the title *Gewalt als
Gottesdienst. Religionskriege im Zeitalter der Globalisierung.* © Verlag C. H. Beck,
Munich 2008. The translation of this work was supported by a grant from the
Goethe-Institut, which is funded by the German Ministry of Foreign Affairs.

GOETHE-INSTITUT

Printed in the United States of America on acid-free, archival-quality paper

Library of Congress Cataloging-in-Publication Data

Kippenberg, Hans G. (Hans Gerhard)
 [Gewalt als Gottesdienst. English]
 Violence as worship : religious wars in the age of globalization / Hans G.
Kippenberg ; translated by Brian McNeil.
   p.   cm.
 "Originally published in German under the title Gewalt als Gottesdienst."
 Includes bibliographical references.
  ISBN 978-0-8047-6872-6 (cloth : alk. paper)
  ISBN 978-0-8047-6873-3 (pbk : alk. paper)
   1. Violence—Religious aspects—Islam.   2. Violence—Religious aspects—
Christianity.   3. Violence—Religious aspects—Judaism.   4. War—Religious
aspects—Islam.   5. War—Religious aspects—Christianity.   6. War—Religious
aspects—Judaism.   7. Globalization—Religious aspects.   I. McNeil,
Brian.   II. Title.
BL65.V55K5613   2010
201'.7273—dc22

                                                         2010018099

Contents

Preface

This book seeks to establish a new paradigm for research in a field that is both highly relevant and much disputed. More than half of all Germans incline, for example, to the view that religions generate conflicts and are therefore intolerant. This opinion is confirmed by a flood of publications that link monotheism with intolerance. On the other hand, we find the no-less-justified view that none of the world religions can allow itself systematically to issue a summons to violence, and that the main tone sounded by all religions is nonviolence. Against the background of this dispute, the present book offers a close examination of some cases that point to a close connection between religion and violence. The examination of eight cases will show which traditions from the ample stock of religious lore have been chosen to justify violence, and in what situations this has occurred. These cases are well known from the newspapers and television; but the reports often omit any reference to genuine religion, or else they conceal this under a different vocabulary. Unlike such presentations in the media, the research in this book plunges into a deep religious current of contemporary politics.

It would have been impossible to carry out this comprehensive program without dialogue with my academic colleagues, and my position as a Fellow of the Max Weber Center for Advanced Cultural and Social Studies afforded excellent opportunities for this. First of all, I should like to thank the doctoral and postdoctoral students and the Fellows: their competence in the disciplines of jurisprudence, history, philosophy, economics, and sociology has influenced my project in ways that I can no longer reconstruct. Without their suggestions and criticisms, I could not have developed the conceptual and methodological instruments that I have employed in the investigation of this subject. The stimulating climate created at the center by Dean Hans Joas was ideal for my work. I should also like to thank Ursula Birtel-Koltes and the staff at the University Library in Erfurt, who got hold of books that were hard to find. Mrs. Birtel-Koltes has also helped with the work of text processing.

It was originally agreed that the German publisher would receive the manuscript of this book in 2003, but my research took longer than anticipated. The subject matter presented itself in shifting forms and with an ever-new vitality that resisted attempts to "tame" it academically. Nevertheless, Ernst-Peter Wieckenberg and Ulrich Nolte never lost interest in this project, and they have accompanied its realization at various phases with helpful suggestions.

The eight cases I have investigated have involved wide reading over a period of many years. Since I am not equally at home in every field, I have asked colleagues with proven academic qualifications to read through what I have written. Manfred Brocker read the chapter on American Protestantism, Ulrike Brunotte the introductory section, Alexander Flores my remarks about the Palestinians, Kurt Greussing the section on Iran, Stephan Rosiny the chapter about the Shi'ites in Lebanon, and Zwi Werblowsky in Jerusalem the section on Israel. I wish to express my profound gratitude to them all; naturally, any mistakes remain my own.

I have delivered parts of this book as lectures on various occasions: at academic meetings in Erfurt and Augsburg, at the Evangelical Academies in Loccum and Bonn-Bad Godesberg, at the Ecumenical Church Congress in Berlin in 2003, at the Catholic Church Congress in Saarbrücken in 2005, and in a research group of the FEST. I also spoke at a seminar in Dhaka in Bangladesh, where my remarks about the Islamic justification for 9/11 provoked such a storm of indignation in the press—"Arrest Professor Hans!"—that the German embassy was afraid that I might not make it safely out of the country.

Patrick Wöhrle, a doctoral student at the Max Weber Center, helped me with the final version of the German book. The Max-Weber-Kolleg Erfurt and the Jacobs University Bremen contributed financially to translating the book into English and editing it.

Except where otherwise mentioned, all translations from German texts in the present book are by Brian McNeil.

CHAPTER I

Introduction: Violence as Communal Religious Action

The intellectual, political, and military response of Western countries to the attacks of September 11, 2001, displayed a helplessness that itself conjures up new dangers. Let me mention only one example. On September 15, 2001, the auxiliary bishop of the archdiocese of Hamburg, Hans-Jochen Jaschke, expressed his indignation that the group responsible for the attacks had invoked God: "Thereby they dishonor the holy name of God. They misuse it for their perverse state of mind. . . . We must not allow criminals to justify their actions in the name of God, to issue a summons to a holy war, and to promise a reward from God to those whom they have blinded. For God's sake, NO!" What we must do now, the title of Jaschke's newspaper article declares, is to *raise on high God's holy name*: "In view of 9/11, I believe that the emergency situation exists in which appropriate, limited, legitimized violence may be used. It can create the preconditions for a rational unity among human beings. A worldwide civilization of love is possible only when it is not threatened by terror."[1]

Today, we know that the military salvaging of God's honor did not create the preconditions for love, but merely added further impetus to the escalation of violence. It is therefore high time to examine the efficacy of the therapy applied and to offer a new diagnosis of the phenomenon of contemporary religious violence.

Ought We Seek to Understand Religious Violence?

Academic disciplines are kept on their toes by unexpected leaps on the part of the objects they investigate. Scholars of religion have been surprised in this way by occurrences of religious violence. In 1978, when the conflict between an American faith community and the U.S. authorities in Jonestown, Guyana, ended with the murder of an American congressman and members of his entourage and the subsequent mass suicide of the community, scholars of religion were confronted by a phenomenon for which they were not prepared—and this was only the beginning. Since then, religious violence has broken out in many different places in the world: other cult wars in the United States, the Islamic revolution in Iran, the civil war in Lebanon, the transformation of the Middle East conflict from one between states to one between faith communities, the attacks on the United States by jihadists on September 11, 2001, and the "War on Terror." All these are studied in the present book. One could easily extend the list of cases (to include, for instance, the Serb wars against Muslims in Bosnia and in Kosovo, the Hindu riot in Ayodhya that led to the destruction of the Babri Mosque, or the conflict in Chechnya). However, I limit myself to the eight cases mentioned here, because a close analysis of a few select instances increases our chances of developing an ideal model for other cases as well. This also makes it possible to look more precisely at each individual arena of violence, at the actors involved, and at the sequence of events.

This subject attracts considerable public interest, and rightly so. For a long time, religions were considered as guarantors of the legal order, but today they are under suspicion of promoting violence and posing a threat to law and order. This is the perspective guiding my inquiry into the individual cases, which are explored as actions rejecting the authority of states, including state sanctions against murder, kidnapping, bodily harm, rape, and crimes against property, in the name of a purported higher, revealed law. The appeal to a higher law thus seeks to legitimate actions that transgress national and international law. The focus of the investigation moves from the individual and rational motives of those who perpetrate violence to the meanings that they and others attach to their actions. This will give us a spectrum of religious views of history and models of action that justify the violation of laws.[2]

The subject is a delicate one. When religious violence manifested itself anew in the events in Jonestown, the American scholar of religion Jonathan Z. Smith was the first to recognize what a tremendous challenge this meant for the claim of religious studies to academic standing, declaring: "[I]f we continue, as a profession, to leave it ununderstandable, then we will have surrendered our rights to the academy."[3]

The link between religion and violence is so controversial because although the constitutions of the secularized states detach political power from religious legitimation, they also place the citizens' religion under their special protection. The two facts are logically and historically connected. At the same time as the first of the constitutions were written and gave legal guarantees of religious freedom at the close of the eighteenth century, philosophers were developing an understanding of religion that transposed its validity from external authorities to the subjective authority of citizens. Only an interiorized religion could achieve civil peace; the state and its means of coercion were incapable of doing this on their own. For such a position, religious violence is a dangerous contradiction: an action cannot be simultaneously religious *and* violent. Smith refers to this troublesome point when he writes that the academic study of religion, which arose in the nineteenth century, has helped domesticate religions and transmute them from a passion to a commitment. It was admitted to academia only because it succeeded in doing so. Today, in view of the panic public reaction to religious violence, this task presents itself anew, and no effort should be spared in the endeavor to understand this violence.

When we attempt to grasp religious violence as a comprehensible action, we risk offering an apologia for it. And Hezbollah's web site sufficiently testifies to the appropriation of academic elucidations of suicide attacks by perpetrators of violence. In order to counter this danger, I shall follow Max Weber in making a strict distinction between two views of what it means to "understand": that is, between the understanding of the motives of those who act and the understanding of the significance of their actions. If we want to understand the *motives of those who act,* the more plausible its motivations, the more comprehensible an action. If we want to understand the *significance of an action,* we must trace the model that orients it; we must then determine the spectrum of alternative models from which this orientation was selected; and we must consider the approval or rejection that is attributed to the model. In what follows, I shall take the second path and concentrate on the significance of acts of religious violence.

Disgust at every attempt to understand religious violence has become even greater after 9/11. Immediately after these events, the columnist Henryk Broder wrote in the German newsmagazine *Spiegel*: "Now all I am waiting for is for some noble soul to get up and say that the attacks in New York and Washington must be seen in connection with the struggle of the Third World against the First World. Shall we place bets that this will happen in the next few days, as soon as the smoke has settled over the ruins on Manhattan?" Broder formulated this question so polemically because he was convinced that: "A fight between the cultures is taking place. . . . What is involved here is a sheer delight in murdering, a delight that now does not even need an excuse."[4] With these words, he deliberately transposed the action into the realm of the incomprehensible and suggested that nothing could—or should—help to explain it. We find a similar line of argument in Wolfgang Sofsky, who had written in 1996 in his *Traktat über die Gewalt* that in seeking to interpret it as a means to an end, one completely misunderstands the character of violence. Sofsky now applied this thesis to the events of 9/11. The (alleged) lack of a letter in which the perpetrators claimed responsibility for their deed clearly meant that terrorism wanted more victims, not just more onlookers. "It was impossible to discern any political goal beyond the desire for destruction. The attack did not mean anything. It was an act of destruction without any ulterior purpose. . . . The terrorist's war . . . wants to kill a great number of people, to spread fear, to paralyze people's life through fear."[5]

Sofsky writes that religion played no role here beyond the "overcoming of the fear of death."[6] He calls the phenomenon of violence he distills in this way a "massacre"; it is impossible to explain it. He is no doubt correct in saying that the significance of violence in the modern era has generally been unrecognized, aside from Georges Sorel's *Réflexions sur la violence* (1908). Hans Joas, too, concludes that violence must not be seen *only* as a means to an end; but this does not mean that one cannot understand it. As a matter of fact, violence gives expression to experiences and meanings that are not generated by a purpose or a norm that is fixed in advance.[7] In this sense, its message belongs to the category of performative actions whose meaning lies in their reenactment of a celebrated model of conduct. Sofsky never even mentions this performative character, however, leading Bernd Weisbrod to accuse him of being a spokesman for an "aesthetic of horror."[8]

The frequently repeated assertion that there was no letter claiming responsibility for the 9/11 attacks, and that the perpetrators were intent only upon destruction, overlooks the videos they left behind, in which they claim responsibility for their actions. On April 15, 2002, al-Jazeera aired a documentary that it had allegedly received from a pro–al-Qaeda production company and that included a separate videotaped will and testament prepared by one of the 9/11 hijackers. A man identified as Ahmed Ibrahim al-Haznawi talks about his plans for attacks in the heartland of the United States. In his statement al-Haznawi said he would help send a "bloodied message" to the world: "The time of humiliation and subjugation is over. It's time to kill Americans in their heartland. O God, revive an entire nation by our deaths. O God, I sacrifice myself for your sake, accept me as a martyr."[9]

Besides this confession, the 9/11 perpetrators left behind a document that guided them in their actions.[10] The existence of this manual appears to justify experts on terrorism such as Peter Waldmann, who maintain that these attackers, like terrorists in general, "were not interested in the actual destructive effect of their actions. These were only a means, a kind of signal, in order to communicate something to a large number of people. We must affirm that terrorism is primarily a communication strategy."[11] Two separate strands in the attack can nevertheless be distinguished. On the one hand, it was planned long in advance and was the fruit of careful reflection. It was intended as vengeance on the United States for injustice that had been suffered. In this sense, it was a rational, intentional action. On the other hand, the attack was staged like a *ghazwa,* or early Islamic military raid, and in that sense, it proclaims itself a performative action that embodies its own meaning.[12]

The performative character of the action was exceedingly sinister in the eyes of the American public and government and gave it the character of something incomprehensible. The U.S. government believed that it could protect the country only by means of equally unconditional violence. In keeping with the exorbitance of the U.S. government's military counterviolence, the spiritual manual the FBI published in September 2001 played no role whatever in the pursuit of the perpetrators and is nowhere mentioned in the detailed report of the investigation of the events preceding 9/11 published by Congress and the president three years later. From the very outset, the countermeasures were not accompanied by any attempt to understand the actions of the perpetrators or to determine the appropriate reaction in accordance with this understanding. It was assumed that only an immeasurable hatred of America and American freedom could have motivated the perpetrators and their backers. They were thought capable of anything at all, and this meant that the military reaction must be as comprehensive and as powerful as possible.

Practices of Religious Violence

The problem of the religious practice of violence was raised in academic literature as early as the 1970s.[13] In 1972, the originals of both René Girard's study *Violence and the Sacred* and Walter Burkert's *Homo necans*—inquiring into the connection between violence and Greek religious ritual and myth—were published. In 1997, Burkert retrospectively observed that the evidence and the interpretations of the two books were partly comparable, since both attempted to uncover a hidden "crime" in existing institutions.[14] The two investigations' points of departure were also similar, namely, sacrificial rituals. In their daily lives, human beings are forbidden under pain of punishment to kill other human beings; but *for precisely this reason,* killing can become a holy act. Girard describes the circular relationship between holiness and violent action as follows: it is a crime to kill the victim, because it is sacred—but the victim would not be sacred if not killed.

The two authors offer different explanations of this link, however. Burkert argues that since aggression against an animal is a communal action, it is a prerogative of the collective and therefore "holy." Girard begins with the biblical account of the scapegoat. When the high priest lays all the guilt and transgressions of the people on a male goat on the Day of Atonement and sends it into the wilderness (Lev. 16:20–22), the destructive forces that have piled up in society are thereby discharged.[15] But whether this is understood as a communal triumph in the bold action of killing or as catharsis of an aggression through the vicarious victim, in each case, communality is constituted or renewed through the ritual of killing.[16]

Scholars who take this line tend to see religious violence as unavoidable and, in fact, as socially productive; but others take a different view. The suspicion that religion and destructive violence are closely linked goes back to the seventeenth and eighteenth centuries, when it was argued that the devastating wars of religion could be explained by the fact that a monotheism treating the worship of other gods as idolatry necessarily led to intolerance and promoted violence. Only an apolitical, inner religion would be immune to this. Since then, this assertion has run like a golden thread through the history of European thought. Even today, opinion polls in all European countries show that a majority of citizens (varying in proportion from one country to another) regard religion as a cause of conflicts and as intolerant, and wish that it had less influence.[17] In the wake of September 11, 2001, there was renewed suspicion that monotheistic religions cause violence.

How Intolerant Is Monotheism?

Jan Assmann, whose academic field is the history of ancient religion, has undertaken in several books to clarify the nexus between monotheism and violence.[18] He interprets the remarkable linkage between Moses and Egypt in the Bible as a faded memory of the reforms by Pharaoh Akhenaton in Egypt, who wanted to replace the many Egyptian deities by the one sun god Aten, or Ra, alone. Assmann draws a distinction between this exclusive monotheism, which denies the existence of other gods, and another type of belief in one God, which postulated a cosmic ordering as the location of all the gods and goddesses who were worshiped; he calls this "cosmotheism."[19] The attempt to replace the latter with an exclusive monotheism failed in Egypt and succeeded only in Israel where, according to Assmann, an open and tolerant belief in God gave way to an exclusive and intolerant belief in one God. Moses' "anti-religion" knew only the true veneration of the one God as opposed to the false veneration of the many: "I am the Lord your God, who brought you out of the land of Egypt, out of the house of slavery. You shall have no other gods besides me" (Exod. 20:2–3). In Israel, this belief was violently imposed. Assmann does not, however, see the biblical narratives of the Golden Calf, the sacrificial competition between Elijah and the priests of Baal, and the violent enforcement of Josiah's reforms as relevant, historically factual instances of violence. Instead, he proposes a "change of perspective in the memory of history," arguing these texts do not tell us how monotheism was enforced de facto, but how its enforcement was remembered.[20] The language of violence that monotheism speaks is a "semantic paradigm" that has taken on a life of its own, but it does not in the least engender violence.[21] Forms of divine worship perceived as false, such as heresy, paganism, idolatry, magic, and apostasy, were excluded only in a symbolic manner. Where violent acts are attested to in Judaism, they are internal, directed against apostates of one's own faith. The principal enemy is the apostate, not the foreign unbeliever, and the first object of religious violence is the apostate. Any violent activity going beyond this occurred only at a later date, and was manipulated: "The semantic dynamite contained in the sacred texts of the monotheistic religions is kindled not in the hands of the believers, but in those of the fundamentalists who want political power and who make use of religious motifs of violence in order to get the masses to support them."[22]

This reconstruction by Assmann has attracted considerable attention. It has the great merit of taking the violent side of Jewish/Christian/Islamic monotheism with renewed seriousness from a historical and a systematic perspective, and of reconstructing a long tradition of violent religious language with great diligence and accuracy. At the same time, however, one must ask critically whether in limiting monotheism's violent record to apostasy, Assmann does not offer too narrow a picture of it.

Blessing as Curse

Some biblical narratives of the promise of the land, which Regina M. Schwartz has investigated, indicate a further source of violence whose origin lies in a particularity of the Jewish faith in God.[23] Cain, the farmer, offered to the Lord a sacrifice of the fruits of the field, while his brother Abel, a shepherd, offered some of the firstborn of his sheep. The text tells us, without any precise explanation, that the Lord looked with pleasure on Abel and his animal sacrifice but rejected Cain and his plant sacrifice (Gen. 4:1–5). Cain is so enraged at this that he murders Abel. We read of a similar, no less impressive instance in the story of how Jacob obtained by trickery the blessing of his blind father, Isaac, by pretending to be Esau (Gen. 27:30–37):

As soon as Isaac had finished blessing Jacob, when Jacob had scarcely gone out from the presence of Isaac his father, Esau his brother came in from his hunting. He also prepared savory food, and brought it to his father, and he said to his father, "Let my father arise, and eat of his son's game, that you may bless me." His father Isaac said to him, "Who are you?" He answered, "I am your son, your first-born, Esau." Then Isaac trembled violently, and said, "Who was it then that hunted game and brought it to me, and I ate it all before you came, and I have blessed him?—yes, and he shall be blessed." When Esau heard the words of his father, he cried out with an exceedingly great and bitter cry, and said to his father, "Bless me, even me also, O my father!" But he said, "Your brother came with guile, and he has taken away your blessing." . . . Then he said, "Have you not reserved a blessing for me?" Isaac answered Esau, "Behold, I have made him your lord, and all his brothers I have given to him for his servants, and with grain and wine I have sustained him. What then can I do for you, my son?"

A similar scenario occurs when the promise is given that the people of Israel will occupy the territory in which the Canaanites dwell. The Israelites do not lay claim to the land because they were born in it, or because they have some kind of rights in it, but because God has promised that they will possess it: "When the Lord your God brings you into the land which you are entering to take possession of it, and clears away many nations before you . . . greater and mightier than yourselves . . . , then you must utterly destroy them; you shall make no covenant with them, and show no mercy to them" (Deut. 7:1–2). This narrative also portrays the one God not as infinitely generous, but as disconcertingly partisan. Not everyone receives the divine blessing; some are stricken with privation and with death, as if there were a cosmic shortage of salvation. Shortage—one land, one people, one nation—is inscribed in the Bible as a principle of unity.

Such narratives have had a more enduring impact on the thinking of believers than abstract ethical demands, and they have been given a place in the repertoire of the monotheistic models of action. Fidelity to this *one* God and the bond to this *one* community are the basis of property rights from which other persons are excluded.[24] This particularism is a powerful presupposition of religious violence.[25] In this case too, however, there is nothing automatic. The biblical God gives to human beings out of his superabundance, and all that he asks in return for his love is faith. It would be idolatry if those who receive the blessing were to turn the particularism of this blessing into a source of violence against those who are not blessed.[26]

Faith Communities as Bearers of Violent Actions

One further reservation about Jan Assmann's affirmations should be mentioned here. The community the Jews founded in Palestine after their return from exile in Babylon spoke a language that was no "semantic paradigm" devoid of practical consequences. After their return from captivity in Babylon in the fifth century BCE, the Jews received from the Persians the privilege of constituting an autonomous legal community. This allowed them to form a body that laid down its own regulations in agreement with the social legislation of Deuteronomy (Nehemiah 10). This community not only knew the Mosaic distinction between the true God and the many false gods; it also linked this to the social distinction between liberation and slavery. It made the words "who brought you out of the land of Egypt, out of the house of slavery" its practical maxim.[27] All believers were obliged to ensure that the members of the community would not become the permanent slaves of foreigners.[28] When the temple in Jerusalem was desecrated in the second century BCE by Hellenistic rulers in alliance with apostate Jews, with the intention of depriving the community of its normative center, Jews rose up violently under the leadership of the Maccabees against collaborators in their own ranks, Hellenistic office bearers, and foreign troops.[29] The Book of Daniel interprets the dramatic events of the desecration and defilement of the sanctuary by adherents of Hellenism as a turning point in the history of Israel and the prelude to a new era of salvation. Unlike that of the Maccabees, however, its message is one of patient waiting. The Books of the Maccabees take a different line: anyone who dies in the struggle against the godless and for the ancestral laws, is counted as a martyr who will be awakened to eternal life. Violence with the aim of defending the Jewish faith community thereby became an exemplary religious act.

This means that as early as the believing Jews of classical antiquity, monotheism supplied a script for violence against unbelievers in a situation where the Mosaic social constitution of the Jewish community had to be defended against an expanding economic slavery and foreign rule in the political realm. In this regard, the Jewish Maccabean revolt is exceptionally instructive, since the believers had recourse to violence only when the threat to the religious ordering of their community also entailed a threat to its social ordering. Accordingly, the Jewish rebels were able to conclude a treaty of friendship with Gentiles such as the Roman senate when this treaty granted the Jewish community independence and self-administration (1 Macc. 8:23–28).[30] The case of ancient Judaism thus shows that the biblical paradigm of violence was applied when the obligatory nature of the community's values had to be defended against external foes; but if rulers who themselves were Gentiles were willing to ensure the existence of the Jewish community, it was even possible to conclude a treaty with them.

This suggests that exclusive Jewish monotheism never in practice achieved the monopoly Assmann attributes to it. It is therefore unsurprising that alongside or within monotheism there existed a belief in one God who was capable of cohabitation with other gods.[31] There were innumerable regulated forms of religious cohabitation between Jews and Gentiles in the pagan cities of classical antiquity. Not only could the Jewish creator God also be venerated by Gentiles as "the Most High," but Jewish citizens also engaged actively in propaganda among their Greek and Roman fellow citizens for their God as the true God of all human beings, a God who even possessed the extraordinary ability to overrule the fate to which all human beings were subject by virtue of their birth. According to this type of Jewish belief in one God, the particular divine powers received a subordinate, but recognized position. This "monarchical" view of monotheism was so solidly anchored in Judaism that Peter Schäfer calls Assmann's exclusive monotheism a "bogeyman that never existed in this way."[32] Schäfer dismisses as absurd Assmann's suggestion (made in all seriousness) that anti-Semitism can be explained as the indirect consequence of exclusive Jewish monotheism.[33] The occurrence of anti-Semitism in Greek cities is much too local in terms of place and time, and too specific, to allow us to see it as only the reverse of genuine Jewish monotheism. Rather, an open and tolerant faith in one God was the basis of the peaceful coexistence of Jews and non-Jews in the religious pluralism of the cities of antiquity. Subsequent to classical antiquity, moreover, the boundary between God and the supernatural powers of this world was fluid for the mediaeval Jewish Kabbalah. It was only in the course of the rejection of such views by philosophers of the modern period that a "purified," exclusive monotheism came to prevail within Judaism.

Similar observations have been made with regard to Christianity. Here, too, scholars no longer assume a necessary connection between monotheism and the persecution of those holding different beliefs. The violence practiced in the Middle Ages against heretics, apostates, Jews, and pagans was not the consequence of a monotheistic tradition of violence and intolerance but was generated by specific local and historical conditions.[34] The generalization from individual cases to a picture of the Middle Ages as a downright "persecuting society" is rejected today on the basis of strong arguments.[35] The historical reality of the Middle Ages was characterized by a plurality—which however must be sought behind a terminology that often sounds a different note. It is true that monotheism generated a greater sensitivity to religious diversity; as Michael Borgolte has shown, it is to this circumstance that Europe owes the "discovery of its plurality."[36] The positions taken by Jewish, Christian, and Islamic authorities against compulsory conversion likewise made a contribution to the understanding of faith as an individual decision; this made the individual and his or her personal conviction a central religious value.[37] For a long time, however, this value did not go as far as the acceptance of a turning away from the faith: after the Christianization of the Roman empire, apostasy was punished as a crime, and the apostate lost his civil rights.

Like Christianity, Islam formulated rules regarding the toleration of other religions. It acknowledged the preceding revelations to Abraham, Moses, and Jesus, but while it respected the Jews and Christians as "people of the book," a series of legal gradations ensured that they did not have the same status as Muslims. Although Muslims could conclude treaties with unbelievers, apostates were persecuted all the more rigorously within Islam and were deprived of their rights.

A close examination of these monotheistic cases of violence shows that they all give the lie to the idea of any kind of necessary link between monotheism and violence. Assmann is correct to say that one must not infer a practice from the language of violence; but the instances of apostasy and of the violent defense of the faith community against its foes also give the lie to the opposite thesis, namely, that monotheism is peaceful per se, and religious violence is never imaginable except as an abuse. There is a link between monotheism and violence, but one must call this contingent: it is neither necessary nor impossible. It depends on the current situation of a faith community.

A look at the modern history of violence in Hinduism shows that this link exists even independently of the monotheistic religions. Sudhir Kakar comments as follows on the religious conflicts that keep on erupting between Hindus and Muslims: "What we are witnessing today is less the resurgence of religion than (in the felicitous Indian usage) of communalism where a community of believers not only has religious affiliation but also social, economic, and political interests in common, which may conflict with corresponding interests of another community of believers sharing the same geographical space."[38] And even Buddhism (where one would least expect it) generates violence. After giving an account of the nerve-gas attack by the Buddhist sect Aum Shinrikyo on the underground in Tokyo in 1995, Mark Juergensmeyer asks how even a religion that teaches nonviolence can justify violence.[39]

Religious Frameworks of Everyday Communal Actions

These findings of the study of religion require us to define more precisely the relationship between faith communities and violent action. My starting point is the fact that religious violence seldom has its cause in purely religious conflicts; usually, it occurs in the context of a clash between secular social interests. Hence the metaphor of religion as a "cloak," or talk of religion as an "ideology" or of the "instrumentalization" or "manipulation" of religion. However, these concepts disguise the nature of the link between the two types of action instead of clarifying it. In point of fact, Max Weber has elaborated a thesis that clarifies the state of affairs and also shows plausibly why one should have recourse to concepts from the sociological theory of action when one analyzes religious violence.

In *Economy and Society,* Weber constructs religion as a specific ordering of community action alongside law, governance, and economy. He avoids defining the essence of religion, limiting himself to investigating the conditions and effects of this kind of communal action:

> The external courses of religious behavior are so diverse that an understanding of this behavior can only be achieved from the viewpoint of the subjective experiences, ideas, purposes of the individuals concerned—in short from the viewpoint of the religious behavior's meaning (*Sinn*). The most elementary forms of behavior motivated by religious or magical factors are oriented to *this* world. "That it may go well with thee and that thou mayest prolong thy days upon earth" expresses the reason for the performance of actions enjoined by religion or magic.[40]

The only possible source of an understanding of religious action is the meaning that the actors ascribe to it. In order to describe this expectation of salvation, Weber quotes the Bible: "That it may go well with thee and that thou mayest prolong thy days upon earth" (Eph. 6:2–3). Meaning is not a formal category representing the mediated relationship of humanity to the world; rather, Weber is following the German historians of religion of his period, who saw "meaning" as the outstanding achievement of religion in a world that, taken by itself, was devoid of meaning.[41]

Accordingly, the difference between religious and nonreligious conduct lies not in the difference between types of action, but in a specific expectation on the part of the actor, which can be linked to various types of action. From this perspective, every everyday action can become religious, provided that the actor frames it with a corresponding expectation of salvation. Since Weber sees the constitutive principle of religion not in a subjective experience of the holy but in a common experience of meaninglessness, the communality is the presupposition for the generation of such a meaning for conduct—community (*Gemeinschaft*), not as the antithesis of society (*Gesellschaft*),[42] but as the bearer of a specific way of looking at the world that processes the experience of absurdity, possesses a certain autonomy, is capable of development, and enters into reciprocal relationships with the other forms of community, such as family, neighborhood, ethnic group, law, and governance. These reciprocal relationships can be favorable or obstructing.[43]

In order to define the extent to which religious expectations inspire social actions, a special kind of concept must be constructed. For this purpose, Weber elaborated the instrument of the ideal types, which, as Karl Jaspers puts it, are "not generic concepts under which reality is subsumed, but concepts of meaning against which reality is measured, in order to grasp it succinctly to the extent that it corresponds to these concepts, and in order to display clearly, by means of these concepts, the de facto existence of that which does not correspond to them. They are not the goal of knowledge . . . but a means to make us as clearly aware as possible of the specific character of the human reality that is under consideration."[44] In the case of the problem of religious violence, this means that one must assume that violent actions will be interpreted in terms of religious meanings, although this does not mean that nonreligious motives, goals, and interpretations are excluded.

Definitions of the Situation and the Choice of a Model of Conduct

I believe that an approach drawing on the theory of action that has been developed by sociologists, following Max Weber, and by American pragmatism offers the most appropriate instruments for the analysis of such cases. Such an approach pays much greater attention to the definitions of the situation and to the interpretative frameworks employed thereby than do explanatory approaches whose point of departure is a "translation" of theoretical, dogmatic, or normative principles into a subjective practice. Situations are not the external field in which intentions that exist outside the situation are put into action; rather, situations are defined only by the actors. Hans Joas observes: "The concept of 'situation' [is] well suited to replace the pattern of goal/means as the first basic category of a theory of action."[45]

Hartmut Esser outlined his approach, which derives from the theory of rational choice, in an essay and subsequently developed it considerably in a number of books.[46] Many of his observations and concepts are helpful in the clarification of our problem. He begins by remarking that there is no direct correlation between people's attitudes and their de facto conduct. What people anticipate they will do in some particular situation, in response to questionnaires about their attitudes, does not necessarily coincide with what they in fact do. The social psychologist Richard T. LaPiere published a study of this as long ago as 1934–1935, based on the case of a young Chinese married couple who visited 67 hotels, auto camps, and "tourist homes" and 184 restaurants and cafés in the United States. With only one exception, they were never refused admittance to any hotel or restaurant because of their Chinese "race"; indeed, they were given specially favorable treatment in 72 cases. When LaPiere wrote to the hoteliers and restaurateurs six months later and asked whether they would admit or serve members of the Chinese race, however, of the 51 percent of those who replied, 91 percent stated that they would not do so—a blatant contradiction of the fact that, with only one exception, the couple had not been refused admittance anywhere.[47] Esser notes that the extreme discrepancy between attitudes and conduct has surprised and disconcerted many social scientists.[48]

Similarly, scientists of religion do well not to assume a causality between religious beliefs and actions. It is only when one acknowledges this discrepancy that one can grasp why there is no necessary connection between an exclusive belief in one God and the practice of violence. Religious convictions do not directly and immediately determine corresponding behavior. If, however, there is no necessary linkage between religious beliefs and violent actions, a different model for this kind of connection must be developed; and this is the intention of the present book.

Esser entitled his chapter on the case of the Chinese couple "Das Thomas-Theorem," alluding to a conclusion reached by William I. Thomas and Dorothy Swaine Thomas in a joint study published in 1928: "If men define situations as real, they are real in their consequences."[49] Every action presupposes a definition of the situation. This is not generated of necessity by the situation itself, however, but is "imposed" on the situation by the subjects. If they then act in accordance with this definition, this "imposition" has real effects. It is true that routine usually saves subjects from having to come up with a definition on their own. When a definition becomes less plausible, however—for instance, as a result of disappointed expectations—the actors can suddenly become conscious that they have still further possibilities of defining the situation in which they find themselves.

They then switch from an "automatic" to a "reflective" mode. This does not mean that they can interpret every situation arbitrarily; they remain dependent on external conditions, and their intentions do not exist independently of the situation in which they find themselves. But the external circumstances do not compel them to accept one particular definition. This opens up room for maneuver, which is foreclosed by the acceptance of a single interpretation. When they undertake a new "framing" of the situation, one criterion of its success is whether it is communicable and recognizable.

Here, the availability of the various scenarios plays a role. Esser speaks of "framing" or "the selection of the referential framework." When the actors create a definition, they rely on established concepts of action and choose one of these as binding. The choice of an "action" can be oriented to purposive rationality, to tradition, or to feelings. The framework can also be established in accordance with values whose validity is based on its opposition to a completely different reality, as happens above all in the constitution of individual or communal identity.[50]

When they construct a framework, actors bind themselves to the "models of the course of social action conserved" in the framework "as knowledge." When actors adopt such a script and take their places in a scenario, they bind themselves to one particular sequence of courses of action—cognitive, emotional, and social. The mode of entering into such models of action is, however, dependent on further principles. For example, an ethics of responsibility and an ethics of conviction will establish different options for conduct once a model is adopted.

Religious violence cannot be explained sufficiently as a misuse and manipulation of religion. The following study situates religious violence in a course of action. It follows step by step the genesis of religious acts of violence and reflects on the situations, interpretative patterns, and scripts used by both the faith community and its enemies. It also investigates the extent to which categories such as cult, fundamentalism, or terrorism help us to understand courses of action and asks whether the application of such categories to certain communities may influence the attitude of media and the state in their regard.

In order to grasp religious violence as a part of a complex drama, the field of investigation will be widened from the individual perpetrator and his motives to the action itself, and from the action to the meaning ascribed to it by members of the faith community in question and by their enemies. We shall also look at other actors, such as organized groups, who remain in the background but play a determinative role in the action's course.

CHAPTER 2

The Growth of Religious Communities in the Age of Globalization

The Ambivalence of Religious Communality

Only a short time ago, people lamented the apparently inexorable onward march of secularization, which was perceived as threatening the moral foundations of society. But when religions proclaimed their return to the public domain—in some cases, with violence—the weaknesses of this supposition emerged clearly. As a reaction to this unexpected quandary, attempts were made to help people understand the indisputable connection between religion and violence. The terms "cult," "fundamentalism," and "terrorism" were seen to define degenerate, manipulated forms of religion, certainly not genuine religious forms. As such, these phenomena were sources of violence. Yet these new categories are combative concepts that declare specific types of faith communities to be inherently violent, and they ignore the conflicts in which these faith communities become violent. Concepts created in this way are not a solution; rather, they are themselves the problem, since they influence the measures the forces of order take against these communities and thereby legitimate the use of violence.

The problem that concerns us here, the ambivalence of religious communality, is not new: it was recognized and discussed by philosophers as long ago as the age of the Wars of Religion. Two mutually exclusive positions were formulated at that time. Thomas Hobbes (1588–1679) maintained that the cause of violence was the publicly performed faith of the Church. The only possible solution was a strong state; as the highest authority on earth, the sovereign must keep faith communities in check and exercise control over public religion. Citizens were free to worship privately only to the extent that they did so in secret.[1] In the twentieth century, Carl Schmitt took up Hobbes's diagnosis anew and asserted that the principal task of the state in the modern age was to depoliticize the longing of the faith communities for salvation.[2]

During Hobbes's own lifetime, a completely different view arose, which held that religious violence would be tamed, not by a strong state, but by a religiosity independent of the Church. In his book on natural law, which was widely read throughout Europe, Samuel Pufendorf maintained that religion is the most important and most solid bond of human society. Without religion, states would lose their social cohesion, since this depends on a functioning conscience on the part of the citizens.[3] Jean-Jacques Rousseau discovered this book and developed its thesis further in the "Profession of Faith of a Savoyard Priest," a section in *Émile; or, Education* (1762), where he writes that in order to recognize one's duties, one needs neither philosophers nor theologians. Similarly, the study of the revelatory scriptures of Judaism, Christianity, or Islam does not result in any corresponding knowledge. "I have only to consult myself about what I want to do. Everything I sense to be good is good; everything I sense to be bad, is bad. The best of all casuists [used here in the sense of "moral theologians"] is the conscience," Rousseau asserted.[4] It is not the judgments of the understanding but the feelings of the heart that are the best teacher of the human being. The "real duties" of religion "are independent of human institutions."[5]

For Rousseau, too, religion is the strongest social bond; but whereas Hobbes is highly suspicious of the conscience, since he is concerned with safeguarding the inner peace of a society, Rousseau views it as almost an infallible authority, which reliably prescribes the maxims of correct conduct independently of the churches. Any potential religious intolerance is excluded from that religion. Two decades later, Immanuel Kant went even further in his philosophical elaboration of the supposition that morality had an evidential character. Thanks to reason, the citizens are capable of deflecting ecclesiastical intolerance and making the historical religions serve the cause of preserving societal unity. These two positions agree in their criticism of ecclesiastical institutions, but they diverge diametrically in their evaluation of the impact made by private religiosity in the public domain: Hobbes discerned in this a potential for societal destruction, but Pufendorf, Rousseau, and Kant saw it as the guarantee of the moral unity of a bourgeois society—always presupposing that religious intolerance is excluded.

On the assumption that the power of communally organized religion had been broken in the modern period, the problem of the ambivalence of the religious bond lost its urgency. For example, the sociologist of religion Peter L. Berger assumed as late as 1967 that religion had a polarizing effect in the modern period. On the one hand, it withdrew into the private sphere; on the other, it became political rhetoric. "The over-all effect of the afore-mentioned 'polarization' is very curious," Berger wrote. "Religion manifests itself as public rhetoric and private virtue. In other words, insofar as religion is common it lacks 'reality,' and insofar as it is 'real' it lacks communality."[6]

For a time, many people may indeed have had the impression that communal religion was losing its relevance; but a different judgment is made today. The continuous growth of faith communities in the United States and the downright explosive spread of Protestantism in Latin America, the Pacific, and elsewhere testify to the changed situation,[7] as does the wave of foundations of mosque communities in Europe, the Middle East, and the United States.[8] This, however, presents the old problem with a new acuteness. In order to clarify what constitutes religious ambivalence today, we must look at the contemporary consolidation of faith communities and at the social forms they take.

Communal Religiosity in Judaism, Christianity, and Islam

It is certainly not the case that all religions have formed *closed communities* of believers over the course of their history. Often, religions have the same boundaries as existing social entities such as the domestic community (the family), the group of relatives (descendants), the tribe, or the nation; in addition, criteria other than the specifically religious (for example, age and gender) have been decisive for membership in a faith community. It also happens that believers may attach little or no relevance to their membership in a faith community as far as salvation is concerned. All this clearly changes when achieving salvation depends on a lifestyle: on conducting one's life according to ethical principles, as in the case of prophetic religions, and on a promise given to the community at large rather than to the individual alone. This applies to Judaism, Christianity, and Islam. Their adherents see themselves as the addressees of the promise given to Abraham in Genesis 12:1–3:

Now Yahweh said to Abram, "Get out of your country, and from your relatives, and from your father's house, to the land that I will show you. I will make of you a great nation. I will bless you and make your name great. You will be a blessing. I will bless those who bless you, and I will curse him who curses you. All peoples of the earth will be blessed in you."

Judaism, Christianity, and Islam share a common belief in that divine promise, and have established a pattern of their communities in agreement with this concept:

- The religious community is the addressee of a pledge of salvation and becomes itself an article of faith of its members; the particular local congregations are regarded as part of an invisible transcendent community of those who are saved ("Israel"; "the Church"; the *umma*). The sacred history of that community is distinct from the history of the world.

- The religious community requests that its members help and assist the fellow believers in situations of need (Max Weber calls this an "ethics of brotherliness").

- At times when the religious community itself is threatened in its existence, its members are expected to be prepared to die for the community and its faith. This readiness is regarded as exemplary (the "cult of martyrs").

- The religious community punishes apostasy. This holds true not only for Islam, but also for Judaism and Christianity. In the Bible, idolatry, blasphemy, the profanation of the Sabbath, physical violence against one's parents, adultery, and homosexuality are subject to severe punishments.

- The religious community claims recognition by the other social orders of its society ("legality"; "legitimacy").

Only where all these five features are found is it possible for the loyalty of the believers to their faith community to diverge from their loyalty to the social ordering of their society. This split between the faith community and society in general enables the rise of religious ambivalence. Only under these circumstances is it possible for a faith community not only to establish a social bond but also to disrupt an existing one.

Judaism

Over the course of their history, the great Abrahamic religions—Judaism, Christianity, and Islam—have developed such characteristics of communality. When after their return from exile in the fifth century BCE, the Jews of Palestine established a legal community of their own in the Jerusalem area, and the Persian rulers granted it autonomy, they had to pledge to the Jewish governor Nehemiah that they would not permit their children to marry non-Jews, would abstain from business dealings on the Sabbath, and would forgo the produce of the land and the debts owed to them every seventh year. In this way, they confirmed the prophets' assertion that the belief that the land of Israel belongs to God forbids all indifference to the distress of a fellow believer and requires that one support the sick, widows, orphans, slaves, and strangers. Indeed, they even had to outlaw the enslavement of fellow believers and the confiscation of their land for debt as a transgression of the covenant with God. The liberation of slaves at regular intervals became a religious commandment.[9] When the religious ordering of Jewish society was threatened by adherents of Hellenism in the second century BCE, those who rose up violently against this threat and died were celebrated as martyrs. At the same time, some who were particularly loyal to the faith and separated from the Jewish city-state of Jerusalem founded the community of Qumran and renewed by means of their rules the biblical obligation of the people of Israel in relation to the poor and the defenseless.[10]

In Israel, the Torah was not reserved to the priests but addressed the entire people. This claim that the document possessed a public dimension made it possible for Jews to adopt for their own communities the legal forms that were in force in cities of the Hellenistic kingdoms and the Roman Empire, such as the Greek association and the Roman *col-*

legium.[11] This meant that the relationships among the members, which had been given a religious codification, now also became legally binding.[12] Many centuries later, a similar legal principle was followed by the Jewish organizations responsible for the "repatriation" of Jews to Palestine. Before the state of Israel existed, immigration to Palestine was supervised by the World Zionist Organization and the Jewish Agency. These two organizations represented the interests of the Jewish people to the authorities of the British Mandate, and even after the foundation of the state of Israel, they continued to exist as corporations with extensive autonomous powers with regard to the settling of Jews in the land of Israel.[13]

Christianity

In terms of communal religiosity, Christianity followed in the footsteps of Judaism. The basic text in Christianity that proclaims solidarity with the needy is found in the Gospel of Matthew. At the Last Judgment, the righteous and the damned hear the following words when they ask why they inherit the kingdom of God, or why they are damned to eternal fire: "Whatever you have done [or not done] for one of the least of these my brothers, you have done [or not done] for me" (Matt. 25:31–46). It is not his external affiliation with the Jewish people that reveals to us the identity of the real brother but only his need: his hunger, thirst, homelessness, illness, or imprisonment. This is the litmus test of faith. In classical antiquity, Christians carried out this task in common, forming associations for this purpose. The prosperous made financial contributions to a common purse, out of which the presiding minister gave support to orphans, widows, the sick, prisoners, and foreigners (Justin, *First Apology* 67.6). Christian communities were also responsible for the funerals of impoverished members. Although Christians were persecuted until the reign of Constantine because of their refusal to take part in the cults of the cities and the empire, they were nevertheless able to organize themselves in this way, since its social usefulness meant that their group was exempt from the otherwise strict prohibition against the unauthorized founding of associations. Like the Jewish communities, Christian communities adopted Roman legal forms and thus established themselves in the civil society of classical antiquity.[14] Their associations also celebrated the memory of the martyrs who had laid down their lives because of their steadfast refusal to offer pagan sacrifices. Up to the present day, in states with modern secular constitutions, the law regarding associations and corporations (which is in continuity with Roman law) continues to ensure that the Christian, Jewish, and Islamic ethics of solidarity is effective on the level of civil society.

Islam

In Islam, too, prayer on its own does not suffice to make a person a faithful Muslim. Here is the basic text in the Qur'an:

> It is not piety that you turn your faces to the east and to the west. True piety is this: to believe in God, and the Last Day, the angels, the Book, and the Prophets, to give of one's substance, however cherished, to kinsmen, and orphans, the needy, the traveler, beggars, and to ransom the slave, to perform the prayer, to pay the alms. And they who fulfill their covenant when they have engaged in a covenant, and endure with fortitude misfortune, hardship and peril, these are they who are true in their faith, these are the truly god-fearing. (Sura 2:177)

In contrast to Christian practices, certain groups of community members have a documented title to support by their brethren in the faith, namely, the poor, the needy, the administrators of the alms tax, slaves (for their ransom), debtors, travelers, participants in a jihad (Sura 9:60), and converts.[15] In modern Islamic thinking, righteousness continues to designate a relationship between unequal persons that is asymmetrical in material terms but involves a societal reciprocity.[16] Well-off Muslims are obligated to commit themselves actively to justice and to the common good (*maslaḥa*) of society, to pay the alms tax laid down by law (*zakat*), and to support the needy with voluntary donations (*zadaqa*).[17] Rulers also act as benefactors of the needy;[18] systems of state welfare have taken over this role only to a very limited extent, and aid to those in need has remained predominantly a matter for the faith community. Today, even more emphatically than in the past, the Islamic mission (*da'wa*) includes the foundation of social institutions.[19] In addition to the powerful and the rich, it is private Islamic associations that take on tasks of distributing welfare, and a number of these associations have demonstratively begun to redefine the boundaries between the public and private spheres, and to see in their religious activities a discharging of public tasks.[20]

Two institutional presuppositions make these activities possible. First of all, private persons are allowed to form associations today everywhere throughout the Middle East. In Egypt, where this has been particularly well researched, around 14,000 private associations (*jamaʿiyya*) were registered in the 1990s.[21] These are voluntary, small, and local, operating primarily in the fields of health and education. Although the Muslim Brotherhood is currently a banned organization in Egypt, its members have been involved in founding innumerable associations. These private associations, which stand between the individual and the state, are a specific trait of contemporary Islamic public life in the Middle East.[22]

Islamic foundations likewise operate in this sphere of civil society, and this too presupposes societal welfare. Prosperous Muslims, including rulers, can donate their personal assets to the Islamic community in such a way that family members or private persons can be the beneficiaries for a time; but through *waqf*—the name of this institution—income from land, rents, industries, or money belongs at some point irrevocably to Islamic institutions and groups.[23] For a long time, Western scholars regarded Islamic states as examples of "oriental despotism," in which the sovereign reigned unchecked over his subjects. More recent studies have pointed out that the Islamic foundations in these countries constitute an autonomous area of public life—though we should keep in mind that neither our concept of "public sphere" nor that of "corporation" is appropriate to the context, and that they can only be employed heuristically.[24]

It follows that solidarity with the needy is a religious value in all the three great Abrahamic religions. But neediness is not itself an immutable category. Neediness and the demands made by an "ethics of brotherliness" change in keeping with economic and social circumstances. In his study of the Latin American Catholic theology of liberation, Walter Schmidt cites the work of Amartya Sen, winner of the Nobel Prize for Economics, in support of this view.[25] Sen refuses to define poverty in merely quantitative terms or to measure progress by means of the growth of the gross national product or the rise in incomes. An economic development worthy of the name consists in something else, something more than this: namely, in the expansion of human capabilities: "There are good reasons for seeing poverty as deprivation of basic capabilities, rather than merely as low income."[26] Sen's insight here opens up a broader perspective on the globalization of markets than an either/or approach (that is, *either* welcoming it on economic grounds *or* condemning it on ethical grounds). The new economic circumstances also entail a change in the religious ethics of solidarity.[27] Social networks and competencies become the most valuable gift that can be given to the needy, since they facilitate their self-realization. The "ethics of brotherliness" anchors the Abrahamic religions in the mechanisms of the global market.

Faith Communities as Actors in Civil Society

The forms of religious communality are even more varied today than in the past. The synagogue in Judaism, the church in Christianity, and the mosque in Islam were never the only social form of communities inside their religions; today, it is even less possible for an investigation of religious communality to be content to study the traditional institutions. The first important factor here is the expansion of civil society. A great number of organizations operate today in the space between the state, the economic sector, and the private sphere. These organizations have various legal forms, and all are characterized by a high degree of self-organization, which diverges from the traditional types. "The actors in civil society in the public sphere also include faith communities, at any rate when they . . . appear in the plural, and hence as competitors, rather than as a state church with a monopoly," Gunnar Folke Schuppert observes. This wide range of legal forms, corresponding to the societal tasks these organizations in fact perform, or claim to perform, ranges from "private" to "governmental," in an "unclear organizational landscape."[28] Thanks to new societal forms, private religiosity is now seen to be increasingly making its appearance in the public sphere. For many years, sociologists of religion focused on the privatization of religion in modern society, until José Casanova, Grace Davie, and others reversed this by showing that even private religion is not restricted to the private sphere. Rather, religions articulate in the public sphere experiences and claims that have their origin in private experience and judgment but are intended to be shared with others. Casanova argues that this "deprivatization" of religions is basic to the constitution of religions in civil society today. Their public character is fundamentally different from traditional forms of state religion.[29]

Religious communality acquires a high degree of relevance in this dimension of civil society. This is true even of Europe, despite Peter L. Berger's dictum that the whole world has become immensely religious today with the exception of Europe.[30] The English sociologist of religion Grace Davie has formulated the difference between Europe and the United States in her affirmation that a divergence between "believing" and "belonging" is characteristic of Europe. A dramatic decline in church attendance may thus coincide with a widespread diffusion of views connected with religious faith, making Europe an exceptional case. This divergence is explained, Davie contends, by a new "vicarious" form of religiosity, in which although religion may be highly valued as an actor in civil society, this does not correspond to active membership in any church.[31]

Contemporaneously with the consolidation of religious communality, a concept was developed in the United States that sheds a great deal of light on this phenomenon. The concept of "social capital" is linked above all to the name of Robert D. Putnam, professor of public policy at Harvard. In his research into the effectiveness of the regional governments responsible for a broad spectrum of tasks in the public domain that were created in Italy in the 1970s, Putnam discovered surprisingly large differences in the implementation of the reforms. In the north, they were a success, but they tended rather to be a failure in the south of the country. Putnam attributes this discrepancy to different social histories, going back to the fourteenth century, and sees it as an instance of path dependence: where you get to go depends on where you are coming from. In northern Italy, there was an ancient tradition of active associations of citizens who were accustomed to take local matters into their own hands; but those who lived in the southern cities were dependent on their landlords and expected their affairs to be settled by "those at the top."[32] The involvement of the north in civic matters constituted "social capital," which proved decisively important for the economic and political success of the regional governments.[33]

Immediately after the publication of his study, Putnam applied his newly won insight to the United States. For example, he regarded the increasing tendency over the previous two decades for Americans to go bowling alone, rather than with others, as symptomatic of a loss of social capital, and he published an article about this entitled "Bowling Alone," which later became a book. Putnam interpreted the phenomenon of the solitary bowler in the light of Alexis de Tocqueville's classic work *Democracy in America* (1835–1840), in which the French observer remarked that American democracy depended on the readiness of the citizens to form associations of every kind: "Wherever at the head of some new undertaking you see the government in France, or a man of rank in England, in the United States you will be sure to find an institution or association."[34] Given the erosion of Americans' involvement in civic affairs, Putnam sought to employ Tocqueville's insight as a gauge of what is achievable by the self-organization of citizens, whose potential is portrayed as almost immeasurable:

When Tocqueville visited the United States in the 1830's, it was the Americans' propensity for civic association that most impressed him as the key to their unprecedented ability to make democracy work. . . . Recently, American social scientists of a neo-Tocquevillian bent have unearthed a wide range of empirical evidence that the quality of public life and the performance of social institutions (and not only in America) are indeed powerfully influenced by norms and networks of civic engagement. Researchers in such fields as education, urban poverty, unemployment, the control of crime and drug abuse, and even health have discovered that successful outcomes are more likely in civically engaged communities. . . . Social scientists in several fields have recently suggested a common framework for understanding these phenomena, a framework that rests on the concept of *social capital.* By analogy with notions of physical capital and human capital—tools and training that enhance individual productivity—"social capital" refers to features of social organization such as networks, norms, and social trust that facilitate coordination and cooperation for mutual benefit.[35]

This discovery of a new kind of capital and of its almost miraculous effects caused a sensation. It almost seemed as if a political scientist had discovered the independent variable upon which both the success of political activity and the quality of a society depended—and at no extra cost.[36] And it seemed that one must act at once, since the social capital was rapidly dwindling. The faith communities were the only exception here, and they gave Putnam a reason to hope: "Religious people are unusually active social capitalists," he observes. "Religious involvement is a crucial dimension of civ-

ic engagement. Thus trends in civic engagement are closely tied to changing patterns of religious involvement."[37] Both Republican and Democratic
members of Congress saw this diagnosis as endorsing their positions—the
former saw it as confirmation of the superiority of private initiative and the
market to measures taken by the state, and the latter saw it as confirming
the stimulating effect of social legislation. It thus came about that in 1996,
the two parties jointly decided on a reform of the welfare laws, although
the new legislation was effectively implemented only under the subsequent
administration of George W. Bush from 2001 on. Notwithstanding that
the U.S. Constitution prohibits any financing of religion by Congress (and
subsequent interpretation by the Supreme Court has extended this prohibition to financing by the individual states), it was henceforth possible for
government to give financial support to the charitable work of faith communities in allocating funds for the needy.[38]

The Social Capital of Faith Communities

Putnam understood the term "social capital" to refer to "networks,
norms, and social trust that facilitate coordination and cooperation for
mutual benefit." This definition follows a new approach in American social science research in the 1980s.[39] James C. Coleman was the pioneer
here: he had defined social capital as a specific resource alongside economic capital and human capital, and had seen this as a special precondition
of the success of social actions.[40] This "relational capital," which must not
be confused with nepotism, attains its value only by remaining continuously in circulation. The more intensively someone builds on personal
relationships and trusts in them, the greater is this relational capital; the
less someone builds on them and trusts in them, the smaller the relational
capital.[41] This is the point where religiosity and social capital intersect. If
solidarity with the needy belongs to the practice of faith, the network that
thus comes into being is a source of social capital for the needy and a con-
cretization of the religiosity of the believers.

Sociological analyses of these networks soon added a further dimension to the theory of social capital, one also important for the investigation
of religious networks. It concerns the opportunities available to the actors
in various networks. The more links someone maintains to distant clus-

ters of networks, the greater the likelihood that he will realize the goals of his action. The first to observe this ("strength of weak ties") was Mark Granovetter in his research into the job market. When one applies for a job, one's chances are improved by knowing people from social clusters other than one's own. The more links of this kind a person has, the easier it is for him to get hold of relevant information, and the more successful his search for a position.[42] In view of the tendency of religious networks to form many mutually independent clusters, Granovetter's thesis is particularly compelling with regard to this field. The encounter of persons who do not know each other is preceded by a tacit commonality of worldviews and ethics that enable, stimulate, and structure relationships. This suggests that we should also follow Hartmut Esser in drawing a distinction between a "relational capital" and the "system capital" that it presupposes. Examples of system capital are the mutual social control and attention of the members; an overarching trust in the willingness of all the members to cooperate and in the functioning of the system as a whole; and the overarching validity of values, norms, and morality.[43] All of this perfectly applies to religious networks.

M. Rainer Lepsius's studies of the process of institutionalization help us define system capital more precisely. He argues that processes of institutionalization isolate central ideas, specify these with regard to specific contexts of action, and endow them with validity. Those who act in accordance with this process can integrate more and more social areas into the sphere where these ideas are valid.[44] This is the best way to define the system capital of a faith community. Belonging to a religion locates the activity of the individual in a context of salvation history, thus laying the foundations for an a priori trust that dares to step outside local boundaries.

Here a word of warning is necessary. One should not be too quick to draw the conclusion that social capital is always and under all circumstances productive for civic society. It is indeed true that the transactions mediated by social capital promote the maintenance of social rules, as well as mutual trust and support, and give access to goods in short supply. As Alejandro Portes notes, however, precisely this effect can generate threats to the ordering of civil society if the participants monopolize the resources for their own group, exclude members of other groups, put pressure on one another to conform, limit individual freedom, or isolate themselves in ghettos or gangs.[45] Similarly, the deprivatization of religion, as analyzed by Casanova, need not necessarily benefit the common good: it can also lead to a conflict with the state and legal order and to the formation of a "counterpublic."[46]

Putnam refined his concept in view of these objections and drew a distinction between a social capital that has an outward orientation and constructs bridges between social unequals and a social capital that has an inward orientation and establishes a commonality between equals. One type constructs bridges, while the other type of social capital binds and homogenizes.[47] These two types have fundamentally different effects on civil society. One can expect positive societal effects from a bridge-building social capital, and negative societal effects from a homogenizing social capital. Putnam cites Ashutosh Varshney's study of India as an example of how homogeneous communities are more inclined than heterogeneous communities to present a danger to civil society.[48] According to this research, the violence between Hindus and Muslims has declined where common civil-societal associations bridge the gulf between members of the two communities. However, Putnam correctly adds that in practice, most communities simultaneously develop the two functions of social capital. This means that what is true of religion applies to social capital as well, namely, that it can have an ambivalent effect on civil society. Since it is possible to monitor both functions empirically, the corresponding results are also a reliable indicator of the predominance of one or other aspect in the case of faith communities.

Cultural Enclaves and Diasporas

New concepts have been elaborated recently for communities formed by means of religious networks in order to distinguish these from established societal forms. Two of these concepts—the "cultural enclave" and the "cultural diaspora"—require discussion here, since they stem from differing perspectives on the new societal forms of religious communality.

Treating the cultural enclave as a type of religious communality goes back to the work of the ethnologist Mary Douglas, who attempted to offer a systematic definition of the societal distinctiveness of tribes and ethnic groups by investigating their internal ordering with regard to two variables: the amount of pressure the group puts on the individual, and how obligatory the rules and norms are that the individual must observe. This led her to classify societal units in terms of group pressure and of the obligatory nature of social rules and norms (which she calls "group and grid"). In her typology, a "cultural enclave" is a group that strictly isolates itself from the external world and pressures all its members to do so as well. Within such a group, however, there is little in the way of hierarchical structures; the tendency is rather for members to turn to charismatic authorities.[49]

Emmanuel Sivan has taken up this concept and studied it systematically by comparing cases from the three Abrahamic religions.[50] The result is a rich phenomenology of a "strong" religiosity. The conception of salvation history interprets the contemporary situation as exile; the believers lead their lives in an age in which unbelief, apostasy, and heresy are dramatically increasing, while the true divine order of things is losing its authority and people follow norms and laws that they themselves have created. Arrogance and hubris rule the world outside. The enclave must be protected against the external world by thick walls of fidelity to the faith. Established dichotomies between light and darkness, purity and impurity, justice and tyranny define the relationship between the enclave and the world of godlessness. Under these conditions, religious authority can no longer be assigned according to the criteria that were valid in the past; the believers must find their way through the possessors of an extraordinary charisma. Above all, it is the fighters for the faith or the martyrs who deserve veneration. It is inevitable that charismatics sometimes break even with sanctified traditions, and this does not damage their prestige. On the contrary, the enclave with its societal tasks must make itself independent of the "world outside" and its "weak" religion. It is animated by the idea of attaining cultural sovereignty over the lives of all its members through territorial hegemony, and this is why social institutions such as hospitals, schools, communications media (newspapers, radio, and television), institutions for the arbitration of legal disputes, and services ensuring safety in the local area are built up.

The concept of the cultural enclave overlaps in part with that of the sociomoral milieu, which goes back to Lepsius, who employed it to explain one particular pattern of conduct by electors in the history of

Germany.[51] He found that societal units in which religion, neighborhood, region, the economic and social situation, and cultural orientations were largely identical usually voted according to one particular pattern. Their vote served to give political expression to their shared worldview and to the morality based on this worldview. Martin Riesebrodt has adopted the concept of the "sociomoral milieu" in order to analyze the Evangelical and Shi'ite fundamentalism.[52] The concept of the "cultural enclave" adds the criterion of territorial demarcation and control to the characteristics of the "sociomoral milieu."

With this theory, Sivan successfully identifies precise metaphors for the practices of those faith communities that set themselves against the dissolution of collective morality. He thus reveals the contemporary meanings of interpretative patterns and scripts for actions that seem archaic. Well-known traditional metaphors lose their inherited frame of reference and become a "utopian" image of the world that allows believers in every imaginable place in the world to interpret their situation, to act accordingly, and to bind their faith to a territory. Territorialization is a characteristic of this form of religious communality; but it is highly problematic, since the control of neighborhoods also entails a limitation on the public authority of the constitutional state. Salwa Ismael has demonstrated this in the case of a morally rigorous Islamist neighborhood in Cairo, showing how traditional religious morality is transformed into a public order enforced with violence. The state and the faith community are rivals for cultural hegemony.[53] Religious "frontiers" have come into existence, in which a struggle for supremacy over morality is taking place.

Another concept that captures a further kind of limitation on the national and constitutional order by processes of segregation is that of the cultural diaspora. James Clifford has taken up the concept of "diaspora" and given it a specific meaning in relation to that of "minority."[54] The term "diaspora" derives from the attempts of social scientists to do justice to the transnational character of culture. Clifford takes the case of the inhabitants of a town in Mexico whose friends and relatives have moved to a town in California. Despite the distance between these two places, the migrants maintain contact so effectively that it is possible to speak of a single community. Modern technologies of transport and communication turn the crossing of boundaries—which once irrevocably separated people—into a new kind of experience of communality. The migrants who live in the United States continue to elaborate their own identity in relation to the land of their origin, giving their biography a transnational structure. Their loyalty and their link to their old homeland continue to exist, despite the relocation of their life to the American society that has taken them in.

It is obvious that in such cases, the three-generations model of integration—according to which the first generation lives for a short time in the new country and then dies, the second faces hardship, and the third prospers—can no longer function. Instead of a gradual absorption of the migrants into the dominant culture, they now find a life in two cultures. The concept of "minority" is inappropriate to such groups; the national state cannot integrate such transnational groups into its own self-understanding. Clifford speaks of a globalization from below, or of an "alternate" cosmopolitanism. Means of communication and transportation make it possible for migrants to maintain relationships to the country, the place, and the people from which they come, even across great distances, and this means that the "foreign country" becomes a place where people live at the intersection of several different social circles. The case of this Mexican community may still sound rather exceptional, but this is certainly not the case with faith communities. They regularly cross over the borders of the national state, thereby becoming transnational. The state thus loses the ability to control them.[55]

The Ethics of Brotherliness: Between Responsibility and Conviction

In order to understand the connection between territoriality and religious ethics, one must also look at the societal phenomenon of the neighborhood. Max Weber sensed that a religious "ethics of brotherliness" would become even more important under modern market conditions. In order to demonstrate this, he turned to the phenomenon of the neighborhood, which is one of the forms of community that he relates to economic activity in his book *Economy and Society*. He discusses first the household community, then neighborhood, religion, law, and domination, placing neighborhood *before* faith community. Weber analyzes each of these great societal orderings and powers as types of communal action, and identifies the actors' subjective expectations of meaning.[56]

The link that brings together the neighborhood and the faith community is the emergency assistance. When households get into difficulties, the neighborhood is asked to help. This is true both in rural villages and in the apartment blocks of a big city. There too, the neighbor is also a helper in need, so that "neighborhood is the typical locus of brotherhood."[57] In reality, brotherliness is certainly not the norm between neighbors; often enough, this "ethics of the people" is ignored due to personal hostility or a conflict of interests. Indeed, neighbors can become particularly bad enemies. Nonetheless, "The essence of neighborly social action is merely that somber economic brotherhood practiced in cases of need."[58]

This is the starting point for Weber's discussion of the faith community, which constitutes an independent instance of communal action driven by a longing for an extraordinary salvation. The community turns to mediators of the hoped-for salvation, such as the magician or shaman, the priest or ascetic saint, or the prophet. The paths of salvation to which these charismatic figures seek to win adherents and that they represent are transmuted by the laity into practices of their own: magic and ecstasy, cult and an ethic of law, ascetics or an ethic of conviction. In the course of this differentiation, the prophetic type of congregational religiosity also comes into being.[59]

In this way, the faith community develops alongside the neighborhood association as a second type of congregation.[60] This occurs because the faith community assumes the neighborhood association's obligation to aid those in need and translates it into the injunction to "brotherliness."

Congregational religion set the co-religionist in the place of the fellow clansman. "Whoever does not leave his own father and mother cannot become a follower of Jesus." This is also the general sense and context of Jesus' remark that he came not to bring peace, but the sword. Out of all this grows the injunction of brotherly love, which is especially characteristic of congregational religion, in most cases because it contributes very effectively to the emancipation from political organization.[61]

It is above all in the prophetical faith communities that assistance and aid to those in need are detached from spontaneous neighborly reciprocity and become the demands of a religious ethic. Indeed, these can take on the radical form of a specifically religious "attitude of love" or "communism of love"—which in turn contributes to the disenchantment of the world's realities.[62] "The more a religion of salvation has been systematized and internalized in the direction of an ethic of ultimate ends [*Gesinnungsethik*], the greater becomes its tension in relation to the world," Weber writes.[63]

Ethics of Responsibility and Ethics of Conviction

Weber regarded the transformation of neighborly reciprocity into a religious "ethics of brotherliness" as so fundamental to the development of modern culture that he returned to it specifically in his famous "Intermediate Reflection" (*Zwischenbetrachtung*) of "religious rejections of the world and their directions." His treatment there is condensed and more dramatic. Religiosity centered on salvation transforms the old economic neighborhood ethics into a relationship between siblings in the faith. The obligation to help widows, orphans, the poor, and the sick becomes a fundamental ethical commandment, and one's own salvation depends on its fulfillment.[64] The extent of the obligation is defined by the way in which the experience of the irrationality of the world is processed.[65] When believers regard reality in principle and everywhere as the reality of an incomprehensible suffering, the ethics of brotherliness bursts through all societal barriers and becomes universalistic. The more consistently it is practiced, the greater it is in tension with the structures and powers of the world; and the more this conflict leads to the consolidation of the autonomous political and economic laws of the world, the more irreconcilable is the dissonance between the religious value of brotherliness and the reality of the world. Paradoxically, this makes the religious ethics of brotherliness an engine for detaching social structures and powers from all the expectations placed in them in the search for meaning.

How is one to behave under "conditions of the world that are inimical to brotherliness"? One is compelled afresh to make a decision.

For there seems to exist no means of deciding even the first question: Where, in the individual case, can the ethical value of an act be determined? In terms of success, or in terms of some intrinsic value of the act *per se*? The question is whether and to what extent the responsibility of the actor for the results sanctifies the means, or whether the value of the actor's intention justifies him in rejecting the responsibility for the outcome.[66]

A widespread misunderstanding holds that the distinction between an ethics of responsibility and an ethics of conviction denotes an antithesis between conduct based on ethics and conduct based on power politics. Wolfgang Schluchter has vigorously refuted this and has shown that Weber does not regard the ethics of responsibility and the ethics of conviction as related to different values. There can be *no* ethical action *without* a conviction. Consequently, an ethics of responsibility can exist only where belief in the validity of *particular* absolute ethical values on which conviction about an action is based is already present.[67] This, however, means that the two types of ethics are equal in rank. When brotherliness is practiced as a principle of conviction, the actor takes no responsibility for the positive or negative consequences of what he does. When brotherliness is practiced as a principle of responsibility, deviation from the pure norm is justified with reference to the consequences for other persons. The merit of the ethics of brotherliness can thus underwrite either an action oriented to conviction or an action oriented to responsibility.

One key to understanding religious violence lies in the "ethics of brotherliness" of territorialized faith communities. Instead of dissociating religious violence from genuine religion by employing terms such as "cult," "fundamentalism," or "terrorism," the present study seeks to explain it on the basis of tensions between faith communities, on the one hand, and governmental, legal, and economic structures, on the other. This requires further research. First of all, we must explain the way in which religious communality is independent of other societal structures or powers such as the state, the law, or the market. All the Abrahamic religions have developed communal forms that lay claim to autonomy. Through the adoption of legally sanctioned societal forms, solidarity among believers—a requirement of the religious ethic—acquires a more binding character, both within the community and in relation to outsiders. Moreover, in the age of globalization, the growth and the differentiation of civil society have made it possible for faith communities to develop new forms of institutionalization. Where faith communities resist the moral autonomy of Western individualism, there is a tendency to territorial segregation and transnational networking. The cultural enclaves and diasporas that result can resist integration into the national state and develop a new type of societal power.

In *On Violence,* Hannah Arendt argues against the view that power is a matter of the state and is based on force. Instead, she seeks to draw a sharp distinction between the two. The force used by the state is intended to compel obedience; up to this point, she follows Max Weber. But then she qualifies her position by saying that the same is not true of power. She writes: "An individual never has power at his disposal." Power "is in the possession of a group, and remains so only as long as the group stays together. If we say of someone that he has power, this means in reality that he is empowered by a particular number of persons to act in their name."[68] According to Arendt's definitions, faith communities can be bearers of power even when they are not themselves part of the state.

The religious ethic of Abrahamic faith communities demands that believers be ready to support their community and its members with their property and, in extreme cases, even with their lives. This ethic has proved capable of taking the form both of an ethics of responsibility and of an ethics of conviction. The situation, and the interpretation of the situation by believers, indicates what has to be done. Threats to the autonomy of the community can lead the believers to replace the ethics of responsibility by a martial ethics of commitment.

CHAPTER 3

Conflicts with Alternative
Religious Communities in the
United States in 1978 and 1993

On November 18, 1978, an event in Guyana, a small and impoverished socialist country in Central America, provoked worldwide horror.[1]
The members of an American faith community called the "Peoples Temple" had committed collective suicide after some of them had attacked a
delegation of concerned parents and politicians, killing five persons. The
Peoples Temple was founded in Indiana in 1955 by the preacher and heal-
er Jim Jones (1931–1978). In the early 1970s, in order to avoid the nuclear
holocaust they were anticipating, they moved to California, which they
thought would be a safer place. There, they found perfect conditions for
recruiting new members. Many who belonged to the baby boomer generation had been disgusted by the Vietnam War and had turned their backs
on American culture, finding in California the ideal conditions for an alternative communal life. The community gathered around Jones did not
practice the racial separation customary in many other parts of the United
States: it had both white and black members, and this was deliberate. A
new community was to arise, transcending the social differences of race,
as well as of gender, age, and possessions. Although Jones sympathized
with communist countries, his was not a political program—the Peoples
Temple was more of a cultural enclave.

Drawing on the Judeo-Christian tradition, Jones had a worldview that offered his followers an explanation of their bleak situation.[2] It was impossible for the present world to be the work of a benevolent God; it was the work of an evil god who degraded and tormented human beings with racism, poverty, sickness, oppression, and ignorance. As the person who had insight into this situation, Jones saw himself as a redeemer. By proclaiming the truth, he undertook redemption from the prison of this world. The members of his community labored intensely to put an end to the degradation of blacks, women, old people, and the poor. They also took seriously the word of the Lord in relation to outsiders: "What you have done to these poor persons, you have done to me" (Matt. 25:40, 45). They organized health care at home for the poor and the sick, which brought in money. Further sources of income were donations and growing wine grapes. This "apostolic socialism" was also a commercial enterprise.[3]

In the eyes of his followers, Jones was the bearer of a spiritual power and, as such, was above the norms that otherwise applied to members of the community. All the members of the community were obliged to break with the dominant American culture and to find direction solely in Jones and his charisma. Jones claimed the right to have sex and children with women in the community—a practice that became a source of legal conflicts when women with children wished to leave the community. In the first years, though, Jones enjoyed great prestige, and he was included in a 1975 list of the hundred leading pastors in the country. He received numerous honors. The tide began to turn when the periodical *New West,* on the basis of statements by persons who had left the community, prepared a report about financial misdealings, beatings, coercion, murder, and "brainwashing" in the community. When Jones got wind of it, he attempted to take legal steps against the publication. He was unsuccessful, and the article was published on August 1, 1977. He then moved with nine hundred of his followers to Guyana, where, in 1975, he had already sent a small advance guard of the "Peoples Temple" to found the settlement of Jonestown. They were welcomed there with sympathy as representatives of a movement for black liberation.

Brainwashing on Trial

The emigration of Jones and his followers intensified a conflict that was already smoldering in California. Parents and relatives of young members of the community were endeavoring to get their children out of the community and back into their families, but this proved virtually impossible through normal legal means. First of all, young people come of age in the religious sense before they come of age in the legal sense; and secondly, freedom of religion is strictly protected by the U.S. Constitution. Parents and relatives are able to obtain guardianship of their adolescent children in religious matters only when the faith community to which their children belong demonstrably engages in practices contrary to the law, thereby losing its protected status. This is how we must understand the accusations leveled against the "Peoples Temple" by *New West* and other media: the intent was to undermine its status as a religion.[4]

Born of the initial spontaneous opposition to groups such as Hare Krishna, the Unification Church, or Scientology on the part of concerned parents and relatives, from 1971 on, a movement came into being that aimed to warn the public of the threat posed by "cults."[5] Unlike "sects" (which split off from existing and recognized church communities), "cults" were new foundations—and this very fact provoked suspicion and fears.[6] In addition to the affected families, defectors and other opponents of the groups were active in this opposition movement, which was consolidated into a "Cult Awareness Network" (CAN). The term "cult" became the embodiment of reprehensible religion, a polemical concept. To classify a community as a "cult" was to deny it any seriousness, to unmask it as a pseudo-religion.[7]

The association of the term "cult" with the practice of brainwashing was to prove momentous for further developments. The term "brainwashing" had originated during the Korean War, when imprisoned American soldiers made statements of such a nature that every right-thinking American was convinced that they must have been uttered under duress. In 1975, this concept was substantially widened in the sensational trial of Patricia Hearst, the publisher's daughter kidnapped by a militant left-wing group. In the course of her captivity, she changed sides and was photographed with other members of the group during a bank raid with a weapon in her hand. When she was arrested and brought to trial, the Hearst family lawyers argued that her actions were the result of a brainwashing. In the photograph, she merely looked like a perpetrator; in reality, she was still a hostage. The court accepted this line of argument. In the trial's aftermath, this type of interpretation made its way into judicial disputes about "cults."[8] After courts had admitted the possibility of a brainwashing, parents (supported by CAN) began to have their children "de-programmed" against their will, asking psychologists to use force and complete isolation to liberate their children from their links to various groups. These psychologists earned good money from the very fact that they promised to heal—and in turn, they gave generous donations to CAN.

The coalition of opponents then opened its doors to other groups and views. Christian fundamentalists joined in and broadened the interpretative framework by seeing the deviation from the norms of monogamy and private property as a diabolical conspiracy against Christianity and the values of the humane world. This led to a confrontation between two religious scenarios, each with the potential to intensify conflict: on the one hand, a faith community that broke with the norms of bourgeois American society, and on the other, opponents who regarded such a breach as a sign that the power of evil was growing.

Murder and Suicide

Concerned relatives of members of the Peoples Temple and other opponents asked Congressman Leo Ryan for his support in their attempt to free their relatives from the clutches of the group. Fourteen relatives and journalists accompanied him on his flight to Guyana in November 1978, as well as a former lover of Jones who had left behind a child in Jonestown. This woman maintained that another man was the child's father and that she should therefore have custody. Jones saw the arrival of this group in Guyana as a sign that the community's end was near, and he found confirmation of his foreboding when the group left and sixteen members of the community—including some who were indispensable for its existence in Guyana—decided to leave Jonestown and fly back with them. Annie Moore, a nurse, expressed her deep disappointment about what occurred in a farewell letter. She wrote that Jim Jones had shown them that they were all equal, and that they could live together without any differences. What a wonderful place Jonestown was, where children could play in the jungle and develop freely, and where old people were accorded a dignity that they did not possess in the United States. She concluded her farewell letter by saying that the members of the community had died because they were not allowed to live in peace.[9] Her sister Rebecca Moore, who was not in Jonestown (where she had lost another sister and a nephew), also attacked the persecution the community had suffered. Later, however, on looking back, she also castigated the violence that was practiced within the group itself.[10]

In a conflict situation of this kind, apostates play a principal role. As former members, they appear to the outside world as particularly credible witnesses to what is going on in the community. When an apostate justifies himself by saying that it was mental coercion that had lost him the respect of his family, he both clears himself of a disgrace and provides evidence of how depraved the "cult" is. Since an apostate has the stronger battalions on his side, his testimony increases the pressure to persecute and thereby contributes to a transformation of the community's situation.[11] Conversely, the apostate is often the first object of the community's wrath. At the airfield in Jonestown, loyal followers of Jim Jones attacked the group of apostates with weapons as they were leaving. Congressman Ryan and three persons died; eleven others were wounded. This was followed by the "white night" in which the members of the community committed suicide with poison or turned their weapons on each other. In his sermons in earlier days, Jones had contemplated suicide in such a situation: he held it to be a more dignified solution than submission to the destructive powers of this world. Indeed, he made the members rehearse and simulate it. Nine hundred and eleven persons lost their lives, voluntarily or against their will. The corpses were brought back to the United States, but there was no forensic investigation. An undignified tug-of-war ensued over the place of burial; no state or city was willing to assume the responsibility.

Escalating Acts of Violence

The fact that the violence was directed not only against internal and external enemies, but also against themselves, attests to the extent to which leading members of the Peoples Temple had linked their lives to the existence of the community. Jones had founded a community that rejected fundamental norms of American culture, and this led American religious spokesmen for that culture, such as Billy Graham, to affirm that the only way to understand Jones was as one of the false Messiahs of the Last Days predicted in Matthew 24.[12] For its part, the community interpreted persecution as an attack on its existence. Events took a particularly fateful turn when the concerned relatives succeeded in winning over powerful allies within the established order—the press, investigating officers, a congressman. The greater the threat to the existence of the community, the more it saw itself in an all-or-nothing situation. All in all, John R. Hall surely draws the correct conclusion from these analyses when he says that the cause of the violence lay not in the essence of the "cult" itself but in the course of the conflict between the Peoples Temple and its enemies.

A report by the American Civil Liberties Union as early as 1977 had pointed out the escalating effect that labels can have: "A religion becomes a cult, proselytizing becomes brainwashing; persuasion becomes propaganda; missionaries become subversive agents; retreats, monasteries and convents become prisons; holy ritual becomes bizarre conduct; religious observances become aberrant behavior, devotion and meditation become psychopathic trances."[13] David Chidester has coined the apt term "cognitive distancing" for this kind of rhetoric. The repertoire of religious self-description is systematically rewritten. The personal conviction of the community members is turned into the consequence of psychological coercion; the form of community building is denounced as un-American; Jones is unmasked as a false Messiah; and the Peoples Temple is dismissed as a noxious manipulation of religion.[14] The resistance put up by cornered men and women becomes something inherent to the "cult," and "Jonestown" the paradigm of the "cult" as such. Jonestown was dangled as an awful warning before the eyes of every adolescent who toyed with the idea of joining a similar group. If proof were still needed of how dangerous alternative communities are, this was supplied by the collective suicide, which confirmed and sealed the devastating verdict. Jonestown—the worst case—became the normal case, and "cult" became the equivalent of self-destruction. The concept of brainwashing or mental coercion played the key role here. Even after the American Psychological Association dissociated itself (on the basis of a professional report) from its own members, who had argued in reports presented to the court that group members had been brainwashed, anti-cult organizations continued to spread this explanation.[15] The result was that this interpretation had a determinative influence on the course of events in Waco, Texas, fifteen years after Jonestown.

Conflicting Scenarios in the Waco Battle

On February 28, 1993, the Federal Bureau of Alcohol, Tobacco, and Firearms (ATF) mounted a violent surprise attack on an Adventist community in Waco, Texas. This group was suspected of acting against the law. It was accused of converting semiautomatic weapons into automatic weapons. The transgression concerned not the illegal possession of weapons but the lack of authorization. In addition, the group's leader, David Koresh, was accused of child abuse. Both accusations had been spread by a representative of an anti-cult organization who had received the relevant information from an apostate.[16] The accusations were subsequently dropped in the judicial investigation into the events at Waco.[17]

In the aftermath of Jonestown, "cults" enjoyed the right to the free exercise of religion only to a limited extent.[18] When the Davidians heard of the approach of the law enforcement unit of the ATF—a convoy of eighty vehicles, including a unit of seventy-six heavily armed police officers—they took up their weapons and defended their community. Texas law permits people under certain circumstances to resist arrest, provided that the authorities use inappropriate force.[19] During the onslaught, four police officers and six members of the community lost their lives. When not even this led the Davidians to surrender, the FBI took over the case and laid siege to the site. Significantly, this was a "Hostage Rescue Team" (HRT), since the FBI planned its strategy on the basis of the "liberation of hostages" (although some of the officers involved were aware of the different nature of the situation). The siege lasted several weeks. The thoughts and actions of the operational command concentrated totally on a single problem: how to free the "hostages," above all, the children, from the power of the "cult" leader. They employed instruments of "stress intensification": the electricity was cut off and the site was lit up garishly at night and bombarded with repulsive noises from gigantic loudspeakers. When the besieged did not give up, the Clinton administration attorney general, Janet Reno, finally ordered a forcible eviction. On April 19, the "liberation commando" forced its way onto the site with tanks and sprayed tear gas into the buildings. Fire broke out. Seventy-four community members, including thirty-three young persons under twenty-one, died of gunshot wounds or in the flames; David Koresh was one of them.

The authorities later asserted that all these people had died in a collective suicide like that at Jonestown. This seems doubtful, but we cannot completely exclude the possibility that the fire was set by the Adventists themselves. Traces of fire accelerators were found in several places, and shouts from the site that were recorded on tape seem to point in this direction. A meticulous reconstruction by Kenneth Newport illustrates the contradictions without resolving them.[20] At any rate, the theory of a collective suicide cannot be dismissed out of hand, since the beliefs of the Waco Adventists included the idea that at the end of time, the world would be purified by a fire in which the godless would perish but the righteous would be saved. This belief could explain why some members of the community deliberately refrained from leaving the burning building in order to escape from the fire.

The Extraordinary Behavior of a Messiah

From the perspective of those involved, the events unfolded in an completely different manner. Let us take a closer look at the faith community in Waco, which originated with the New England Baptist preacher William Miller (1782–1849), who proclaimed that the second coming of Jesus would occur in 1843–1844. A "great disappointment" was inevitable, but it spurred Miller's followers to spread the teaching that a final extension had been granted so that people might repent.[21] Accordingly, the movement continued to exist in various groups, one of which called itself "Branch Davidians." They founded a community settlement called Mount Carmel near Waco, Texas, in 1935. Over the years, they set up a communal infrastructure with an infirmary, an old people's home, a school, and other institutions.[22] In this, they resembled other Adventists, who have founded and operate a great number of educational establishments, hospitals, and old people's homes worldwide. Such activities are often viewed as characteristic of postmillenarian groups who are working towards a gradual improvement of society as a whole, but this is not the case with the Adventists. They do not want to Christianize the world but to create an independent Christian cultural enclave that is as self-sufficient as possible.[23]

In 1981, a gifted young interpreter of the Bible named Vernon Howell (1959–1993) joined the group in Mount Carmel. In the Book of Revelation (5:2–5), there is a question: "Who is worthy to open the book and to break its seals?" The answer is: "The Root of David." Howell regarded himself as the "Root of David," and he changed his name to David Koresh. The group already believed in a continuing revelation through prophets, and people were thus willing to believe him. Just as God had entrusted a special mission to the Persian ruler Cyrus (Koresh in Hebrew), who is therefore said to be "anointed," or a "Messiah," in the Old Testament, so too Koresh believed that he had been entrusted with the special task of raising up the house of David anew. The Messiah whom he claimed to be was not Jesus Christ who had returned, but a son of David who had been announced in Psalms 40 and 45: the righteous one on whom the sins fall (Ps. 40:13), or the anointed one who marries the many virgins (Ps. 45:12.15). Koresh behaved accordingly: whereas the married couples in the community were obliged to separate, and all its members were obligated to a life of sexual abstinence, Koresh claimed and practiced the right to have sex and children with women of the community. These children, he asserted, would receive a privileged place in the coming kingdom of God.

The Unmasking of an Immoral Cult

Another interpretation of these same events was spread by a married member of the community, Marc Breault. When he realized that a young girl was visiting the sinful Messiah Koresh in his room, he was so indignant that he and his wife left the community in disgust. He then contacted the organized opponents of cults and sounded the alarm.[24] If people remained devoted to the community despite such repulsive goings-on, this could only be the consequence of mental coercion. It was also Marc Breault who was behind the accusations of child abuse and of infringements of the law regarding weapons.

Two reporters from the local *Waco Tribune-Herald* newspaper seized on his stories of and wrote a series of articles entitled "The Sinful Messiah." A new "cult" had been discovered. The first of these articles appeared the day before the first attack on the site on February 27, 1993; the second on the day after the attack, March 1. Others followed during the siege, increasing the pressure to employ force against the community. Opponents spread rumors that there was a risk of a collective suicide like the Jonestown one, and the FBI action force believed that they had to act quickly.[25] The concept of the "cult" determined their thinking and acting to such an extent that Davidian survivors later brought to trial asked the court to stop using it, since it would prejudice the jury.[26]

The religious dramatization of conflicts with faith communities has a long history in the United States. This is owing in part to the specifically North American experience of Protestantism.[27] In America, from the seventeenth century onward, many religious groups that deviate from standard Christian doctrines have arisen under the leadership of charismatic figures. Despite an initial vehement rejection, these "sects" (e.g., the Baptists and the Methodists) succeeded over the centuries in achieving recognition and moved from the periphery to the center of American religious life. But communities that combined a rejection of the world with a lifestyle that contradicted the maxims of traditional morality were felt to be particularly scandalous. For example, the Mormons' practice of polygamy prompted a flood of publications dealing in a highly imaginative manner with the sexual details of their marriages; and the Supreme Court declared in a judgment that while the American constitution protected belief, it did not protect religious actions contrary to established law. Like the Mormons, Catholic institutions too were the object of tell-all stories and books unmasking convents as places where nuns were kept as sex slaves. Such rumors about new faith communities have been so regular since the last quarter of the nineteenth century that Philip Jenkins speaks of cycles.[28] Similar stories circulated in France in the eighteenth century during the Enlightenment.

Around 1900, the term "cult" came to stand for all bourgeois reservations with regard to deviant religious groups. The prototype was the exotic religions such as Voodoo that were becoming known in America at that time. "Cult" was a polemical neologism for non-Christian religions: cults were the perverse opposites of Christianity. In addition to moral categories, medical categories were soon employed in order to make the abnormal comprehensible—were these persons not psychopaths who needed treatment? Two periods during the twentieth century saw the diffusion of new religious movements and communities that were regarded as abnormal and were the butt of public hostility, the years from 1910 to 1940 and from 1960 to the mid 1990s. The formative phase of such communities was regularly followed by a phase of the uncovering of scandals. The media reported disgusting practices, and government agencies took action against the groups. One voice heard with particular clarity in the choir of the enemies of cults was that of the Christian fundamentalists, most of whom accepted premillennialist teachings and assumed that the course of history would bring an increasing undermining of Christian doctrines and values by the power of evil. They saw no implausibility in classifying charismatic figures with unconventional messages as false prophets and Messiahs of the Last Days.

Koresh's Apocalyptic Interpretation of the Siege

During the weeks of the siege, David Koresh endeavored to interpret the crisis of his community through the Revelation of John. He taught that the seer of Revelation had foreseen the events of Mount Carmel: when the Lamb opened the fifth seal of the book of God, John saw under the altar the souls of those who had been slain and who cried out for vengeance. He heard the assurance addressed to them that they must be patient only for a short time (*chronos mikros*), until the end of all things would come (Rev. 6:9–11). Koresh saw this as a vision of the members of the community who had been slain in the first attack and related it to the ensuing situation of siege. But when would the "short time" be over? Four days before the second attack, he received the desired answer in the form of a revelation: it would end once he had written down his interpretation of the seven seals of the Revelation of John. In a letter, he informed his lawyer (who was outside the site) that he would leave the site with his followers as soon as he had done this.[29] He also asked the lawyer to forward the letter to James Tabor and Phillip Arnold.

These two biblical scholars had already offered their cooperation to the FBI during the siege. As exegetes specializing in apocalyptic and well informed about the Adventists, they were interested in the events at Mount Carmel and spoke about them on the local radio. The Davidians heard their accounts on battery-driven radios. Tabor and Arnold wanted to help the FBI understand the biblical interpretations better and thus gain insight into Koresh's interpretation of the situation and his willingness to surrender. They also wanted to discuss Koresh's interpretation of the Book of Revelation with him. However, the FBI refused this offer, since they regarded the letter as a delaying tactic. Attorney General Janet Reno knew nothing of the existence of this letter when, after some hesitation, she took the decision some days later in Washington, DC, to go ahead with the forcible eviction.

The Spiral of Violence Continues

The violence did not end with Waco. Exactly two years later, on April 19, 1995, an enormous explosion destroyed the Federal Building in Oklahoma City.[30] The perpetrator, Timothy McVeigh, chose the date deliberately: the "Christian Identity" movement to which he belonged believed that a conspiracy in Washington, DC, was also responsible for the bloodbath in Waco. Jews had taken control and had deceived white Americans about the true character of their administration. *The Turner Diaries* by William Pierce, published under the pseudonym of Andrew Macdonald, was a bestseller in this milieu.[31] It relates how after a liberal Congress passes a law to prohibit the possession of weapons, legions of FBI agents swarm out across the land to disarm free citizens. Only one small, resolute group of whites resists. They make a bomb and bring it on a truck to the FBI Building in Washington, DC. Seven hundred people are killed when it explodes, and a telephone caller tells the *Washington Post*: "White America shall live." One detail makes it quite clear that McVeigh sympathized with these ideas: like the hero of the *Diaries,* he blew up the building with a bomb consisting of a mixture of ammonium, nitrate, fertilizer, and heating oil.

The Importance of Translating Worldviews

In order to clarify how the violence at Waco had come about, the U.S. government ordered an inquiry and asked scholars of religion to contribute expert opinions. In his statement, Larry Sullivan drew attention to the tacit assumptions on which the actions of the operational command were based.[32] The strategy of the "liberation" of "hostages" did not fit the religious situation of the believers on the site. The fixed idea that religion is a private matter made those responsible blind to the kind of religion that can mobilize a group and get it to carry out communal actions. The authorities regarded Koresh's long-winded explanations and hours-long sermons as "Bible babble." They held that a religion that comes into conflict with the law cannot possibly be genuine. In this way, the law enforcement officers failed to realize that they themselves were playing a role in Koresh's apocalyptic drama, namely, the role of the bloodthirsty Babylon, God's foe. Those who view religion as primarily a private matter are neither willing nor able to perceive it as a framework for communal actions.

A report for the Department of Justice by another scholar of religion, Nancy Ammerman, made a similar diagnosis of the FBI's mistakes. Initially, she had shared the view that Koresh must be a religious charlatan, but when she looked more closely at his teachings, she recognized that they were a variation of what other millenarian groups also believed. She too altered the direction of her investigation and studied the FBI and its assumptions. FBI agents regarded the theology and morality of David Koresh as wrong because they understood religion as an internal and morally exemplary conviction and knew very little about the history of religion. The only way they could make sense of what they saw was by means of the stereotype of the "cult."[33]

In their investigation, James D. Tabor and Eugene V. Gallagher came to the conclusion that the FBI could have defused the situation had it accurately defined the type of faith community involved.[34] This is supported by the fact that three years later, the FBI followed the recommendations of the Waco Commission. The Montana Freemen were another Christian group who believed that they were living in the Last Days and who regulated their lives by a law of their own, the "Common Law." When the Freemen came into conflict with federal authorities over tax offenses, this confirmed their conviction that the federal government was the "Babylon" of the Revelation of John, and hence a satanic power. One of their ranches was besieged by the FBI for months on end. But this siege was not like that of the Branch Davidians. This time, the FBI appointed people to mediate between the community and the authorities, and experts who had investigated millenarian communities were consulted. As "worldview translators," they advised the FBI to avoid doing anything that the community might regard as a confirmation of its own interpretation of the situation. And in fact, the conflict was resolved without violence, through negotiations.[35]

During a review of these events two years later, in which a special unit of the FBI and scholars of religion took part, both sides acknowledged the role of scholars as "worldview translators."[36] Two points in particular had become clear to the participants at this meeting. Since every millenarian group has its own view of the world, and thus of its own situation, those in authority must understand this worldview before they can assess whether the community will use violence only in self-defense, or whether the community itself will launch a violent attack.[37] Christian millenarianism does indeed expect violence; but only a few millenarist groups consistently call for the active use of violence. It is recommended that law enforcement agencies consult experts to distinguish between the two types of groups and, in the case of a community that tends more to be on the defensive, to negotiate a solution to the conflict.[38]

Religious Models of Action and Violence

In response to Jonathan Z. Smith's demand that we not simply accept the assertion that an incomprehensible cult is prone to violence, a number of American scholars began investigations that led to a considerable change in the manner in which violence was explained, first in the case of the Peoples Temple in Jonestown and then in that of the Adventists in Waco. It was recognized that the main cause of the violence was not the communities themselves but the way in which the conflict between them and their opponents unfolded. Hall has summarized the results as follows: "The key to understanding mass suicide at Jonestown lies in the recurrent dynamics of conflict between religious communities claiming autonomy and external political orders. In the general case a demand to submit to the external order forces a choice within the community between the sacred and evil. The choice brings religious conviction to a question of honor, and is the seedbed of martyrdom."[39] Hall followed this study with another analysis that includes Waco. There too, the conflict was intensified and accelerated by the interaction between a community that interpreted its experiences as signs of the Last Days and powerful opponents (including media and governmental authorities) who suspected them of crimes and took violent action against them.

The analytical model he developed could shed new light on other cases too. In order to understand violent actions, it is not enough to look at the faith community in isolation: we must look at the course of the conflict as a whole. If we do, as the cases of Jonestown and Waco reveal, we perceive the presence of actors who had hitherto remained obscure, although they contributed to the violent turn of events. We also find concerned relatives who defamed the group as enemies of civilized society and employed legal means against them; apostates who gained a high profile in the media thanks to the disreputability of the group to which they themselves had previously belonged; media that turned individual events into sensational scandals and published accounts of atrocities; and governmental authorities who took violent action against the groups because of alleged breaches of the law. What all these actors had in common was the view that they were dealing with a "cult" and not in the least with religion.

When the opponents spoke of a "cult," they thereby communicated that they were dealing with a harmful pseudo-religion that deserved to be rejected, opposed, and eliminated. The classification encouraged those who desired to put a violent end to what the group was doing, while the communities concerned interpreted the escalating situation in terms of their salvation-historical worldview and acted accordingly. Looking at the course of conflict as a whole, we can see both the interlocking and the differentiation of both sides' scenarios. "Cult" is such a central concept, then, that if we are to understand the escalation of violence, we must take it into account when we look at the course of events. The use of this term has come under suspicion of being itself an instrument employed to evade the question of a possible link between violence and an allegedly genuine religion. As Catherine Wessinger writes:

When we label a group with the pejorative term *cult,* it makes us feel safe because the violence associated with religion is split off from conventional religions, projected onto others, and imagined to involve only aberrant groups. As we well know, however, child abuse, sexual abuse, financial extortion, torture, terrorism, murder, and warfare also have been committed by mainstream believers. . . . The pejorative stereotype of the "cult" helps us avoid confronting this uncomfortable fact.[40]

Naturally, religions *can* take on a violent form. The problem is that the designation "cult" limits this possibility to specific groups, thereby itself becoming a polemical instrument employed to deny them their right to existence, to demonize them, and to combat them.

A model for action focused on the course of the conflict is the best way to explain the links that can arise between religions and violence, since the perpetrators of violence are not the only ones to influence the course of events. In the first place, there is the faith community itself. In the cases of the Peoples Temple and the Adventists of Waco, the faith communities were cultural enclaves. For its members, the community was a protected place, and it seemed to them that their lives depended on its continued existence. Members were subject to a strong pressure to conform and were led by an unconventional religious hierarchy. Secondly, there were the opponents. Apostates, the organized anti-cult movement, the media, the judiciary, and the police authorities acted in accordance with their own interpretations of the situation and their competencies. The federal state made its appearance as the guardian of individualism, the family, and private property—the true American values. The opponents castigated deviations from these values as something metaphysically evil. Apostasy from these immoral communities was greeted and promoted by powerful organizations, who were in turn supported by the media and the state. The heuristic model of an eschatological community that rejects the world and is combated by apostates and official bodies could be useful in the investigation of other models of religious violence as well. The expectation of an increase in violence in the Last Days and the experience of persecution have generated cycles of violence on the part of the state and religious violence in response.

CHAPTER 4

Every Day 'Ashura, Every Tomb
Karbalā: Iran, 1977–1981

The first entire country to become an arena of religious violence in the twentieth century was Iran, from 1977 to 1979. The demonstrations and street fighting against the Pahlavi regime made use of the concepts of history and the rituals of the Twelver Shi'a and thoroughly modernized them. An annual procession in the month of Muharram was meant to keep alive the memory of the murder of the third Imam, Husain, on the orders of Caliph Yazid near Karbala in what is now Iraq in 680 CE. In the month of Muharram, which fell in December and January 1977–1978, the processions swelled to become enormous political demonstrations against the Shah's regime. When the clergy in Qom, a stronghold of Shi'ite learning, joined their students in demanding that the regime grant the rule of law and freedom, the army used force against them and shot many of them on January 9. The leading clergyman in Qom then declared that those who had been shot were martyrs, and that the government was the enemy of God. Forty days later, when the memorial service prescribed by ritual was held on February 18, the dead were commemorated as martyrs. When the army advanced on the demonstrators and once again people were killed, memorial services for the martyrs were held once again, forty days later. A "chain of martyrdom" accompanied the deterioration of the old order. At intervals dictated by the ritual, the uprisings spread across the land in a kind of snowball effect, until the Shah's regime was swept away because of its own violence.[1]

Newspaper reporters give us glimpses of the ceremonies of mourning that commemorated those who had been shot. For example, Arnold Hottinger, the correspondent of the *Neue Zürcher Zeitung*, wrote as follows about an assembly in Isfahan at the beginning of 1979:

The speakers [in the mosque] follow one another, and their listeners are repeatedly given the opportunity to shout out their cries and slogans, as is certainly in keeping with the religious tradition of the ceremonies of mourning. A mixture of religion and politics is presented: the speakers, mostly clergy but sometimes also laymen, speak of the pioneers of the Shi'a who laid down their lives. This leads them almost automatically to speak of the bloody sacrifices that "we are making today for freedom." The people mourn Husain and promise that they are ready to sacrifice themselves for him, like so many others of his companions and successors. The speaker adds: "This is the meaning of our struggle against the Shah to establish an Islamic republic." (*NZZ*, January 7–8, 1979)

The speakers praised the deaths in the street battles as lives laid down for Husain, and those present promised in reply that they were willing to make a similar sacrifice. Another source reports a woman participant as saying: "Khomeini has said that whoever dies in the struggle against the Shah's regime dies the death of a witness, martyrdom—naturally, this applies only to the one who consciously takes part in the demonstration, not to one who happens to be shot while passing by."[2] The speakers here are not in the least members of the uneducated, traditional classes, but young educated urban dwellers. After the unrest broke out, an Iranian woman who lived in the West returned to her country and kept a diary in which she recorded her experiences and her motivations. Omol Bani relates enthusiastically that Imam Husain's death as a witness has been reinterpreted by Ali Shariati, and that this has greatly intensified the willingness to fight. In her thoughts, she herself lives in the age of Husain. In the darkness of ignorance, an angry son is born of the little house of Fatima, the daughter of the prophet Muhammad and wife of 'Ali—Husain, who rises up against the rule of the palaces and the exploiters: "The only weapon this man has is his own death. But he comes from a family that has taught him the art of dying rightly. This is *shahada*."[3] *Shahada* designates the first of the five pillars of Islam: "I bear witness that there is no god but God, and that Muhammad is the messenger of God." However, it also designates testimony in the sense of martyrdom, and was therefore a slogan in the struggle against the Shah's regime.

Unlike the concept of sacrificial death in other cultures . . . *shahada* is not a death which the enemy forces upon the revolutionary and imposes upon him. It is the welcome death which a fighter himself chooses in full consciousness of his situation. . . . *Shahada* is a challenge to all the centuries, to all the generations: "If you can kill, then kill; and if you cannot kill, then die!" (a quotation from the Iranian intellectual Shariati)[4]

Martyrdom is not a fate that overtakes a person. It is a freely chosen action.

A Shi'ite Ritual of Revolution Is Performed Anew

The events to which this idealization of dying was linked lie far back in the past. They occurred in connection with the struggle for the succession to the deceased Caliph Mu'awiya. 'Ali's party believed that Husain was entitled to the succession to the Prophet, but when he set out in the year 60 after the Hegira (680 CE) to assume this office in Damascus, he was intercepted and besieged in the Iraqi city of Karbalā by the general of the Caliph Yazid, who had taken power in the meantime. For days on end, the troops prevented him and his followers from getting access to water, so that they nearly died of thirst. Then, on Muharram 10, the day of 'Ashura, they attacked the little group and killed Husain together with his family and some who remained faithful to him. Only four years later, his adherents held a penitential march on that same day. They lamented what had happened and accused themselves of complicity in abandoning the Imam. The oldest element in these memorial celebrations, which soon underwent a considerable elaboration, was Husain's request for a drink of water, which was refused.[5]

Celebrations on the day of 'Ashura were organized above all after Shi'ism became the state religion in Iran in the sixteenth century. European travelers, who visited Persia in growing numbers from the beginning of the seventeenth century on and were fascinated by what they saw, inform us about the Shi'ite practice of marching with lamentations through the streets of their town or city quarter on Muharram 10, the anniversary of the murder of Husain. We are also told about the societal composition of the processions. The committees that organized the celebrations relied on the clientele of a rich patron, on a neighborhood group, on the religious followers of a respected clergyman—or on all three together. The processions were thus based on already existing relationships of loyalty.[6] In practice, the processions were usually performed by craft guilds.

A Demonstration of Willingness to Die

The participants in the procession were inspired by the idea that the events of the past were once again present in the days of 'Ashura. A report from the beginning of the twentieth century quotes a participant as saying: "Today is the day of 'Ashura, and these events took place in Karbalā."[7] The slaughter of Husain and his followers was reconstructed on the streets in a way that profoundly moved the onlookers. One particularly striking feature was the men who scourged themselves with chains and sabers until the blood flowed. These men wore shrouds in order to emphasize that they were willing to sacrifice themselves; and they were ready to demonstrate this in practice too, in street battles there and then—for the European travelers agree that when the processions met each other, they assailed and fought each other. One early account summarizes all the distinctive features of these encounters:

Likewise, all the people from the neighboring towns take part in these processions with long and thick clubs in their hands, in order to use these at the given time against the other processions that they may chance to encounter—not only for the sake of precedence, but also (I believe) in order to depict the battle in which Husain died. And they firmly believe that the one who stands firm in his place in such a skirmish, since he is dying for Husain, goes directly into Paradise. Indeed, they believe that the gates of Paradise stand open throughout the entire period of their 'Ashura, and that all the Mohammedans who die in these days will be brought in there immediately.[8]

Other travelers confirm these words point by point: that the fighting broke out over ritual objects, that they fought with clubs, that the fighting was due to the rivalry of the different processions to get precedence, that it portrayed the events of Karbalā, that it was suppressed by the state, that those who died in these fights were considered martyrs like the martyrs of Karbalā, and that people believed that the gates of Paradise were open in the days of 'Ashura. All these features show that the 'Ashura celebrations belong to the type of periodical, collective rituals of revolution, and that like such rituals, they too temporarily suspend the legal order.[9]

These rituals of revolution are widespread, and their interpretation is a matter of controversy. For a short period, these rituals turn upside-down the existing asymmetrical relationships between men and women, between rulers and subjects.[10] Many British social anthropologists were once convinced that such rituals had the function of purifying a society from the aggressions of some of its members, thereby stabilizing the hierarchical structure.[11] The ethnologist Victor Turner (1920–1983) examined this hypothesis by means of field studies in Africa, and he dismissed it. He recognized in the rituals of revolution the presence of two antithetical types of societal relationships: on the one hand, a hierarchical structure of positions and roles, and on the other hand, an undifferentiated communality, which he calls *communitas*. Both societal types—the structure and the *communitas*—make their own independent claims to validity: "For individuals and groups, social life is a type of dialectical process that involves successive experience of high and low, communitas and structure, homogeneity and differentiation, equality and inequality."[12] When hierarchies become rigid, however, social movements can draw on the experience of communality and overthrow them.

In Iran, too, the ritual street battles in Muharram provided a setting for staging the tensions latent in everyday life between the different loyalty groups in the Iranian cities. This had consequences for the significance that the historical events of Karbalā acquired. Historically speaking, the conflict between Husain and his enemies was a confrontation between two parties (later called Sunnites and Shi'ites) about the legitimate caliph; but in Iranian society, the battles were fought between Shi'ites. Now, it was the sacrifice for one's own loyalty group that had an exemplary religious character—no longer the sacrifice for the community of all the Shi'ites. The drama of Karbalā was staged as the readiness to sacrifice one's life for one's own group.

The remembrance of the past events was kept alive in another way too, by means of a Passion play. The martyrdoms of Karbalā were depicted on the stage: in addition to the martyrdom of Husain, those of his companions 'Abbas, Qasim, 'Ali Akbar, and others. Each act of the play illustrates anew that the redemption that Husain's death brings is effective only when one takes him as the model for one's own action:

O Shi'ites, Husain gave his head for you. Smite yourselves on the head out of grief for the king of the East and of the West. Husain made his life a ransom for the Shi'ites. Now strew your life on Husain's path.[13]

The actors in the play continually address each other with the words: "May I be your ransom."[14] This is more than a mere cliché: the corresponding concepts of *feda* (ransom, ransom money, etc.) and *qorbān* (sacrifice) speak to deep-rooted societal expectations. Both in the past and in the present, the security of the individual has been guaranteed not so much by the government as by the solidarity of the group to which one belongs. When people become dependent on others as a result of war, debt, or other reasons, the only thing that helps them is ransom by their own group. This is why the Passion play presents ransom as a moral obligation incumbent on all those who belong to a loyalty group. When some people want to discourage him from martyrdom, 'Ali Akbar cries out in indignation:

Behold, my father is left without companions and lamenting. He has no one in this wilderness to bring (him) aid.[15]

It is however not permissible for simply anyone to bring this aid. In the Passion play, this is reserved exclusively to young men, and the myth of the sacrifice of Ishmael inculcates this point: "The life of the son is worthy to be sacrificed for (his) father."[16] Women have another task, namely, to give their consent to the path to sacrifice on which their sons set out. Before the Imam sends the two young men 'Ali Akbar and Qasim out to the battlefield, he sends them back to their tent: "It is your mother who must give her consent to this action."[17] 'Ali Akbar's mother still hesitates, but when Qasim's mother tells her that she will certainly allow her son to take part in the battle, she too utters the decisive words:

Place your hope in God the righteous judge, go and sacrifice (your) life for (your) father.[18]

The exemplary religious action remains linked to the decision taken by others. It is embedded in a societal world in which loyalty groups dominate and compete with one another.[19] Readiness for sacrifice is the presupposition for societal survival. As yet, the believer lives in a world that is full of injustice (*zulm* = tyranny); this will change only when the Imam Mahdi emerges from his occultation and fills the world with justice (*'adl*).[20]

The Tyranny of Westernization

The European expansion that became ever more noticeable in Iran from the nineteenth century on soon had momentous consequences, in a new interpretation of the 'Ashura ritual. When Nazir al-Din Shah (r. 1848–1896) granted an Englishman the tobacco concession for the whole of Iran in 1891–1892, a storm of protest broke out in the country. Bazaar merchants and craftsmen, clergy, and intellectuals declared the shah to be a tyrant like the usurper Yazid. At the high point of the dispute about the tobacco monopoly, demonstrators clothed in shrouds marched through the streets in order to proclaim publicly their willingness to die, if need be, in the struggle for a just social order.[21]

This interpretative pattern declined in importance in the 1920s and 1930s. After Reza Shah Pahlavi came to power in 1925, he employed every legislative instrument available in order to deprive the Shi'ite faith community of legitimacy. The clerics, who had previously been exempt from military duty, could now be drafted; their influence on the legal system and the schools was cut back, they were forbidden to carry out the bloody Shi'ite rituals, and the religious foundations were subjected to state control and regulations. A law about clothing forbade women to wear the veil and men the traditional garb. The only exception was the clergy—for in this way, it would be possible to distinguish them externally from the laity. The goal of all these measures was to expel Shi'ism from the public life of Iran and to stigmatize it.[22]

The End of Traditional Village Societal Forms

The marginalization of the Shi'a was well advanced by the time that the son of Reza Shah Pahlavi (r. 1925–1941), Mohammed Reza Pahlavi (r. 1941–1979), whom the United States had brought to power, undertook a radical modernization of the country at the beginning of the 1960s. Of all the various reform measures of the "White Revolution" of 1962, the land reform was particularly far-reaching and had the most serious consequences in the long term. Until that date, the traditional large landholders had owned immense territories, which were cultivated by dependent peasants. The harvest was divided between the landlords and the peasant farmers according to a traditional ratio that took into account the possession of one of the five factors of production: land, seed, draught cattle, water, and physical work. If (as was frequently the case) the peasants had nothing to contribute apart from their manpower, they were left with only one-fifth of the harvest.[23] Every impartial observer must regard this sharecropping as the embodiment of injustice and exploitation.

The agrarian reform, recommended and conceived by American experts, destroyed this system. The farmers received the property rights to the fields that they cultivated, although with the stipulation that they must compensate the former landholder. The former owner was compensated by a state-owned bank, which the new owner then had to repay. A rationalization of cultivation was intended to make it possible for the peasant farmers to pay these credits back. The intention was to create a new class of farmers who sought to earn money. However, this reform ignored the many agricultural workers—estimated at 40 percent of the village families—who did not possess any customary right to the sharecropping, but belonged to the village community and formed working teams (*boneh*) with the peasant farmers, receiving for this a share in the harvest. Thanks to the introduction of machines, these agricultural workers lost their employment and were obliged to move to the cities. The experts had included this in their calculations, since the increasing oil revenues would bring an industrialization of the country and thereby many new jobs; but things did not turn out in this way. Too few new jobs were created, and those that were created made demands that did not match the low-level abilities of those who had moved to the cities. Worse still, the landless were soon followed by many of the new farmers—the expectation of an agricultural revolution had been deceptive. Instead of more agrarian products being produced in Iran itself, even grain came to be imported, paid for from oil revenues. In the end, the land reform had destroyed the societal forms of the villages, but without the simultaneous emergence of an industrial society. In the cities, this led to an explosion of the number of inhabitants and of the slums.[24]

The Growth of Shi'ite Networks

In Iran's overpopulated cities, it was religious institutions that were most qualified and most willing to take care of those who had been uprooted and disappointed. Looking back on the 1960s and 1970s, Said Amir Arjomand observed a noticeable increase in religious activities; there had been a mushrooming of religious associations, which migrants joined.[25] The legal reforms had gravely weakened the Shi'ite institutions, but they still had income and assets, as in the past. Accordingly, the progress of the Western modernization in the countryside drove the uprooted persons in the cities into Shi'ite networks, which, despite all the government measures, had remained close to the poor, many of whom had been steamrollered by the economic developments in Iran and found social Shi'ism attractive. Instead of being embedded, as previously, in rural societal forms and relationships of loyalty, they formed a faith community.

From the very outset, the land reform that was enacted by the Shah's regime and the further program of modernization (the "White Revolution") had also encountered opposition on the part of the bazaar merchants and craftsmen. Among the city dwellers too, the modernization brought advantages only to certain social classes, while others were affected adversely by it. Craftsmen and merchants in the bazaars were largely excluded from the oil wealth, but they were suddenly forced to compete with firms that received state subventions, operated factories that produced goods for everyday use that had previously been made in the bazaars, and sold these products outside the bazaars in modern shops. The discontent exploded in June, 1963, when a great protest demonstration against the Shah's regime was held in the Shi'ite month of grief, on the 'Ashura day (Muharram 10 = June 5, 1963). The Shah's troops dispersed it with bloodshed.

Karbalā Becomes the Model for Action Today

Clergy took part in the revolt in 1963. Alongside the predominantly apolitical clergy, a politically active group had formed, which entered the public arena. Ruholla Mussaui Khomeini (1902–1989) played a prominent role as the harshest critic of the Shah in this group. After the bloody confrontations, he was forced into exile, first in Turkey, then in Najaf in Iraq.

Najaf was an appropriate place for his activities, since the tomb of Imam 'Ali drew Shi'ite pilgrims from all over the world. It was a center of Shi'ite scholarship, where the younger generation of clergy from many countries studied. In exile, Khomeini elaborated his radically new theory that the state form of monarchy was incompatible with Islam. As long as the Imam Mahdi remains hidden, only a "government of the jurist" (*velayat-e faqih*) is legitimate.[26]

A genuine renaissance of Shi'ite theology took place in Najaf in the 1960s, especially with regard to the conception of martyrdom.[27] In 1963, the Shi'ite clergyman Ayatollah Taleqani declared that death in the struggle against the Shah's regime was an act of martyrdom, and laid claim to the core metaphor of Sufism, *fana* (annihilation of the self in God), for this action. Anyone who is led by the knowledge of the truth to be willing to sacrifice himself, in order thus to realize the truth, is a martyr, and this also applies to those killed during the demonstrations in 1963. It is indeed true that there was a tension between this transposition of a conception of Islamic mysticism to death in the struggle for an Islamic societal order, on the one hand, and the predominant rejection in classical Islam of every form of taking one's own life, on the other. But laying claim to the mystical concept of "annihilation" for such an act (as was done shortly afterwards by Sunni adherents of the jihad in Egypt too) meant that the intention of the acting person became decisive for the religious legitimacy of his action. One may speak of a dying in the jihad only when this completely corresponds to the intention of the one who acts (*niyya*). A conscious and intentional death in the struggle against the impure, unjust world was ethically exemplary and, when seen from the perspective of the apocalyptic end of history, a victory. And in any case, it was not a reprehensible suicide.

Young theological students from Iraq, Iran, and Lebanon, who believed it was necessary to mobilize the faith communities of their countries against the increasing cultural Westernization, adopted this concept of martyrdom. Even a deliberate destruction of one's life in the struggle against the powers of godlessness was no longer taboo: on the contrary, it was elevated to exemplary status. Theologians who kept in touch with one another even after their studies in Najaf, and who had considerable influence on public life in their native countries, such as Baqir al-Sadr in Iraq, Musa al-Sadr and Sayyid Muhammad Husain Fadlallah in Lebanon, and

Khomeini in Iran, brought about this transformation of the Shiʿite tradition into a religious activism. In all their sermons and writings, they taught that Shiʿites must never again abandon Imam Husain, as had once happened in Karbalā. Instead of ritually lamenting, the believers should rise up like Husain to fight against injustice. But we no longer hear that the consent of the women of the family is necessary for such a decision: the action has become utterly individual, and all that counts is the pure intention. It belongs to God—and here and now, to the Shiʿite authorities—to discern the purity of a person's intention. In this way, a religious practice embedded in loyalty groups became an action that was subject to the judgment of the faith community.

The new generation of clergy moved away from the earlier view that the believers must above all learn how to bear injustice patiently. Khomeini's gradual ascent in the course of his exile to the role of the highest Shiʿite cleric, the *marjaʿ at-taqlīd* (Arabic "authority"), to whom both laity and clergy owe obedience, sounded the death knell of political abstinence.[28] He summoned believers to fight actively against injustice and on behalf of "the humiliated" (*mostazʿafin*). For a long time, Shiʿites had been bidden to conceal their identity, as long as the Imam Mahdi had not yet emerged from his occultation and they were living in a dangerous world full of injustice and falsehood—but now, Khomeini demanded that they abandon this practice, in view of the attack on the faith community of the Shiʿa. Instead, they must be ready to fight and to die.

From Concealment to the Public Profession of Faith

Concealing one's faith (in Arabic *taqiyya* or *ketmān*, literally, "caution," "fear," "concealment") was typical of the Shiʿite way of life at an early date, as we see in affirmations of the imams:

He who has no *taqiyya*, has no faith; a believer without *taqiyya* is like a body without out a head.[29]

This, however, does not determine what exactly was demanded in practice. Ignaz Goldziher holds that this was an absolute obligation,[30] but Etan Kohlberg has argued against this position. He writes that even for the Shiʿa, *taqiyya* is not in every situation an obligation, but only when a candid profession of the faith would harm the imam or his community. The exception to this rule is constituted by actions that belong to the distinctive characteristics of the Shi'ite legal school; but since the Shi'ite legal tradition differs from the other Islamic legal schools only on small and rather marginal points, the *taqiyya* would only seldom have been a religious obligation irrespective of the situation.

This means that the requirement of *taqiyya* remains rather unclear, if one compares it to the clear maxims of an ethic for the laity. This prompted Egbert Meyer to study the occasion and the sphere of application of the *taqiyya* in the works of Shi'ite theologians more closely. His finding is that they treat *taqiyya* in connection, not with ethics, but with the coming of the Imam Mahdi. "Until the appearance of the imam who is to return, when that which is true will gain the upper hand once and for all, *taqiyya* is an action which is worthy of consideration at all times."[31] This means that there is an inherent link between the occultation of the Mahdi and the practice of concealment. As long as the Imam is hidden, *taqiyya* governs the conduct of the believers on purely rational grounds. In turn, the occultation of the Imam Mahdi itself is linked to the practice of *taqiyya* (literally, "caution"). When the twelfth and last Imam went into hiding, this was justified by reference to his fear of his enemies: the Imam was obliged to shelter from them. Reason dictated the concealment. However, the opposite is also true: if the believers await the imminent return of the Imam Mahdi, the end of the concealment is likewise at hand.[32] It will cease definitively only when the Mahdi appears. But if the Shi'a itself is endangered, no concealment is permitted.[33] This danger existed in Iran under Mohammad Reza Shah Pahlavi. In this situation, Khomeini summoned the believers to distinguish a correct *taqiyya* from a false *taqiyya*. In such a situation, the believers were obliged to fight for the truth. *Taqiyya* was no longer an option for their conduct; the time to rise up had come.

Westernization as Poison, Infection, and Temptation

Academics and intellectuals also belonged to the opposition to the Shah's regime. Secular opposition figures in Iran had recognized that the growing numbers of those who had lost their rights through the land reform and modernization measures formed a revolutionary potential for a change of government. As long as the Shi'ite clergy were apolitical, the chances for a secular Marxist alternative were good; but the new Shi'ite activism confronted the secular opposition with a new situation. Some of its members turned their backs on Marxist atheism, while retaining the Marxist criticism of society—with the difference that they now understood themselves as Husain's comrades-in-arms, as *mojahedin*.[34] They conferred a new prestige on the Shi'ite view of history and the Shi'ite ethos in the educated middle classes. Two of their spokesmen made a particular contribution to the change of position on the part of educated persons.

The Iranian writer Jalal Al-e Ahmad (1923–1969) diagnosed the situation of his country as *gharb-zadegī*: Iran was the victim of a poison or infection (*zadegī* means both of these) through the West (*gharb*). Healing required the removal of the external poison and a strengthening of the body's defenses, and the Shi'a of Iran was regarded as the appropriate remedy.[35] The other pioneer thinker from the educated middle classes was Ali Shariati (1933–1977), the son of a clergyman from Mashhad and a fervent admirer of Al-e Ahmad. He had spent some time studying in Paris, where he had read Frantz Fanon's *The Wretched of the Earth*, which he later translated into Farsi.[36] Fanon argued that the peoples of the Third World should not merely expel the colonial rulers from their countries. It was only by killing these rulers that they could liberate themselves from something much worse, namely, the inner dependence on them. This violence had a "detoxifying" effect, liberating the colonized person from his inferiority complex and rehabilitating him in his own eyes. For Fanon, therefore, violence was the only effective instrument for the liberation from oppression.

Ali Shariati sympathized with this anti-colonial glorification of violence and connected it with a new interpretation of the early Shi'a, with which his professors of Islamic studies in Paris had acquainted him.[37] In this view, Ali's party, the Shi'a, in its early period had engaged in a militant struggle for a just social order and against an unjust order, before the Shi'a degenerated into a "black" religion of penitence and self-flagellations. The official "black" Shi'a represented by the clergy was a distortion that must be replaced by the genuine militant "red" Shi'a. When the Shah's regime executed young resistance fighters who were friends of Shariati's in 1972, he declared them to be martyrs whose action had consisted of two elements: the blood they shed and a message. Six years later, one of the rousing slogans of the rebellion against the Shah's regime was generated by his ideas: "Every day 'Ashura, every tomb Karbalā."[38]

In this connection, we must look at the characterization of the United States as the Great Satan. William Beeman has freed this from a mistaken interpretation that helped to give Iran an assured place in the Evangelical scenario of the Last Days as the dwelling place of evil.[39] In Islam, however, Satan is not the same figure as the Antichrist in Christianity. He is not the ruler of the world at the transition to the eschatological millennium—for in Islam, that is the role of the *dajjāl*. Satan is the seducer who turns people aside from the way of God, exactly as we know him from the story of the temptation of Jesus (Matt. 4:1–11). The temptation comes from outside, and is a test where one must prove one's worth by fighting it off. This view is a fundamental element in the Shi'ite worldview, which sees the origin of moral impurity, not in the human being, but as coming from the external world.[40] Scantily clad women, sexual permissiveness, pornography, alcohol, Western music—all these turn Muslims aside from doing what is right. Western culture appears as the great seducer that does everything in its power to sully the inner human being.

Stagings of Martyrdom

The resistance to the aggressive war that Iraq fought against Iran from 1980 to 1988, with the support of the United States, was a testing ground for the new religious practice. In order to resist the assault on its territory by its hated enemy, the Islamic Republic drafted even the poorest of the poor, and indeed even children, for military service, promising them the honorific title of "martyr" and financial support for their families. The insidious plan did not expect the children to fight with weapons: rather, they were to use their little bodies to set off landmines, thus clearing the path to the front line for the army.[41] One little boy who threw himself under a tank with a hand grenade was celebrated as a national hero. Iran officially commemorated this Mohammad Hosein Fahmideh with pride.[42] Willingness to die was proclaimed the test of faith, and martyrdom became a prominent topos in the political self-portrayal of the Islamic Republic.[43]

The late Iranian journalist Freidoune Sahebjam recorded a story told him by a thirteen-year-old Iranian boy in 1982 that almost beggars belief. He and a thousand other children ran over the minefields of Khuzistan in order to clear the path for the Iranian troops. Before he set out, mullahs in the barracks had promised him and his companions that if they were lucky, they would meet the Imam Mahdi in person. And so it was: as mines exploded on all sides around the boy, and his companions were blown to shreds alongside him, he suddenly saw nearby a white horseman bearing the banner of Islam and pointing in the direction of Iraq, shouting: "Run, children! Run over there!"[44] The boy miraculously survived and was taken prisoner by the Iraqis. But since it was a disgrace for a martyr to survive, he could not return either to Iran or to his mother, who was already receiving a pension both for him and for her husband and other sons who had fallen in battle.[45]

There are also accounts from the other side of the front line, from the Iraqis, which are equally difficult to believe. Christoph Reuter cites a journalist's report of an Iraqi machine gunner who heard a sound like a swarm of locusts coming closer and closer and eventually realized that it came from the mouths of thousands of children chanting: "Ya Karbalā, ya Husain, ya Khomeini!" As the children drew near, the machine gunner shot them down as if they were row upon row of bottles, and yet they still came on in waves from behind trenches and hills, clambered over the dead bodies, and ran toward him until they almost rolled over him and he fled from his position. After this onslaught, the journalist, who happened to be on the scene, and a colleague counted more than 23,000 dead bodies, until night came and they had to stop counting. Around the necks of each of the dead children hung a key: "In order—so it was said—that they would be able after their martyrdom to open the gate to paradise."[46]

Last Wills of Martyrs

In the accounts from the war between Iran and Iraq, the martyr's death has a double significance, both military and religious. On the one hand, it is a contribution to the defense of the country, an action that Durkheim in his study of suicide called the altruistic suicide and that he attributed to moral pressure exercised by the troop on the individual soldier.[47] In his presentation of the recent history of the military suicide attack, Joseph Croitoru concludes that the first cases in the Middle East imitated Japanese models, and that the genuinely Islamic element is therefore rather small.[48] However, this element must not be ignored, even if the reference to the well known "Assassins" of the eleventh and twelfth centuries does not take us very far. Tilman Seidensticker has shown that there were accounts of Islamic suicide attacks in the eighteenth century, in the context of the European expansion in South and Southeast Asia. These accounts, which have been overlooked up to now, indicate that the Assassins were not the only precursors.[49]

The wills of martyrs, which were widespread on the Iranian side in the war between Iran and Iraq, give us information about the second dimension, the religious. Werner Schmucker has examined roughly 175 such wills written by Iranian soldiers in 1980–1981. These were subsequently published by third persons in newspapers and periodicals, and were also brought out in the form of anthologies. According to Imam Khomeini, "These wills make one shudder and wake up."[50] Representatives of the Islamic Republic and relatives of those killed were equally interested in these wills. The published texts consist of two parts, the will in the strict sense of the term and a biography written by a third person, often a journalist. The wills were written by soldiers who sensed that their death was approaching and often took the form of a letter. The structure follows the legal formulae of the legacy in inheritance law. After an invocation of the name of God (*bismala*) and verses from the Qur'an comes a justification of the sacrifice of the soldier's life. The martyr gives himself a place here in the passion narrative of the Shi'ite saints. He has heard Husain's despairing cry in the Passion play—"Why have you abandoned me?"—and he has responded: "I am at your command!" He does not abandon Husain. This part of the will, often written in the form of a prayer, is meant to bear witness to a passionate commitment to the sacrifice of his own life, a sacrifice that is affirmed voluntarily and joyfully. This is immediately followed in the will by a declaration in the first person singular, addressed to his parents, brothers and sisters, his wife, the nation, or the Islamic world, explaining the meaning of his death. Then come requests for forgiveness of his faults, as well as material dispositions.

The martyr's sacrifice serves both the good of society and his own self. This deed is a kind of "injection of blood for the organism of society as a whole," an investment in the "divine revolution," vengeance and retaliation.[51] In the eyes of the one who acts in this way, it is a barter with God in which a worthless life is exchanged for an eternal life. Through this action, the self is disciplined and the desiring soul (*nafs*) is extinguished. This is accompanied by an expiation of all guilt.[52] Here we can see the transposition of maxims of Islamic mysticism to dying in battle. This transposition had its origin in the Islamic renaissance in Najaf, and was not truly compatible with the rigorous rejection of every kind of self-killing in classical Islam. Above all, this interpretative pattern goes far beyond the framework of military expediency and ennobles the real war between Iran and Iraq, making it an event in salvation history. Here, the annihilation of the self preached by Sufism takes place. In the real war (in Islamic terminology, in the little jihad), one is offered the chance of spiritual self-disciplining (the great jihad). This view was also put forward in the 1980s by the Egyptian author Abd al-Salam in his book *The Neglected Duty*, and we find it once again in the attacks of September 11, 2001.

Farhad Khosrokhavar points out the contradiction inherent in this conception of the warrior. On the one hand, we have the aggressive militant warrior who loses his life in the battle against the enemies of God; and on the other hand, we have the witness who suffers in defense, who sacrifices himself for the truth and thus attains redemption. It was above all Ali Shariati who drew a systematic distinction between dying for the faith and death in war, since dying for the faith is not generated by any kind of necessity to defend one's country, but by the free decision of the individual to renounce the world of *jahiliyya* and to become a sacrifice for Husain. The community to which this decision is related is no longer a territorial entity. Khosrokhavar links this with the transnational Islamic community in whose name the members of al-Qaeda act. The kind of individualism that finds expression in the section of the Iranian martyrs' wills that justify their death is heading towards a detachment from national necessities and the assumption of traits of a universal religious ethics of conviction. This means that we could speak of an adoption and transformation of western individualism.[53]

The Category of Fundamentalism

Since the 1978–1979 Iranian revolution, "Islamic fundamentalism" has conventionally been regarded in the media and in politics as dogmatic, intolerant, and violent. Since it threatens the bases of a peaceful coexistence in human society, no holds are barred in the fight against it, even if this should entail the infringement of established law. Mark Juergensmeyer, an expert in the field of fundamentalism, has made a critical examination of this rhetoric. His conclusion is that one must study "antifundamentalism" in order to comprehend the terrified reactions to fundamentalism.[54] Neither he nor the researchers at the Fundamentalism Project of the University of Chicago have identified the exercise of violence as a constitutive characteristic of fundamentalism. After the publication of five volumes containing a wealth of empirical studies, three of these researchers have drawn an interim conclusion that describes this phenomenon as follows:

Fundamentalism, in this usage, refers to a discernible pattern of religious militancy by which self-styled "true believers" attempt to arrest the erosion of religious identity, fortify the borders of the religious community, and create viable alternatives to secular institutions and behaviors.[55]

They do not assert that such groups *could not* become violent; the point is only that their militancy is not necessarily martial. These groups too speak a language of violence, but this does not lead necessarily and inevitably to a practice of violence. The rhetoric of violence does not ineluctably lead to de facto violence.[56] In this case too, one must also bear in mind the dynamic of the conflict. When violence is used against fundamentalist groups, or they believe that their existence is threatened, their attitude to violence changes, and they can employ violence to protect religious communality: "Fundamentalist violence, per se, is a response to government oppression and/or to the growth or empowerment of social groups deemed threatening to fundamentalist interests."[57] In such exceptional situations, the use of violence can be a religious precept, and the believers use every means to defend their community, as the Maccabees once did—as a performative act of faith that gives proof of their willingness to die for the truth.[58] It is only an "antifundamentalism" that interprets this as a community that is intolerant and violent as a matter of *principle*.

When fundamentalists come to power, as in Iran, their relationship to violence can change. Like the Jacobins of the French Revolution (to whom Shmuel N. Eisenstadt compares them), they can launch a violent transformation of society in keeping with their own ideas. In this process, they follow a political program that is typical of the tensions of the modern period.[59] Iran is not unique here: the attempt to shape society in accordance with religious principles has made its appearance in democratic states too.[60]

The United States Remains the Captive of
Its Own Assumptions

When U.S. President Jimmy Carter championed the respect for human rights during his period in office (1976–1980), not a few Iranians hoped that the necessary change of system in their country would occur peaceably. The outcome was completely different, since the U.S. administration took the side of the Shah—a decision that made it a partisan of the violent Caliph Yazid in the eyes of the Shi'a. All the fury that had built up against the Shah's regime now erupted against the U.S. administration. Puppets depicting Carter were burnt in the streets of Teheran, and the U.S. embassy in that city was occupied for more than a year.

Looking back, Gary Sick, who was a member of the National Security Council under President Carter with responsibility for Iran, has related how difficult it was for those with political responsibility to make sense of the events in Iran—the contradiction between what was happening under Khomeini and the Western tradition of secularizing revolutions was too blatant. No one had been able even to guess that a revolution was beginning. "We are all prisoners of our own cultural assumptions, more than we dare to admit," he adds self-critically.

Khomeini's call for the establishment of a religious philosopher-king, the *velayat-e faqih,* and clerical management of political institutions according to religious law was so unexpected, so alien to existing political traditions that it was less a surprise than an embarrassment. The participation of the church in a revolutionary movement was neither new nor particularly disturbing, but the notion of a popular revolution leading to the establishment of a theocratic state seemed so unlikely as to be absurd.[61]

Nevertheless, these self-critical words are still based on an interpretative pattern of the "cognitive distancing" type that we have already seen in the persecution of cults in the United States, namely an intentional disassociation from something for which one has a share in responsibility. They ignore the fact that the type of modernization conducted by the United States was one cause of the rise in the numbers of those who had suffered degradation, and then found protection in the Shi'ite networks, and interpreted their experience in the concepts of the Shi'ite tradition of suffering. Instead, Iran is demonized and becomes the location of something utterly incomprehensible. A comparison from the science of religion may be somewhat daring, but it will help to illustrate this point. We know from research into the persecutions of witches in the seventeenth century that most of those accused of witchcraft were women to whom the "victim of witchcraft" had refused at some earlier date to display a solidarity that tradition demanded. The "victim" therefore feared the resentment of these women and charged them with responsibility for some misfortune that had happened to him or her. Accusations of witchcraft were preceded by a breach of moral obligations on the part of the "victim of witchcraft."[62] Something similar may have played a role in the demonization of Islamist Iran by the United States. The United States was a contributory factor to the genesis of the Iranian hostility—which it now persecutes as something demonic.

CHAPTER 5

"The Party of God" Intervenes in the War: Lebanon, 1975–2000

One of the most respected Shi'ite clerics in Lebanon, Sayyid Muhammad Husain Fadlallah, proclaimed the Islamic revolution in Iran in 1978–1979 an "earthquake."[1] Suddenly, something that had hitherto been unthinkable—the enforcement of Islam as religion *and* as state—was now within the realm of possibility. This epochal event mobilized the Shi'ites in Lebanon too, who had enjoyed close family and religious ties with the Iranians for many generations. They led the apolitical life of a poor rural population in the Bekaa Valley on the border with Syria and in the south on the border with Israel. However, it was impossible to have the same success in Lebanon as in Iran, since (as Fadlallah was very well aware) the general conditions were too different. Seventeen (from 1996 onward, eighteen) faith communities (plural *tawā'if*) were officially recognized in Lebanon,[2] which has been governed since 1860 by the large faith communities according to a proportional system. Since 1943, the highest offices in the state have been allocated according to the following ratio: the office of the president of the state goes to the Christian Maronites, that of the prime minister to the Sunnis, and that of the president of parliament to the Shi'ites. This rather insignificant office was given to the Shi'ites only because of the large landowners in their ranks, not because of the size of their share in the total population, which would in fact have entitled them to a much greater share in government. The Peace Accord of Ta'if (1989), which put an end to the civil war that had raged since 1975, did not entail any considerable change to this societal order, despite the enormous increase in the prestige of the Shi'ites from the 1960s onward; the only difference was that now the Christians and the Muslims received an equal number of seats in parliament.

In the mid 1970s, the societal order lost its equilibrium when Palestinians who had fled to Lebanon became active in the political and military spheres. The instability grew when Israel invaded southern Lebanon in 1978 and advanced as far as Beirut. In 1982, Syria likewise intervened. The civil war spread in a total of seventeen individual wars in which the local faith communities fought with and against one another in shifting coalitions, alternately supported and opposed by Israel, Syria, Iran, France, and the United States.[3] Traditionally, Lebanese Christians could rely on the support of France and the United States, and occasionally of Israel, while the Sunni Muslims and the PLO could rely on Arab states. Initially, the Shi'ites had no such protective power; this changed only with the advent of the Islamic Republic of Iran. Syria too looked after Shi'ite interests. Israel withdrew its troops in 2000; thereafter, it occupied only a small part of the country.

The Structural Power of the Lebanese Faith Communities

In the twentieth century, faith communities in Lebanon were still autonomous entities whose leaders resisted all attempts to introduce a state family law that would be independent of religion. In this, they were continuing an old tradition. The law of the preceding state, the Ottoman empire, made that state essentially Sunni, with the result that it granted a limited legal autonomy to the non-Islamic communities; but the Shi'ites were the only group that were not given any autonomy. Even after the collapse of the Ottoman empire in the aftermath of World War I, the faith communities retained their competence in legislation and jurisdiction with regard to birth, death, marriage, divorce, adoption, and inheritance. Their structural power was increased further by relationships between patrons and clients and by the concentration of the various confessions in particular regions. This wide-reaching autonomy allowed them to take their military defense into their own hands during the civil war and to maintain militias. This meant that the violence they practiced in the civil war had a religious legitimation, either Christian or Islamic: they were all profoundly marked by a martial ethos.[4] In the Peace Accord of Ta'if, the religious leaders once again thwarted the attempt to anchor in state law at least a possibility of choice between a civil and a religious family law.[5]

One consequence of this societal order was the dependence of the Lebanese on their faith communities, irrespective of whether or not they were personal believers. In a certain sense, the situation in Lebanon was the mirror inversion of the situation of Christianity in western Europe. In most western European countries, we typically find a crumbling of links to church communities, accompanied by a continuation of views connected to religious faith, what Grace Davie has called "believing without belonging." Samir Khalaf has shown that the relationship in Lebanon is exactly the opposite. On the one hand, empirical data indicate a decline in individual religiosity in Lebanon, but on the other hand, the attachment to faith communities and the intensity of the social relationships within these communities are on the increase.[6] Not even academics and intellectuals were an exception to this rule: in the choice of their marriage partners or of the teachers of their children, they gave the preference to coreligionists. Why did this happen in Lebanon? We shall look for an answer to this question by investigating the Shi'ite community. Precisely the least prestigious of the faith communities owes its ascent to the growing uncertainty and dangers, although one must also bear in mind that the success of the Shi'ites in Iran and their solidarity with their Lebanese coreligionists made a considerable contribution to this success.

The Mobilization of the Shi'ites and the Disappearance of Their Imam Musa al-Sadr

Like the Christian Maronites to the north of Beirut, the Sunnis in the cities, or the Druses in the mountainous regions, the Shi'ites too had formed regional sociomoral milieus in the Bekaa Valley on the border with Syria and in the south of the country. The rapid economic development between 1950 and 1975 transformed these milieus. Alongside the traditional classes of landowners and dependent peasants, a middle class of merchants and academics came into being, and Marxist ideas penetrated the Shiʿite community. An expanding agrarian capitalism drove many Shiʿites from the countryside into the cities, especially Beirut. These changes were speeded up when the Shiʿite community in Tyre appointed the cleric Sayyid Musa al-Sadr as its head in 1959. He had been born in Iran and had studied in Najaf and Qom. He came from a highly respected family that could trace its genealogy back to the third Imam Husain, and he was related to powerful families in the Iranian clergy. Another factor in his appointment to a position in Lebanon was the fact that some of his ancestors had emigrated long ago from the Lebanese region to Iran. When the Lebanese parliament established a Shiʿite supreme council, al-Sadr defeated a candidate of the Shiʿite landowners and was elected its first head.[7]

The situation of the Shiʿites in southern Lebanon worsened in the 1970s, when Palestinian fighters used the region as a base for military attacks on Israel. Although the Shiʿites believed that the struggle of the Palestinians was justified, these clashes put a strain on the relationship, since Shiʿite villages suffered the most under the Israeli reprisals. Now, however, the Shiʿites were no longer willing to submit to their fate as in the past. In his sermons on the Shiʿite tale about their origins in Karbalā, Musa al-Sadr abandoned the ideal of a passive endurance of injustice. Like other Shiʿite clergy in Najaf, the city of the theologians in Iraq, he too had come to take an activist view: the Shiʿites should stop lamenting the injustice that had been inflicted on Husain and his followers, and they should no longer restrict their remembrance of Karbalā to mourning, processions, self-flagellations, and Passion plays in the month of Muharram. Rather, they should become noncompliant, men of vengeance who revolted against the tyranny. They should no longer be content merely to cultivate their emotions—they should *act*.

In his speeches, Musa al-Sadr employed metaphors chosen from the repertoire of Shiʿite tradition, metaphors that justified decision-making and responsibility. For example, he declared on ʿAshura Day in 1974 in an Islamic educational establishment:

A great sacrifice was needed to shake consciences and stir feelings. The event of Karbala was that sacrifice. . . . Imam Husain put his family, his force, and even his life, in the balance over against tyranny and corruption. Then the Islamic world burst forth with this unprecedented act, this revolution. This revolution did not die in the sands of Karbala, it flowed into the life stream of the Islamic world, and passed from generation to generation, even to our day. It is a deposit placed in our hands so that we may profit from it, that we draw from it as from a source a new reform, a new position, a new movement, a new revolution to repel the darkness, to stop tyranny, and to pulverize evil. Brothers, line up in the row of your choice: that of tyranny or that of Husain. I am certain that you will not choose anything but the row of revolution and martyrdom for the realization of justice and the destruction of tyranny.[8]

The demand was drastic: the Shi'a must not remain a mourning ritual. It must change, and give an answer to social distress.[9]

The new activism found its first expression in demands made to the Lebanese state. In 1974, in a speech to 75,000 persons in the Bekaa Valley, Musa al-Sadr accused members of the government in Beirut of neglecting the elementary necessities of life for the Shi'ites, such as schooling or a water supply. In the same year, he founded the "Organization of the Disenfranchised" (harakat al-mahrūmīn), and a year later, the armed movement Amal (this word means "hope"; its letters are an abbreviation for "Lebanese resistance movements"). This movement was founded before the Revolution in Iran, and many of the later Iranian revolutionaries were trained here in Lebanon.[10] All those who joined Amal committed themselves to a charter that rejects (in the name of God) the separation between societal and political life and religion that is customary in Europe.[11] The wonderful order of the cosmos is the proof of God's existence. The second maxim in the charter is the re-establishing of the true Islamic communality,[12] based on jihad in the sense of working on one's own self and on society. In this first phase of Shi'ite activism, jihad is not restricted to the case of the violent struggle in defense of Islamic territory, but is understood as a comprehensive struggle to apply the Islamic order both in the conduct of one's own life and in society.[13] This leads to the further goals of fighting against the lack of freedom and against poverty, against imperialism and Zionism, and for Arab national patriotism. Amal sees itself as a movement of people who are concerned about the future and take responsibility on behalf of the disenfranchised. It does so in the spirit of 'Ashura, with its revolutionary opposition to falsehood and injustice.

Through this movement, the Lebanese Shi'ites began a struggle for the "just order." And they had every reason to do so: the Shi'ites were more numerous than the other faith communities of the country, the Maronite Christians, the Druses, and the Sunnis, but they were socially and politically despised. This too prompted them to define their situation in the light of the passion narrative of Karbalā, while however deducing new revolutionary options for action like the Shi'ites in Iran. In the coming years, the Shi'ite community itself founded the social institutions that it would actually have expected the state to provide. This innovation was especially plausible under the circumstances of the civil war, since the Shi'ites could not expect that the Lebanese state would guarantee even the most elementary requirements of life, nor that it would protect them against military attacks. This made it wholly logical for the Lebanese Shi'ites in this period to begin the foundation of benevolent associations that devoted themselves to activities such as the care of the sick and education.

When Israel invaded southern Lebanon for the first time in 1978, Amal took on the task of protecting the villages. At that time, the secular political groups among the Shi'ites, including Marxist groups, lost the competition with Musa al-Sadr's religious movement; the interpretation of the world as "full of injustice" smoothed the transition from Marxism to the Shi'a. Thanks to Musa al-Sadr's achievement in leading the community safely through the difficult 1960s and 1970s and strengthening its self-awareness, he was greatly venerated, and this found expression in the address "Imam," in which the meaning "Mahdi" (the Islamic Messiah) resonated quietly.

This made it all the more horrifying when this man one day mysteriously disappeared. After a meeting with President Mu'ammar Gadhafi in Libya in August 1978, Musa al-Sadr was never seen again. The Libyan authorities asserted that he and his companions had left the country in the direction of Rome on Alitalia flight 881 on August 31, 1978, but he never arrived in Rome. Many rumors about these events have circulated up to the present day; it is highly probable that the Libyan leader Gadhafi was personally involved.[14] His followers, however, interpreted his disappearance in the conceptual language of their expectations of the end-time: because of the overwhelming power of his enemies, the true Imam has gone into hiding. Soon, he will appear again and bring about a just order of society. Many of his adherents even call themselves *sadriyyin*, as if they had stopped at the hidden Imam in the way that has so often occurred throughout Shi'ite history. Even as late as 1998, I have seen posters in Beirut with the picture of Imam Musa.

The Birth of Hezbollah, the Party of God

Amal saw itself as a Lebanese nationalist movement, which, despite all its criticism of the distribution of power in the country, did not fundamentally call into question the social order in Lebanon. After the success of the Iranian revolution, however, more and more voices were raised in support of an Islamization of Lebanon. There was a definite parting of the ways in 1982, when Israel advanced further into Lebanon beyond the areas that it already controlled: while Amal under the leadership of Nabih Berri joined the "National Salvation Committee," Husain al-Musawi, a former schoolmaster, and like-minded persons founded an Islamist offshoot of Amal in Baalbek. Other Shi'ite groups split off at the same time and became supporters of a Shi'ite Islamism.[15] Whereas the leaders of Amal wanted to resolve the conflict with Israel via political agreements and treaties, the new group gave the priority to armed resistance to Israel and the struggle for an Islamic order.

In 1982, with the help of Iranian revolutionary guards sent to assist Lebanon in the war against Israel, Husain al-Musawi succeeded in founding the nucleus of a new organization, the "Party of God" (Arabic *hizb Allāh*), whose name alludes to a verse in the Qur'an:

Whosoever makes God his friend, and His messenger, and the believers—the party of God, they are the victors.
O believers, take not as your friends those of them, who were given the Book before you [i.e., Jews and Christians], and the unbelievers, who take your religion in mockery and as a sport.   (Sura 5:56–57)[16]

Initially, the new Shi'ite group kept a low profile. Despite what its name suggests, it was not tightly organized. Hezbollah was a loose network of clergy and their students, above all from the Bekaa Valley, with diverging religious, local, and political loyalties. Later, clergy from Beirut joined, and the group became established in southern Lebanon too. All the divergences within Hezbollah were counterbalanced by the authority of Khomeini and by another clergyman who was highly revered by the Shi'ites, Sayyid Muhammad Husain Fadlallah.[17]

Fadlallah was born in Najaf in Iraq in 1935 and grew up there. Hezbollah regarded him as their spiritual authority, although he himself had no desire to take on the responsibility of leadership. He saw the Iraqi Ayatollah Khu'i, not Ayatollah Khomeini, as the binding authority and the "source to follow."[18] It was only in 1995 that he himself attained this highest grade of Shi'ite authority. Like Musa al-Sadr, Fadlallah possessed the charisma (*baraka*) of the *sayyid,* the descendant of the Prophet. In 1966, he left Najaf, where Khomeini was in exile at that time, and moved to Beirut, where he became the head of a growing community of Shi'ites who had fled from the Israeli military attacks in the south of the country. In Beirut, he founded a *husayniyya,* an institution dedicated to the remembrance of the martyrdom of Husain that included a mosque, a youth club, a school, a hospital, and a newspaper publishing company. His sermons united the anti-imperialistic rhetoric of the nationalists with Islamist situation analyses: Israel wanted to seize Lebanon and posed a threat to Islam as a whole. In this way, Fadlallah made a significant contribution to the shift in solidarity on the part of the Lebanese Shi'ites from the pan-Arabic communality to Islamism. He died in 2010.

The war in Lebanon entered a new phase in 1982 when the Israeli army advanced as far as Beirut in order to destroy the Palestinian Liberation Organization. The Israeli army did indeed withdraw in 1985 from the regions south of Beirut, but it kept one zone under its control, including areas adjacent to the territory it had already occupied in 1978. Another event in 1982 was the arrival in Lebanon of troops from the United States and France, at the request of the Christians; these soldiers saw themselves as "peacekeepers," although they took the side of the Christians. In the following years, Lebanon witnessed the hijacking of planes, the taking of hostages, and bomb attacks.

In all this violence, a new type of death in battle emerged, the self-chosen death as a martyr. Since this was practiced at the same time in the war between Iran and Iraq, we must assume a connection; at any rate, it was not yet practiced when Israel first invaded southern Lebanon in 1978. Now, in addition to those who fell in the fight against Israel and were venerated as martyrs (*shuhadā,* the "battle martyrs"), those who had brought about their deaths with their own weapons were also venerated as martyrs (*istishhādiyūn,* "self-killing martyrs").[19] The first attack of this kind took place in November 1982. The Israeli high command in Tyre was the goal of a suicide attack in which seventy-four persons died—a few weeks after an incident in Nabatiyya which had cost the Israelis the last remnant of sympathy on the part of the Shi'ites of southern Lebanon.[20] A group called Islamic Jihad ("Struggle") claimed responsibility for this deed. In April 1983, the U.S. embassy in West Beirut was attacked, following the same pattern. Even more destructive were the attacks by suicide bombers on the barracks of the American and French troops in Beirut on the morning of October 26, 1983, when 246 Americans and 58 Frenchmen lost their lives. Western media and public opinion were shocked. In her novel *Inshallah,* Oriana Fallaci paints in almost obscene tones the terrible sight that awaited the helpers. Excerpts from the telephone call in which once again a mysterious Islamic Jihad claimed responsibility have been published.[21] The representatives of Hezbollah, who went public only at a later date, denied any responsibility for the attacks and insisted that those who were responsible were not in any sense an organization. This may in fact be true; it is possible that the Arabic name was employed only in order to interpret the act as a military action against the occupation of Lebanon, an action that was legitimate in religious terms. The type of organization of these early groups has been compared to a cluster of grapes: individual cells operated independently of each other, linked only loosely via persons in the background.[22] The concept of a "telephone chain" has also been invoked. Two further attacks on American institutions followed in Kuwait and Beirut in December 1983 and September 1984.

It was only three years after its foundation that Hezbollah went public with "An Open Letter" to "the disenfranchised in Lebanon and the world"[23] on February 15, 1985, the first anniversary of the death of Sheikh Raghib Harb, a cleric from southern Lebanon who had been killed by an Israeli commando.[24] The Open Letter declared Raghib Harb a martyr and a model for all upright Muslims, and presented the Party of God as a part of the "Islamic nation in the world" and as a protagonist in the struggle against the injustice that Muslims suffered throughout the world. Hezbollah did not want to have one specific armed section, since each individual must become a soldier when the summons to the jihad demanded this. Hezbollah goes so far as to claim to be the advocate of the disenfranchised and the humiliated all over the world and to fight on behalf of them all against tyrannical and arrogant states. The principal enemy is the United States and its ally Israel, who are accused of responsibility for the attacks on Lebanon, the destruction of villages, the killing of children, and the massacres of Palestinians in the refugee camps of Sabra and Shatila, as well as for the profanation of sacred places. The only possible response to such aggression is the willingness to make sacrifices, since the only way to regain dignity is through bloody sacrifices. In this letter, Hezbollah also defended the attacks on the U.S. embassy and the barracks in 1983 as righteous punishment, without however claiming responsibility for these acts.[25] The intention was to compel the Israelis, the Americans, and the French troops to withdraw. When this took place in 1985, the celebrations were great.[26]

No one had ever previously imagined that a handful of Muslims who were prepared to stop at nothing could succeed in driving American, French, and Israeli troops from the country. But that was what happened! Sayyid Fadlallah praised their action as an "uprising against their own fear." Martin Kramer has summarized his view as follows: "The great powers inspire 'alarm and fear' among the oppressed, who have no more than 'children's toys' to mount their opposition. By conquering their fear through acceptance of the virtue of martyrdom, the oppressed can evoke alarm and fear among their oppressors."[27]

Martyr Operations Between Individual Decision and Communal Responsibility

In tables that give an overview of suicide attacks throughout the world in the twentieth century, Robert A. Pape lists five attacks in Lebanon against American and French troops in 1983–1984; eleven against military bases established by Israel between November 1982 and June 1985; and twenty against the South Lebanese army, which was supported by Israel, between July 1985 and November 1986.[28] In his list, however, Pape leaves open the question of when the attack was the work of a military death squad and when it was a martyr operation.[29] At any rate, this overview shows that these attacks were organized and not spontaneous individual actions by especially convinced Muslims, although this is how they were frequently remembered.

Hezbollah lost a total of 1,281 of its fighters in the war against the Israeli army between 1982 and 2000. They died in military clashes, and each of them was honored as a *shahīd*. In addition, there were those who were killed by their own weapons in martyrdom operations (*al-'amaliyāt al-istishhādiya*): *al-ishtishhādī al-mujāhid*. There were only twelve of these, less than a third of all the suicide attacks.[30] In a later declaration about its identity and its goals, Hezbollah lavished particular praise on the special willingness of its fighters to die. They had inflicted grave military and mental damage on the enemy, and at the same time strengthened the morale of the Islamic nation.

There was, however, one difficulty in Islam with regard to a self-killing of this kind: in Islam, suicide is an unforgivable sin, and anyone who commits it goes to hell,[31] even when it is committed in battle.[32] This means that convinced Muslims would be the first to have scruples in the preparation and the carrying out of such operations, as a leading Hezbollah cleric openly admitted in an interview with the Persian newspaper *Kayhan* in 1986: "The Muslim fighter needed answers to many questions," said Shaykh 'Abd al-Karim 'Ubayd, a Hizbullah cleric. . . . "Is resistance to the occupation obligatory on religious grounds? What about the question of self-martyrdom?"[33] For an Islamic warrior who kills himself, the fine line between eternal salvation and eternal damnation is narrow and dangerous. In addition to an explosives expert, it was always necessary to have a cleric, whose duty it was to authorize the interpretation of the act as martyrdom. Sayyid Fadlallah's comment was cautious and balanced. He himself denied that he had assured the Shi'ites who attacked the barracks that they would fall in the jihad and go to paradise; he said that he had never delivered a fatwa (a legal judgment) on this subject. At the same time, however, he made public statements that could also be understood as approval. In one address, he asked the rhetorical question: What is the difference between one who goes to war and knows that he will die after he has killed ten persons, and one who dies while he is killing them?[34] For Fadlallah, however, this form of combat was clearly restricted to situations of war and to enemy soldiers.

The lower clergy, whose authority was Khomeini, had far fewer reservations: the director of an Islamic institute in Tyre declared his conviction that those who had carried out suicide operations against the enemy were now in fact in paradise.[35] Iranian theologians had long taken a clear position that was the product of theological reflection. As early as 1963, as already mentioned, Ayatollah Taleqani gave a speech in Najaf in which he praised the conscious self-sacrifice of the martyr as a self-annihilation in God, thereby transforming a spiritual practice of the Sufis into a legitimation of suicide. Later on, in the 1980s, Khomeini sanctioned this position by means of a fatwa.[36] Finally, in the war between Iran and Iraq, he summoned young men and even children to sacrifice their lives in defense of the Islamic Republic. The most significant development for the Muslims in Lebanon was the individualization of the martyr's death as an exemplary act of faith. As yet, the testimony of faith and the defense of Islamic territory against an invader, jihad and *shahāda,* were linked here: although the martyr's death was the action of an individual, in Lebanon it still remained linked to the defense of the country against foreign aggressors.

This kind of self-killing always needs the approval of the religious authorities and of one's coreligionists, for otherwise it would not be martyrdom, but merely suicide. Over the years, however, the criteria for drawing this distinction had changed. In the Passion play, which was performed by the Shi'ites in Lebanon too, it was not possible for everyone who was willing to lay down his life in the fight against the unbelievers to become a martyr. In this tradition, women were excluded from martyrdom, and men were permitted to choose it only if they were not yet married. Many Shi'ite clergy in Lebanon were still maintaining this position in the 1980s. Martin Kramer suggests that in view of the early age at which men in the Lebanese Shi'ite community got married, this meant that candidates were available only from a very narrow agegroup.[37] But these restrictions had already been relaxed, or abandoned altogether, in the 1980s. Khomeini held that it was no longer necessary for parents to give their assent to the involvement of their children in martyrdom operations. Fadlallah agreed and declared in an interview that girls and boys were obliged, even without the consent of their parents, to take part in the armed struggle.[38] The Egyptian text *A Neglected Duty* (1981) presents a similar position. Its author, a Sunni, does not regard the parents' assent to the act of martyrdom as necessary, since the struggle is an individual obligation. It is not necessary to ask one's parents and family for their assent.[39] As had already happened in Iran and in Egyptian jihad groups, so now in Lebanon martyrdom has become a decision taken by the individual—and no longer only by men, but also by women. The assent of one's family is no longer absolutely necessary; even in the case of a married man, his wife's consent is not needed. This detaches the decision from the family and makes it completely dependent now on the assent of the faith community.

When we look at the acts of violence in this way, we recognize the importance of the role played here by the faith communities. It was only thanks to the authorization by the clergy and the assent of the coreligionists that an act of violence could become a sacred action. The founder of Hezbollah, Husain al-Musawi, stated this with remarkable frankness in an interview with the Iranian newspaper *Kayhan* in 1986. He and his followers, he said, had given Islamic Jihad "political and moral support so that it would not look as if their actions were of a criminal nature. In this sense, if it had not been for our propaganda, their actions would have been condemned by the public as criminal acts. We have tried to make the public understand that their action was in the nature of jihad, launched by the oppressed against the oppressor."[40] Fadlallah attributed a further significance to this violence. The global arrogance of the West was a global paganism, and only intrepid Islamic fighters could put the fear of God into the West.[41] By overcoming his own fear and provoking terror and dismay in the unbelievers, the perpetrator sacrifices himself for the power and greatness of God.

The withdrawal of the United States and France and the partial withdrawal of Israel from Lebanon meant a gradual end to the martyrdom operations, the last of which were carried out in the nineties against the Israeli army. Fadlallah had already declared publicly at the end of 1985 that such operations should be carried out only when they would bring about a political or military change that was proportionate to the suffering that a human being experiences when he turns his body into a bomb.[42] He believed that this proportionality no longer existed after the withdrawal of the Americans, the French, and Israel.

Hezbollah as an Actor in Civil Society

The decision to sacrifice one's life for the community was both a personal one by the fighter and a decision by his religious reference group.

This meant that the responsibility for the act must also be borne by the faith community. From the 1980s on, a whole network of Shi'ite institutions had come into existence, financed by the *zakāt,* the voluntary alms *zadaqa,* and the fifth part of profits that Shi'ites owed to their spiritual leader; money also came from Iran. In this way, the Shi'ite spiritual leaders became the founders and heads of social and economic institutions that grew steadily as the years went by.[43]

In 1982, in response to the renewed Israeli invasion of Lebanon, the Shi'ites set up a "Martyrs Foundation" in order to give support to the families of Islamic fighters who had been killed in action.[44] By the end of the civil war in 1990, 1,281 had fallen, including twelve suicide martyrs. Because of its charitable, non-profit-making character, the Martyrs Foundation of Hezbollah was officially recognized by the Lebanese state in 1988.[45] Many other social foundations that were set up in the 1980s did extensive work in the rebuilding of houses that had been destroyed in the war, in the construction of mosques, schools, and clinics, in the provision of water and electricity, and in garbage disposal in the run-down Shi'ite quarters of Beirut.[46] Such services certainly bound those who benefited from them to the Shi'ite institutions, but it would be naïve to think that this was their real goal. Dima Danawi is wrong to see them as the carrot that (together with the stick) was intended to win over the Lebanese to the militant Shi'a: the suspicion that the social activities were the product of political tactics fails to recognize the internal momentum of the Shi'ite activism. As shown above, support of the needy is a religious duty for Muslims. The charitable activities were not restricted to their coreligionists, but helped Lebanese Christians too, since the development of these social institutions went hand in hand with a policy of "opening up" vis-à-vis the other Lebanese faith communities.[47] The case of Hezbollah allows us to observe how a homogenizing social capital can turn into a bridge-building social capital. The situation of the country, at war with Israel, played a role too, since Hezbollah boasted of being the only party in Lebanon that had never abandoned its resistance to the Israeli occupying power. As an especially consistent resistance organization, Hezbollah sought contact with the Christian churches in the country and was respected even by non-Shi'ite Lebanese. Further evidence of its claim to represent the interests of the country was the participation by Hezbollah in the parliamentary elections in Lebanon and its efforts to form coalitions with other religious groups.

In this social matrix, it was possible for a new form of communal religiosity to emerge, centered on the cult of the martyrs. Not a few of the almost 1,300 Shiʿites who had fallen in battle were married, and left widows and children. The Martyrs Foundation was charged with the support of these families, and Danawi's study presents a vivid picture of the kind of help they received. Above all, this was thoroughly organized. The foundation ensured that the families received preferential treatment in the Hezbollah hospitals, which had a higher standard than the state clinics. Similarly, the orphans received free tuition at one of the Hezbollah schools. The intensity and the manner of the propagation of Shiʿite religiosity in these schools can be seen in a survey carried out by the foundation in the schools and educational institutions, in which 85 percent of the children who were asked what they wanted to become later on replied: "engineer," "doctor," or "martyr"; more than 50 percent wanted to become martyrs.[48] The conventional explanation of the self-chosen martyrdom is that this must be the fruit of despair, but this is untenable when one bears in mind that these schools are often better than the state schools and that non-Shiʿite families too send their children to them. Here, martyrdom is rather the expression of altruism, of a willingness to sacrifice one's own life for the community. There is evidence from Palestine that the great heroism displayed by Islamist groups filled believers with pride and gave them a consciousness of strength.[49] The children's answers look like evidence of such a view in Lebanon too. The Shiʿite faith community, once wretchedly poor and depoliticized, had gained power and prosperity through its activism. This, however, does not exclude the possibility that the perpetrator himself may have had a different motive. Individual studies of suicide attackers have shown that the desperate situation of many young people in the Middle East is fertile ground for martyrs.[50]

One branch of the Martyrs Foundation took on the task of preserving the remembrance of the dead. Memorabilia were often placed in small museums in the apartments of the deceased. Halal Jaber describes her visit to Salah, the widow of a martyr, who proudly displayed the video of the events in May 1995, when her husband drove a car full of explosives into an Israeli convoy and killed twelve Israeli soldiers. She and her husband came from southern Lebanon, and had been forced to flee from the Israeli troops. Salah was informed about the plan in advance, but she could not prevent her husband from carrying it out, nor did she wish to do so. His photographs adorned the walls of the living room.[51] In other cases, as in Iran, the family displayed the will the martyr had drawn up before his death.

Within the framework of the Martyrs Foundation, one institution took care of the bereaved of both the suicide martyrs and the military martyrs and ensured that a benefactor would be found to act like a "godfather" to the children as they grew up. A women's project looked after the women, and another institution with both salaried employees and voluntary workers took care of the needs of the families. Although the great majority of those who received this aid were Shi'ites, Lebanese Christians were certainly not excluded from these services as a matter of principle. In this connection, we should note that there were also Christians, from Orthodox families and less frequently from Catholic families, who got involved in the struggle against the Israelis and their Lebanese allies, and lost their lives thereby. Joyce M. Davis has studied the case of one such Christian woman martyr.[52]

Faith Communities in Times of Crisis: A Source of Identity and Solidarity

At the end of the Lebanese civil war, the faith communities were even stronger than they had been at its beginning. This was especially true of the Shi'ites.[53] Before the war, members of one and the same faith community had been scattered over the country, but the escalating violence encouraged the tendency to draw together in one territory. The faith communities were disentangled in territorial terms and laid claim to sovereignty over a territory of their own.

In this context, Hezbollah acquired even more powers. It extended its jurisdiction from family law to other disputes and set up its own court system, with possibilities of appeal on several levels, in the regions where it was dominant.[54] This made Hezbollah, like other faith communities in Lebanon, the source of a new communalism. Samir Khalaf has offered the following diagnosis of the internal dimension of this process: in Lebanon, religious loyalties became the source of communal solidarity and a power that both bound people together and separated them into different communities. According to Khalaf, people seek protection in their faith communities in situations where they are threatened by war and violence:

More and more Lebanese today are brandishing their confessionalism . . . as both emblem and armor. Emblem, because confessional identity has become the most viable medium for asserting presence and securing vital needs and benefits. It is only when an individual is placed within a confessional context that his ideas and assertions are rendered meaningful or worthwhile. Confessionalism is also being used as armor, because it has become a shield against real or imagined threats. The more vulnerable the emblem, the thicker is the armor. Conversely, the thicker the armor, the more vulnerable and paranoid other communities become. It is precisely this dialectic between threatened communities and the urge to seek shelter in cloistered worlds which has plagued Lebanon for so long.[55]

Khalaf's prognosis is gloomy. The local faith community becomes a total institution; identity is reterritorialized; and the condition and the future of Lebanon are determined not by a living civil society but by the conflict between hostile communities.[56]

Once again, we are confronted here by the same ambivalence that we have seen when we looked at the forms that religions take in civil society. It is indeed true that the power of the faith communities has increased, and that one contributory factor in the case of the Shi'ite was the glorification of the resistance to Israel and of martyrdom; but one must not overlook the opposite trends, which Stephan Rosiny has well described with regard to Hezbollah:

In addition to their guerilla war, the success of Hezbollah is based on three further factors. Through a tight-knit network of educational institutions, social-charitable offers of assistance, and measures to establish an infrastructure, Hezbollah succeeded in winning over the allegiance of considerable portions of the Shi'ite population. Through their competent work in parliament and in local administrations, they have won respect beyond the boundaries of their own confession. And finally, they conduct an elaborate information and propaganda activity.[57]

Precisely because the social bond is not primarily based on calculations of political usefulness, but is rooted in a religious definition of the situation, the strengthening of religious communality can also promote an ethics of conviction that attaches a higher value to the protection of one's coreligionists and to the national independence of Lebanon than to the risky continuation of a violent struggle against Israel. The religious practice of Hezbollah, known as jihad, should not be narrowed down to military attacks on Israel or other enemies; it includes all those actions that contribute to the establishment of an Islamic civil order. Despite its transformation into a Lebanese charitable network, however, Hezbollah kept its place on the U.S. and Israeli lists of terror organizations. In the summer of 2006, when some Israeli soldiers were kidnapped and Israel responded not (as had usually been the case) with negotiations for their release, but with a war intended to excise the "cancer" of Hezbollah from the body of Lebanon,[58] the other face of jihad resurfaced, namely, that of the armed struggle. As in the case of the insubordinate American cults, it is only the attempt by the authorities to bring a faith community into subjection through the use of violence that starts the pendulum in that community swinging in the direction of violence.

CHAPTER 6

Israel's Wars of Redemption

Through its surprising victory in 1967, Israel gained control of East Jerusalem, including the Temple Mount, West Jordan, Sinai, the Golan Heights, and Gaza. As "occupied territories," these were placed under martial law. International law forbade annexation, although the status of the former British-mandated territory was not yet wholly regulated.

Article 2 of the first chapter of the Charter of the United Nations states:

3. All Members shall settle their international disputes by peaceful means in such a manner that international peace and security, and justice, are not endangered.

4. All Members shall refrain in their international relations from the threat or use of force against the territorial integrity or political independence of any state, or in any other manner inconsistent with the Purposes of the United Nations.

The UN Charter thus prohibited an ancient practice.[1] Contemporary legal opinion would have to regard the violent occupation of Canaan by the tribes of Israel, or the conquests of huge areas in the Middle East and North Africa by early Islamic armies, as illegal, and would therefore see religion as instigating breaches of international law. "Conquest no longer constitutes a legal title to the possession of a territory."[2] When a territory is occupied by another state today, this must be only a temporary situation, and the rights of the military administration are restricted; also, the settling of civilians in the occupied territories is forbidden. Article 49 of the Fourth Geneva Convention of 1949, which is binding also on Israel qua member of the United Nations, prescribes:

The Occupying Power shall not deport or transfer parts of its own civilian population into the territory it occupies.[3]

An Ambiguous UN Resolution and the Transformation of the Middle East Conflict

After Israel's victory in 1967, the UN Security Council confirmed in Resolution 242 that Israel was not allowed to annex the occupied territories. In order to achieve a just and lasting peace in the Middle East, the first step would be the mutual recognition of all the states involved; and, secondly, "withdrawal of Israeli armed forces from territories occupied in the recent conflict." The link between the withdrawal and the recognition of Israel remained unclear. In French, which enjoys equal status with English at the United Nations, the text reads somewhat differently: "Retrait des forces armées israéliennes des territoires occupés lors du récent conflit." Does this mean that Israel must withdraw from "territories" or from "*the* occupied territories" as a whole? Is Israel required to return all occupied territories as the French version suggests, or is there some latitude for negotiation? The answer can be found in the drafting process of the English version on which the Security Council voted. The definite article was omitted deliberately in order to allow Israel to have a secure border that need not be the same as the Armistice Demarcation Lines of 1949.[4] In the 1970s, the debate about the exact meaning of words was accompanied by a shift in power in Israel; and in the 1980s, the same debate was accompanied by a new orientation in U.S. Middle East policy.

Despite the legal situation, the Labour Party government annexed both the Golan Heights and East Jerusalem after the victory and made them subject to the law of the state of Israel, without however attempting in any way to have the Arab inhabitants of East Jerusalem vote on the new status or to grant them Israeli citizenship (as had happened in 1948, when Arabs in Israel's territory were granted citizenship under certain conditions). Meron Benvenisti writes that although Israel was a democratic society, it was now convinced that it could act in accordance with principles that did not need the consent of either the population directly affected or the international community of states.[5] Benvenisti, a political scientist, was deputy mayor of Jerusalem under Teddy Kollek from 1971 to 1978, with responsibility for Arab East Jerusalem. He has given us the most detailed and reliable data about the developments in the occupied territories.[6]

Most of the members of the Israeli government saw the occupied territories of the former British mandated area as an object that could be exchanged—land for peace—but they wanted to wait for a peace treaty with the neighboring Arab states before deciding on the exact extent of the territories that would be returned. Already on September 1, 1967, however, a conference of Arab states meeting in Khartoum passed a resolution that stated a threefold "no":

The Arab Heads of State have agreed to unite their political efforts at the international and diplomatic level to eliminate the effects of the aggression and to ensure the withdrawal of the aggressive Israeli forces from Arab lands which have been occupied since the aggression of June 5. This will be done within the framework of the main principles by which the Arab States abide, namely, no peace with Israel, no recognition of Israel, no negotiations with it, and insistence on the rights of the Palestinian people in their own country.

In response, General Yigal Allon, a minister in the Israeli government, drew up a plan to exclude areas around Jerusalem and the Jordan Valley from any future restitution, for reasons of security, and to settle Jewish inhabitants there.[7]

Developments in the 1970s soon took a different direction. Religious Zionists interpreted the military occupation of territories that had once belonged to the biblical land as a stage in the messianic process of the restoration of Israel, and they began to settle there.[8] It was no longer the requirements of the military security of the state that dictated their action, but the desire to prevent a renewed partition of the biblical land. By 1977, they had established almost eighty settlements in the occupied territories, with some 11,000 inhabitants; a further 40,000 lived in East Jerusalem and the new municipal districts there.[9] When the Likud Party came to power in 1977, the new government aligned itself with the settler movement and itself took charge of the further process of settling. The new prime minister, Menachem Begin, justified this by saying that one cannot annex territory of one's own, but only foreign territory—and Judea and Samaria were the land in which Israel had originally come into being.[10]

When a Republican administration came to power in the United

States in 1981, this brought a new orientation on this question there too. Under President Jimmy Carter, the attitude of the United States to the Jewish settling of the occupied territories had still been hostile. A legal opinion of the Department of State affirmed on April 21, 1978, that Israel had occupied Gaza, West Jordan, the Golan Heights, and Sinai and had set up Jewish settlements there, although it was not entitled to do so.[11] A different view was taken by President Ronald Reagan, who declared shortly after taking office in 1981: "I disagreed when the previous administration referred to them [the settlements] as illegal—they're not illegal."[12] A decade later, Secretary of State James Baker explained the change in the U.S. position on the legal question by saying that whereas the settlements had once been called illegal, now weaker terms were used: they were only an obstacle to peace. The territories were "disputed" but not "occupied," since not only the Palestinians, but also Israel had justified claims to them (*Washington Post,* September 18, 1991). As a consequence of this new position, the United States has repeatedly prevented the United Nations from exercising pressure on Israel to apply the Fourth Geneva Convention. High-ranking Israeli representatives welcomed the changed view of the U.S. government—in 2002, for example, Dore Gold, Israel's ambassador to the United Nations from 1997 to 1999, alluded to "disputed territories." The term "occupied territories" was unacceptable to Israel, since it called into question claims to the land that it believed were justified.[13] The term "liberated territories" began to be used in Israel.[14] In this way, U.S. foreign policy from the 1980s on has supported Israel's religiously grounded claims to the Holy Land. When Prime Minister Ariel Sharon visited Washington in 2004, President George W. Bush declared that the annexation of parts of the occupied territories by Israel was irrevocable and that it was not possible for Palestinian refugees to return there.[15]

The substance of the Middle East conflict had changed over the course of the years, from a territorial conflict between the state of Israel and the neighboring Arab countries of Egypt, Lebanon, Syria, and Jordan into a conflict between Israelis and Palestinians about the legitimacy of Jewish or Islamic claims to the land. In order to understand this development, we must look not only at the political actors, but also at the religious voting milieus to whom they owed their electoral successes. This applies not only to Israel, but also to the Palestinians and to the United States. I begin with Israel.

Secular Zionism and Its Ultra-Othodox Opponents

Jews certainly did not always agree that the foundation of a state of their own was legitimate in religious terms. Long before the state of Israel was founded in 1948, there were divergent opinions on this issue. When the emancipation of the Jews from the ghettos in Europe in the nineteenth century did not lead to their recognition as citizens with equal rights, and anti-Judaism and anti-Semitism became widespread, a younger generation of Jews who were already acculturated turned to Zionism. Only a state of their own, they believed, could guarantee Jews the protection that European states withheld from them. Accordingly, in 1897, the First Zionist Congress in Basle resolved: "Zionism seeks to establish a home for the Jewish people in Palestine secured under public law." But behind this demand for a national Jewish state—a demand couched in the language of contemporary politics—there lay hidden a force that was not coextensive with the national state. Max Nordau, the author of the Zionist program, asked how it was possible for a people to survive for eighteen centuries without a fatherland. Was this the effect of a "magic potion"? No, it was the effect of "the messianic promise."[16]

A state of their own—this sounded sweet to the ears of the discriminated and persecuted Jews, but many Orthodox Jews regarded it as utterly heretical. In the period before redemption, exile (*galuth*) is the form in which the Jewish people exists, and the test of the Jewish faith is precisely to refrain from taking independent action to put an end to this state of affairs. The ingathering of those scattered abroad is exclusively the task of the Messiah, and anyone who undertakes this task on his own initiative wants to "force the end to come" and has thereby fallen victim to a satanic temptation. This view was often expressed in the Jewish tradition, although it never became truly binding; for example, the Babylonian Talmud mentions vows whereby Israel obligates itself not to go up to Jerusalem to the Wailing Wall, and not to rise up against the peoples of the world (Ketuboth 111a). But when the return to Palestine suddenly became a real option, Orthodox opponents of Zionism wanted to make this view a binding dogma.[17] Vivid narratives evoke the pernicious character of such attempts, such as the anecdote of the rabbi who makes an agreement with Satan in the harbor of Istanbul. Satan says that he will allow him to travel undisturbed to the Holy Land, but when the ship reaches the coast of Palestine, the rabbi sees him standing on the shore, and Satan mocks him, saying that it was only his overseas representative that had made the pact with the rabbi. These Orthodox Jews held that all one was permitted to do in the Holy Land was to pray or to study the Torah; agriculture was forbidden, and in view of the terrible holiness of the soil, anyone who transgressed this precept must reckon with the worst punishments. There is no sliding transition between the history wrought by human beings and the age of salvation.[18]

Adherents of this view had emigrated to the Holy Land in small groups, though only in order to study the Torah there and to pray. In 1912, while still in Europe, they founded their own organization, "Agudath Israel," and called themselves *haredim*. This designation ("those who tremble before God") was taken from a passage in the Book of Isaiah: "Hear the word of the Lord, you who tremble at his word" (66:5); in the Middle Ages, it was equivalent to "especially pious."[19] A subgroup calling itself the "Guardians of the Wall" was formed in 1939. They, not the soldiers, were the true protectors of the land. The *haredim* were convinced that they were living in a double exile in Palestine: under the rule of Gentiles (British and Turks/Arabs) and dominated by unbelieving Zionists.[20] Numerically, they were a minority in a minority, 30 percent of the Orthodox Jews, who in turn amounted to only 15 percent of all the Jews. Nor did they disappear after the foundation of the state of Israel. Samuel Heilman calculates that the community had some 550,000 members in the 1990s.[21] Their condemnation of the state of Israel did not change as a result of its military successes. One ultra-Othodox rabbi reacted to the military triumphs of Israel in 1967 by calling them a temptation by Satan.[22] Later, in the early 1990s, ultra-Othodox Jews took part in the peace talks between the Palestinians and Israel—but on the Palestinian side! Rabbi Moshe Hirsch, the "foreign minister" of the "Guardians of the Wall," was an advisor to the Palestinian delegation. He saw himself as a Palestinian who was a Jew and fought against the state of Israel; in 1995, he became minister for Jewish Affairs in the Palestinian National Authority, and even received a salary for this, to the annoyance of the Israeli government.[23] The *haredim* wanted to limit Judaism to the religious dimension until the coming of the Messiah. Until then, the political dimension belongs entirely to the Gentile peoples.

A Salvation-Historical Interpretation of the Zionist Settlement of Palestine

Paradoxically, however, the very same orthodox Judaism was also the birthplace of a religious legitimation of secular Zionism. The Hasidism of eastern Europe had long been accustomed to regard future salvation as a reality even now, in the time of exile. After an ecstatic visit to Heaven in 1752, the Baal Shem Tov (literally, "Master of the Good Name"; abbreviated to "Besht") wrote a letter asserting that even today, although the coming of the Messiah still lies in the future, the possibility of a mystical encounter with God already exists.[24] This meant that a new, autonomous stage appeared between exile and redemption, namely, mysticism.[25] The pious (*hasid*) and the upright (*zaddik*) person can rise to the status of a mediator between the believers and God. This function is based not on his learning but on the power of his prayer.

This conception generated a revolutionary interpretation of secular Zionism similar to Hegel's "cunning of reason." Its originator was Rabbi Abraham Isaac Kook (1865–1935), who moved to Palestine in 1904 and became its first Ashkenazi chief rabbi in 1921. Kook had no sympathy with the Orthodox condemnation of the Zionist settlers as apostates who wanted to "force the end." With the authority of a rabbi and a mystic, he taught that the secular way of life of the settlers was a first stage in the process of redemption, and he justified this by means of concepts drawn from the cosmic speculations of the Kabbalah.[26] The sacred has appeared in the profane, in the form of the Zionist settlers; through their return to Zion, they are furthering the process of restoration, the *tikkun,* which embraces the entire cosmos; their turning to Zionism is part of a universal history of salvation and has set the messianic process in motion. It is indeed true that Zionism itself does not grasp its place in the history of salvation; nevertheless, it unintentionally fulfills a divine mission. A "cunning" of salvation history is taking place. (We might note en passant that adherents of American Evangelical premilleniarianism saw the settling of Palestine in a similar light; see below.)

In the *Orot (Lights)* books, which the adherents of religious Zionism read as a revelation, Kook made the land of Israel the pivot and linchpin of his theology of history. In other lands, the Torah cannot unfold its full power; all it can do is to help in the process of perfecting the individual soul. It is only in "the air of the land of Israel" that the Torah takes hold of the soul of the entire nation and determines its practice. The community of Jews outside Israel lives inauthentically; it is only on the pure soil of the land of Israel that the splendor of the Torah exercises its fascination on every person.[27] Since however the land of Israel is so extremely sacred, agricultural work on this land is a dangerous and extraordinary act, which inspires both fear and fascination in the settlers. These teachings by Kook represent a daring attempt to reevaluate the reserve that the Orthodox felt with regard to a settling and use of the land. Kook did not disenchant the settling of the land as a political act, as Zionists did; nor did he condemn it as heretical, as other Orthodox Jews did. Rather, he employed the theology of history to enchant it.

The elder Kook disseminated his teachings from the 1930s on in his yeshiva (talmudic school), the Markaz HaRabKook, initially with only limited success. This changed under his son, Zvi Yehuda Kook (1891–1982), who published his father's writings and further developed his theology of history in sermons, while simplifying it and reversing the relationship between the ending of the exile and the return to Zion. He saw the state of Israel as the real agent of redemption, and he celebrated Israel's Independence Day as a religious feast—weapons were just as important as phylacteries. Today, this yeshiva is one of the largest in Israel, and its former students are active in innumerable institutions both in Israel and in the diaspora.[28]

A "Prophecy" by Zvi Yehuda Kook Shortly Before the Six-Day War

But Zvi Yehuda Kook's fame arose in another manner, which one might almost call fortuitous. On National Day in 1967, three weeks before the outbreak of the Six-Day War, he suddenly switched in the course of a sermon into a lamentation that Hebron, Sichem (Nablus), Jericho, and Anathoth had been torn away from Israel through the UN partition plan of 1947 and the ensuing war. "'They divided my land!' he shouted. Then forcefully, with a fierce love for the Torah and the honor of G-d, he cried, 'And where is our Hevron?! Do we forget this?! And where is our Shechem?! Do we forget about this?! And where is our Jericho?! Do we forget this too?! And where is our Other-Side of the Jordan?! Where is each block of the earth?! Each part and parcel, and four cubits of *hashems's* Land?!'" Soon afterwards, Israeli troops corrected this misfortune and conquered precisely these cities in a miraculous way. Through his sermon, Kook had bestowed a religious meaning in advance on the occupation of territories that belonged to Egypt, Syria, and Jordan. He saw the Six-Day War as a "war of redemption" (*ge'ullah*) that "ransomed" the biblical land of Israel from the unbelievers. This sermon gave him a reputation as a prophet of almost biblical dimensions, although his words had in fact been a ritual lamentation rather than a prophecy. This event is mentioned in every account of the prehistory of the religious settler movement of the Believers Bloc.[29]

Rabbis trained in the Kooks' yeshiva formed the avant-garde of the religious settler movement. They acted in accordance with this definition of Israel's situation and organized on their own initiative actions to take possession of the promised inheritance in Judea, Samaria, and Gaza.[30] Thanks to an agreement made in the 1960s between rabbinic educational institutions and the Israeli Ministry of Defense, it was possible for students to combine the study of Torah with their military service, and there were many young Israelis who wanted to be more religious than the secular Zionists and more political than the ultra-Othodox. It was above all young Ashkenazi intellectuals of the Israeli middle classes who developed sympathy for such a combination. This meant that the antagonism on the part of both secular Zionism and Orthodoxy gave way to a new synthesis between nationalism and religion, between military service and the settling of the occupied territories. In their view, salvation history was marching on independently of the intentions of the actors; and believers who had grasped this could increase the speed of this process through their own cooperation. The settling of the territories occupied by Israel is embedded here in a salvation history and thus receives religious legitimation. Often, messianism is the response to an experience of humiliation and disenfranchisement, but this was not the case here: one can speak of a messianism born of military victory.[31]

Conflict Between the Israeli Government and the Settlers

One early conflict that saw the Israeli government and religious settlers ranged on opposing sides was over Hebron. Orthodox Jews had lived in Hebron long before the partition of the land and the foundation of the state of Israel. When the tensions between Arabs and Jews throughout the land increased in the 1920s, the fury of the Arabs exploded in 1929 in a terrible massacre in Hebron, in which sixty-seven of the Jews who lived in the city lost their lives. The survivors were compelled to leave Hebron, and moved their yeshiva to Jerusalem. Immediately after the occupation of Hebron by the Israeli army in 1967, those who had been expelled and their descendants asked the government or the military authorities for permission to return to Hebron. Rabbi Moshe Levinger, who had studied in the Kooks' yeshiva, made their demand his own and laid down new standards by means of an extraordinary action. He came from an Ashkenazi family who had been forced to flee from Germany in the 1930s. Accompanied by ten other Torah scholars and their families, he celebrated the Passover feast in an Arab hotel in Hebron in 1968.[32] After the feast, however, the families demonstratively refrained from returning to Israel: instead, they remained in Hebron and demanded the right to be allowed to remain. Negotiations with the government followed, and finally the army allowed the refoundation of the talmudic school in its military zone. This was seen as compliance with international law, which prohibited a permanent settling of civilians of the occupying power, whereas temporary military bases were permissible. Later, Jewish families moved into the Arab old city of Hebron, and they subsequently needed protection by the Israeli military against the Arab inhabitants. A new Jewish settlement, Kiryat Arba, came into being on the periphery of Hebron. Other Jewish settlements were established on the same pattern in the years leading up to 1977. And wherever Arabs protested furiously against the Jewish settlers' plans, the latter were protected by the Israeli army.

Gershom Gorenberg has described the first stage of the expansion of the illegal settlements, between 1967 and 1977. The Israeli government was divided on this question, and he notes that it was a confederation of ministers rather than a united regime. One of the tragic heroes of his story, who provides an exemplary illustration of the consequences of this disunity, is Yitzhak Rabin. In 1948, when the *Altalena*, a ship charted by Jewish resistance fighters carrying weapons for the underground group Irgun (led by Menachem Begin), appeared off the coast of Israel and the crew refused to submit to the orders of the newly founded state of Israel, the first prime minister, David Ben-Gurion, ordered that the weapons be seized by force; those responsible were to be taken prisoner. Other officers refused to carry out this order, but Rabin took command and sank the ship; eighteen resistance fighters lost their lives. According to Gorenberg, "The *Altalena* crisis can properly be seen as the moment Israel actually became a state, when a single government overcame the chaos that threatens an emerging nation. Rabin's readiness to confront other Jews had been crucial."[33] Later on, as chief of the General Staff, the same Rabin contributed to the victory in the Six-Day War. In 1975, in negotiations with settlers in Samaria who had recently settled ancient biblical sites on their own initiative, however, he caved in to their demands. "For the second time in his life he faced the *Altalena* test, and unlike the first time, he failed it."[34] Gorenberg sees this as a bad omen for his later fate. "On November 4, 1995, a radical young supporter of the [restitution of Israel in the] Whole Land [of Palestine], Yigal Amir, assassinated Israel's prime minister. It was the final, horrifying act of the tragedy of Yitzhak Rabin: The forces of chaos he had suppressed on the Tel Aviv shore in 1948, and to which he had yielded at Sebastia in 1975, now swept him away."[35]

Punishment for Neglecting the Settling of the "Redeemed Territories"

When Israel was forced after the Yom Kippur War in 1973 to cede to Egypt territories that the Jews understood as belonging to the land of Israel, religious settlers and their rabbis interpreted this as a punishment for failing to take hold of the inheritance. Since Israel had not recognized the meaning of the victory of 1967, God had punished it with a military defeat—this was the "birthpangs of the Messiah." The lesson that God had taught Israel was that the settling of the land of Israel must take priority over everything else.

Gush Emunim (literally, "the Bloc of the Faithful") translated this salvation-historical sequence into action. The period of informal actions was now past; in 1974, the bloc was established as an autonomous organization. The movement drew its strength from a core idea that was both simple and stirring: the messianic historical process has begun—the land of Israel is sacred—the Jewish settling of the land speeds up the redemption—the settling takes priority to following the laws of the state of Israel and international law—the Palestinians have no rights to the land.[36] The Labour Party government that ruled together with other parties from 1973 to 1977 had only reluctantly approved of the settlements in the occupied territories, but this changed when the right-wing Likud Party came to power in 1977. It identified the settling of the occupied territories as its very own task and legalized the settler movement. However, the political autonomy of the settler movement was nothing new in Israel.

Settler movements go back to the time before the foundation of the state, and they subsequently retained the legal status as public corporations that they acquired then. Emigration to Israel was overseen by the World Zionist Organization and the Jewish Agency, which jointly represented the interests of the Jews vis-à-vis the British Mandate authorities. Even after the foundation of the state of Israel, they continued to exist as entities with extensive autonomous powers. The Law of Return in 1950 stated that the new state of Israel was a homeland for all Jews worldwide. Agreements between the Jewish Agency and the government regulated the specific roles of each in the task of settling the immigrants. In 1952, the Knesset passed a law declaring the World Zionist Organization / Jewish Agency a "juristic body" with responsibility for immigration, for integration, and for the settlement projects in Israel. In 1971, however, the two organizations were separated, and the Jewish Agency was given responsibility for the functions in Israel.[37]

The change of government in 1977 meant a new phase in the settlement politics. The government legalized the settling of the occupied territories. From now on, the organization responsible for this task, called Amana (literally, "covenant"), received active governmental support and was able to operate officially in the occupied territories,[38] or (in the vocabulary of the settlers) in Yesha (an abbreviation for Judea, Samaria, and Gaza; the word means "redemption").[39] Beginning in 1979, the individual Jewish settlements have been successively grouped together in territorial legal units that are subject to the law of the state of Israel, not to the regional Palestinian administrations.[40] This created and cemented an unequal treatment of the inhabitants of the occupied territories: while the Jewish settlers had all the rights of Israeli citizens, the Arabs had only a local administration limited by martial law. Behind the façade of martial law, Jewish settlements were set up across the entire territory, and the Palestinians could do nothing to stop this. The intention was to make it impossible ever again to partition the biblical land.[41]

Amana propagated a type of settlement that differed from the kibbutz, the agricultural cooperative.[42] The community settlement (*yishuv kehilati*) consisted of families who earned their income outside the settlement as commuters in the state of Israel. Amana used its financial resources to ensure that convinced adherents of Gush Emunim moved into the new settlements. This, however, was not always the case: surveys of settlers show that the new forms of communality were often more popular than the belief that one was living in the messianic age.[43] Many Israelis found the cheap housing space in a beautiful landscape attractive, independently of their religious orientations. As in other industrialized countries, here too families moved out of the congested conurbations into the outskirts, and Benvenisti speaks of "suburbia" as the third phase of the settler movement.[44] The settlements were also very attractive because of the social and cultural institutions such as schools and hospitals that were available to the settler families.

In 1978, the settler organization Amana submitted to the government a proposal for the settling of 100,000 people in the occupied territories in the course of the next ten years, and Ariel Sharon, then minister for agriculture, made this the basis of government planning.[45] The plan succeeded. The numbers of settlers in Gaza and the West Bank increased dramatically, from 7,000 to 42,000 in 1985, and then to 76,000 in 1990.[46] By the beginning of the 1990s, some 110,000 persons lived in 137 settlements in the territories. In 2006, 440,000 Jewish settlers lived in 205 official settlements in the occupied territories, including the Golan Heights and East Jerusalem. As Benvenisti's map vividly shows, the occupied territories today are a patchwork of Jewish and Palestinian places.[47]

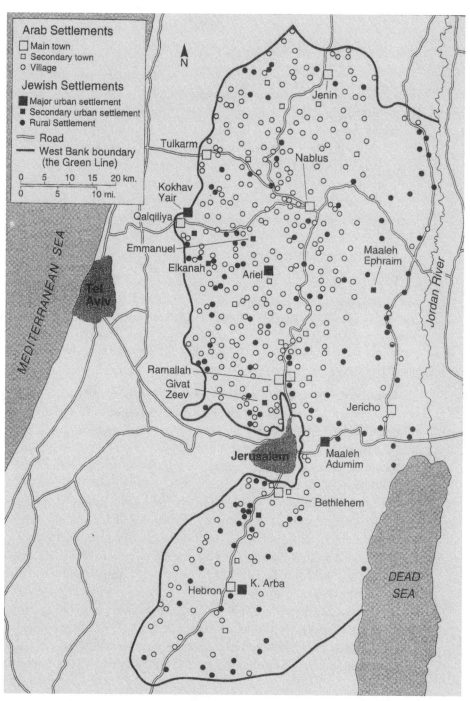

Jewish Settlements in the Occupied Territories

Israel's Martial Law and the Relationship Between Settlers and Palestinians

The settlements were possible thanks to the martial law that had been in force in the occupied territories since 1967. This has a Palestinian prehistory going back to the 1930s, when the British Mandate Authority ruled Palestine by means of Emergency Defence Regulations as World War II loomed closer, and then once again after 1945 in view of Jewish paramilitary activities. Although the Jewish Agency itself had contested the arbitrariness of these laws, the newly founded state of Israel adopted them; all it abolished was their application to Israeli citizens. The Declaration of Independence of the state of Israel in 1948 assured all citizens of equality before the law, irrespective of their religion, but the Supreme Court decided already in the same year that the citizens could not enforce this entitlement by means of an action at law.

Israel has no constitution that might take precedence over legislation that is discriminatory in nature. The declaration of the Establishment of the State of Israel called for equality of rights, but Israel's courts did not deem the declaration to be a source of law. The courts have no power of judicial review of legislation and, therefore, no power to overturn discriminatory laws.[48]

To date, there is no constitution in Israel that guarantees the basic rights of all its residents. The rights of the non-Israeli inhabitants of the country remain restricted by martial law, and the new Arab population was to bear the brunt of such restrictions. The "Arabs of 1948" had been able to obtain Israeli citizenship under certain conditions, but this was refused to the inhabitants of the occupied territories and East Jerusalem. Since Israel thereby acted in accordance with the prohibition of annexation, formally speaking, this legal inequality met with international understanding. But since the number and size of the Jewish settlements grew continually, and the settlers collaborated with the Ministry of Defense in the enforcement of martial law and formed civil defense corps or self-protection groups, there was also an inequality in the exercise of violence between Palestinian inhabitants and Israeli settlers—while the latter were permitted to exercise violence legally, the former contravened martial law if they did so. It was only after the Oslo Accords that regions were formed in which the Palestinian population constituted a legal community of its own under the "Palestinian Authority." Nevertheless, the Oslo Accords did not put a brake on the spread of Jewish settlements. From 1993, the year of the first Oslo Accord, to 2004, the number of Jewish settlers in the West Bank doubled and rose to 231,000 inhabitants in 140 settlements.[49]

The Israeli geographer Elisha Efrat has made a thorough study of the profound transformation of the natural physical landscape of the occupied territories. He writes that today, between 50 and 60 percent of the land is in the hands of Israel or of the settlers, although the settlers make up only 12 percent of the population and population growth among the Palestinians is much higher than among the settlers. The same disparity can be seen in the allocation of water: in the occupied territories, Israel uses 500 million cubic meters of water, but gives the Palestinians only 100 million. The area is criss-crossed by roads that ensure that the settlers have a quick journey to their work in the heartland of Israel, but the Palestinians are forbidden to use these roads. Efrat drew a depressing conclusion from his investigations and analyses:

There are in this region two hostile populations living one on top of the other in enclaves. One gets everything, for ideological reasons and in direct contradiction to theories of logical planning, not to mention political, social, and human logic, while the other gets nothing, and its living space is steadily shrinking.[50]

Since the Jewish settlements were sited in such a way that they dismember the territory of the Palestinians, and the economically more profitable zones (e.g., along the Jordan Rift Valley) were separated from a potential Palestinian state, Efrat doubts that it will ever be possible to set up a viable national Palestinian state there.[51]

Settler Violence Against the Peace Process

The geotheology of Gush Emunim gives the settling of the "land of Israel" absolute priority over every other concern. It is this that decides whether one belongs to the people of Israel and is faithful to the Torah. This view, which has not met with absolute agreement even among its own members,[52] has encouraged a willingness on the part of the settlers to use violence, as has been seen above all in those periods when Israel yielded to international pressure and handed back areas of the biblical land.

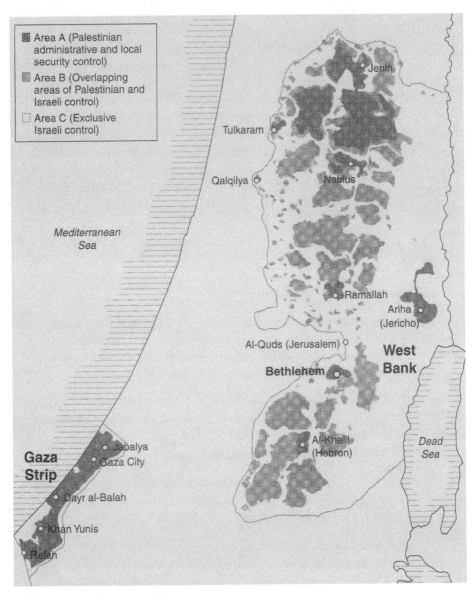

Territory of the Prospective Palestinian State

For many of the religious settlers, the exchange of "land for peace" was and remains a formula of apostasy.

In 1979, the peace accord between Egypt and Israel that had been agreed in the previous year at Camp David was concluded by Anwar al-Sadat and Menachem Begin. One of its provisions was that Israel would withdraw from Sinai, thereby also abandoning the settlement of Yamit. This took place in 1982 and led to grave clashes between settlers and the government. In this situation, some pioneers of the settler movement took the law into their own hands,[53] since they believed that the state of Israel had lost the holiness that Rabbi Zvi Yehuda Kook had once ascribed to it. Gush Emunim was divided into the powerful network of the settler organization Amana with the local juristic bodies and the Settlers Council on the one hand, and an underground on the other hand that was willing to use violence.[54] Indeed, they planned to destroy the Islamic Dome of the Rock on the Temple Mount in 1984,[55] since they regarded the Camp David Accords as a serious sin that could be expiated only by a violent purification of the holy place on the Temple Mount. When the Islamic anathema was finally annihilated and the Temple site was once again pure, a world war would break out. At its end would stand the kingdom of David. They believed that the physical destruction would bring spiritual redemption. This at any rate is how Yehuda Etzion, the head of the group that planned the attack, saw the course of events, drawing on the apocalyptic scenario of Daniel 9:27. True redemption implies that Jews cast away their fear of the Gentiles and fear only the Lord; which in turn means that they expel all the Arabs from the Land of Israel. Such an action is the true proof of faith.[56] The plan was not carried out, because they could not find any rabbi who would give his approval.[57]

The tensions between the settlers and the government of Israel are the expression of a new dynamic in the conflict. From 1948 to 1967 or 1973, the conflict was primarily between Israel and the neighboring Arab states. After this period, it became an intercommunal conflict in the occupied territories between Jewish settlers and Palestinians. The increase in the number of clashes in the 1980s was due both to a growing Palestinian resistance and to the violent actions taken by settlers against Palestinians,[58] which included acts of terror. Settlers carried out bomb attacks on the mayors of two Arab towns in revenge for an attack carried out by

Palestinians in 1980 on the Beit Hadassah yeshiva in Hebron, in which six Jewish students had died. In 1983, settlers attacked an Islamic seminary in Hebron and killed Islamic students. Both these acts of violence had been approved by rabbis. Ehud Sprinzak concludes his researches into this subject by affirming that the use of violence was not marginal in the settler movement, but central.[59] And the Israeli authorities did not always seriously prosecute violence inflicted on Palestinians. For example, in 1988, Rabbi Moshe Levinger shot a young Palestinian who had thrown stones at his car. During his trial, he declared that he had shot into the air and had not wanted to hit the boy; nevertheless, he added that he regarded it as a great honor to kill an Arab. He was sentenced to five months in prison, but was released after only ten weeks.[60]

After the first step in the implementation of the 1993 Oslo Accords, the return of Gaza and Jericho to the Palestinians in 1994, the fury of the settlers and their readiness to resort to violence took on new dimensions. This began with a massacre of Palestinians, and ended with the murder of Prime Minister Yitzhak Rabin. Dr. Baruch Goldstein, a physician born in the United States, carried out the massacre in the Cave of Machpelah in Hebron on February 25, 1994.[61] On this site, where the Jewish patriarchs are said to have been buried and that is sacred to all the Abrahamic religions, mausoleums were built in the Islamic period for Jacob and Leah, Abraham and Sarah, and Isaac and Rebecca. These had been converted into a mosque complex, to which non-Muslims had no access. After 1967, a part of the site had been made accessible to Jews for visits and prayer. The timing of the massacre was not a matter of chance: it was the feast of Purim, which commemorates the vengeance wrought by the Jews on their persecutors in Persia. On the night of Purim, Baruch Goldstein, who lived in Kiryat Arba near Hebron, went to this place for meditation and prayer. He heard Arab youths shouting: *"Itbach al-Jahud,* Kill the Jews!" Israeli soldiers stood by without intervening. Enraged by this humiliation, Goldstein ran home and fetched his machine gun. He entered the building from the Islamic side and fired into the group of Muslims who were holding their morning prayer. After 111 shots, more than 30 people lay dead. Goldstein was seized by the survivors and beaten to death. When the local military authorities heard that shots had been fired in the mosque, they attempted to reach Goldstein, who was their liaison officer, but his pager did not respond. More than 1,000 settlers attended his funeral, and his tomb became a place of remembrance. Friends erected a tombstone with the following inscription:

Here lies the saint, Dr. Baruch Kappel Goldstein, blessed be the memory of the righteous and holy man, may the Lord avenge his blood, who devoted his soul to the Jews, Jewish religion and Jewish land. His hands are innocent and his heart is pure. He was killed as a martyr of God on the 14th of Adar, Purim, in the year 5754.[62]

Goldstein had studied under Rabbi Meir Kahane, and he and his friends from Kiryat Arba sympathized with Kahane's idea that violence against Arabs was the only way to liberate oneself from the ghetto mentality. God's command dooming the biblical Canaanites to be extirpated by Israel (Deut. 7:1–5; 20:16–17) had now to be applied to the Palestinians. They were completely out of place in the Holy Land and must leave it. Punching a Palestinian in the mug was the true sanctification of the name of God (*kiddush ha-shem*). Although the state of Israel banned the Kach Party, founded by Kahane, as early as the 1980s, its ideas lived on among the settlers.[63] One year after the massacre, a commemorative book appeared, edited by Rabbi Ginzburg. *Baruch Hagever* ("Baruch the Man") presents Goldstein's action as a model for every genuine Jew, thanks to his sanctification of the name of God, his (alleged) saving of Jewish lives, his vengeance on the Palestinians of Hebron, his purification of the land from evil, and his struggle for the land of Israel. It treats atrocity as a mystical technique for attainment of unmediated ecstatic and personal experience of the divine. Songs and the Internet pages "Baruch Hagever" keep the remembrance of his action alive up to the present day.[64] Goldstein's tomb has become a place of pilgrimage with the permission of the authorities.[65]

When the second Oslo Accord extended Palestinian autonomy to further towns and villages in the West Bank, the association of rabbis in the occupied territories sounded the alarm: anyone who voted to return the land to Palestinians was like a man who declares his own brothers to be thieves. A rabbinic tradition was brought up to date and widely circulated, to the effect that one who "hands over" (*moser*) or "persecutes" (*rodeph*) a Jew with the intention of bringing about his death must himself be killed.[66] One group of activists assembled before the residence of the prime minister and carried out what is allegedly the worst ritual of cursing known to Judaism, the *pulsa di nura* (Aramaic: literally, "flame of fire").[67] The angel of destruction will strike him; he is damned wherever he goes; his soul is to leave his body directly, and he is not to survive beyond the present month. Yigal Amir, a talmudic student at the Bar Ilan University who had been won over by the commemorative book about Baruch Goldstein, believed that rabbinic statements entitled him to take action. The biblical tradition about Phinehas also played a role: only by killing the Jewish adulterer in the Israelite camp can God's wrath against his people be placated (Num. 25). Yigal Amir killed Yitzhak Rabin at a peace rally on November 4, 1995.[68] Subsequently, Ariel Sharon was threatened with a similar fate when he planned to withdraw from Gaza.[69]

The Palestinians' Resistance Becomes a Terrorist Manifestation of Evil

On June 8, 1977, an Additional Protocol to the Geneva Convention agreed that the rules of this Convention should apply not only to wars between states, but also to a further case:

The situations referred to in the preceding paragraph include armed conflicts in which peoples are fighting against colonial domination and alien occupation and against racist regimes in the exercise of their right of self-determination, as enshrined in the Charter of the United Nations and the Declaration on Principles of International Law concerning Friendly Relations and Co-operation among States in accordance with the Charter of the United Nations. (Art. I, 3)

This meant that the Palestinian resistance organizations too had the right to have their fighters treated in accordance with the Geneva Conventions, provided that they themselves kept to these rules.

The new legal position provoked vigorous negative reactions, which ultimately led to a clear distinction between (justified) resistance and (unjustified) terrorism. Benjamin Netanyahu, subsequently prime minister of Israel, organized two conferences on terrorism for the Jonathan Institute in 1979 and 1983, one in Jerusalem and one in Washington. His brother Jonathan, after whom this Institute is named, died in 1976 when he was the officer in charge of liberating Jewish hostages at Entebbe Airport in Uganda. The declared intention of both conferences was to mobilize the West to fight against terrorism. The organizers were utterly opposed to the idea that one man's terrorist is another man's freedom fighter.[70] Western media had accepted without further ado the terrorists' own account of their motives, with the result that terrorists had been able to present themselves as resistance fighters. That, indeed, was precisely what the terrorists wanted us to think, Netanyahu said, whereas in reality they were destroying innocent lives in an intentional and calculated manner. The 1979 conference in Jerusalem thus adopted a different definition: "Terrorism is the deliberate and systematic murder, maiming and menacing of the innocent to inspire fear for political ends."[71] Terrorists are criminals who use public communiqués in the attempt to help their captured comrades and secure for them the status of prisoners of war. In the background are the Soviet Union and radical Arab regimes; nor is the UNO innocent, since it has justified terrorism and regarded it as a struggle for national liberation. The fight against terrorism can be won only if public opinion and the media in the West abandon their errors.

This appeal made a powerful impact. Subsequently, the United States too opposed the new legal position and threw its weight behind a corresponding new definition of terror. Here, the replacement of "resistance fighter" by "terrorist" is strongly reminiscent of Orwell's "newspeak," which is employed in order to manipulate mental associations. One can also call it an instance of "semantic terror" or of "coercion by a thought police."[72]

Post-Zionism

In his study of the struggle for the Temple Mount, Gershom Gorenberg notes that people not only tell stories: they also live in them.[73] He was disturbed to see how the Middle East conflict was changing, and how this change was promoted by political leaders who carelessly sought the support of religious leaders while denying that the views of the latter might influence them in any way.[74] The religious violence made its move into the heads of statesmen who ought rather to have defended the legal order against religious claims. Newspeak ran rampant: suddenly, there was no longer any Palestinian "resistance," but only "terrorism." At the same time, a spiral of violence was set in motion. Another disastrous factor was that the biblical associations influenced United States foreign policy too:

the concept of the "land of Israel" mobilized sympathy and loyalty in the United States, while talk about "occupied territories" or an "Islamic foundational land" met only with irritated reactions—since after all, the blessing can be given only once. The core understanding of what religion means has been affected by this change, so that, as Gorenberg writes, we are now living in an age in which extremism has been confused with religious authenticity.[75]

The success of the settler movement in Israel shows that the existence of a democracy does not automatically guarantee the rule of law. Nor does it offer protection against the growth and the tolerance of religious violence. The relationship between religious violence and democracy is much closer than is often alleged, for it is precisely in democracies that it is easy for representatives of state institutions to be swept along by swelling religious currents. Even under the conditions of a Western-type state, it is possible that the primacy of human rights over religious claims may cease to be upheld. The Israel scholar Ehud Sprinzak has warned that this danger exists in Israel too.[76] Writers and intellectuals have also dealt with this subject. Amos Oz holds that the behavior of Gush Emunim entails the risk that Israel may abandon the "duo" of Jewish tradition and Western humanism, so that Judaism may be dragged back in a decisive manner to the Book of Joshua, to the days of the Judges, back to the stage of a fanatical, cruel, and closed tribal society.[77]

In view of this transformation of the Middle East conflict, it is easy to understand that the discourse analyses of French- and English-speaking scholars have reached Israel. Laurence Silberstein's overview of these debates shows how publications by Israelis (and by a few Arabs who write in Hebrew), both intellectuals and scholars, reflect on how everyday Zionist concepts are now taken for granted and exercise hegemony over thinking and acting. Everyone can grasp the difference between speaking of "immigration" or "return," of "foreign countries" or "exile," of "Palestine" or "the land of Israel," of "occupation" or "redemption," and of "settlement" or "entering upon an inheritance." Closely linked to the religious vocabulary is the conviction that the hostility of the Palestinians to Israel has no comprehensible causes. An intercommunal conflict is interpreted no longer in legal, political, societal, and territorial categories, but as the manifestation of a well-known hatred of Judaism and anti-Semitism.[78]

CHAPTER 7

Fighting for Palestine as *Waqf*

For a time, mutually contradictory interpretations of the Middle East conflict existed not only in the Jewish camp, but also among the Palestinians. On the one hand, there was the PLO, an umbrella association of several Palestinian liberation organizations founded in 1964, which spoke not only on behalf of Muslims, but on behalf of Arab Christians too, who today number some 50,000 in the occupied territories and 125,000 in Israel. The PLO adopted a charter in 1964, and subsequently sharpened its tone in 1968. This text interpreted the conflict with Israel as the struggle of an Arab people against Zionism, which was seen as one variant of Western imperialism. With the help of the solidarity of all the Arabs and their states, the PLO intended to wage a successful fight for an independent Arab Palestine. Pan-Arab unity and the liberation of Palestine were interdependent. The partition of Palestine by the United Nations in 1947 and the foundation of Israel were illegal acts: since the Jews are a faith community, not a nation, they have no right to a state of their own. The goal of the PLO must be the liquidation of Zionism (Art. 15 of its charter). Jews who lived in Palestine before the Zionist invasion count as Palestinians (Art. 6).[1]

On the other hand, there were the Muslim Brethren, who framed the conflict with Israel differently. In view of the decline suffered by Islam in the successor states to the Ottoman empire after the end of the caliphate in 1924, they believed that the time had not yet come for an armed struggle against Israel; the first requirement was an Islamization of society and of those who were merely nominally Muslims, since an avant-garde of convinced believers would be able to take up the struggle against the godless only when sufficiently large numbers had been liberated from the corrupting influence of the West. The Islamization of one's own society must take chronological and substantial precedence to the armed struggle. The Muslim Brethren, who held this position, were founded in 1928 in Egypt. They formed associations throughout the country in the 1930s, and extended their activities to Palestine after 1945. By 1947, they had twenty-five branches in Palestine, with an estimated membership of between twelve and twenty thousand.[2] This presence of the Muslim Brethren meant that two different attitudes to the conflict existed among the Palestinians: while the Muslim Brethren demanded that they display patience, since Islamization was the priority, the PLO demanded an immediate beginning to the armed struggle.

After the Arab states were defeated in the Six-Day War, however, Arab nationalism declined in prestige and plausibility. Was there any reason why the Palestinians should not find in Islam the communality and the strength which were needed to cope with the partition of Palestine in 1948, referred to as the Nakba (catastrophe)?[3] Increasingly, the political reserve on the part of the Muslim Brethren became hard to sustain. By the end of the 1970s, there were many indications that Muslims of a new generation were no longer willing to follow the maxim that the time was not yet ripe for an armed struggle against Israel. Militant Islamist groups gained the ascendancy in Palestine.[4]

Islamist jihad groups had already made their appearance in Egypt in the 1960s. The present-day culture and society of their country were so corrupt in their eyes that they denied the possibility of a gradual Islamization. This interpretation of the system meant that they parted company with the leadership of the Muslim Brethren, who were politically cautious and worked on a long-term basis, concentrating their activities on the creation of Islamist milieus. These groups were organized as communities (*jamā'a*) of fighters who already practiced jihad. When Dr. Fathi al-Shiqaqi returned to Gaza from his medical studies in Egypt, he joined forces in 1980 with Sheikh Abdulaziz 'Auda, who came from a refugee camp in Gaza and had taken degrees in Arabic studies, Islamic studies, and Islamic law in Egypt, to found a similar group in Palestine.[5] The organization that

Shiqaqi and 'Auda founded and called "Islamic Jihad" (*al-jihad al-islami*) was unwilling to entrust activism to the PLO and the secular independent movements that united under it.[6] Fathi al-Shiqaqi could not accept a situation where Islam was not involved in the armed struggle against the foreign occupation of Palestine. In a retrospect in August 1989, he expressed his dissatisfaction with the Palestinian resistance as follows:

> Those who carried the flag of Islam (the Brethren) did not fight for Palestine, and those who fought for Palestine (the PLO) removed Islam from their ideological framework. However, we, as young Muslim Palestinians, have discovered that Palestine is found at the heart of the Qur'an. Accordingly, we understood . . . that the way of the Jihad in Palestine is the way of salvation for ourselves as individuals, as a group, and as a nation.[7]

Islam and Islamism in Palestine

The politically active Muslims could appeal to a centuries-old rootedness of Islam in Palestine. Before the Prophet and his followers oriented their prayer to Mecca, they had prayed in the direction of Jerusalem. The change in the direction of prayer (*qibla*) did indeed demonstrate Mohammed's turning away from the Jews, but it also showed the great significance that Jerusalem had for the Prophet and that it continued to hold for his adherents.[8] Islamists too praised the land of Palestine as "the first of the two *qiblas*."[9] It was from Jerusalem that the Prophet set out on his heavenly journey, the Mi'raj, and he tied his horse Buraq, which had brought him miraculously to Jerusalem, to the very same wall that is venerated by the Jews as the Wailing Wall.[10] The elaborate buildings of the Dome of the Rock and the al-Aqsa mosque, which go back to the first Islamic century (691–692 and 706–717 CE, respectively), bear witness to the early bonds between Muslims and this city. After Mecca and Medina, Jerusalem is Muslims' third most important pilgrimage site, as is underlined by the names "the noble sanctuary" (*al-haram al-sharif*) for the holy precincts and "the holy" (*al-Quds*) for the city itself.[11]

As Roger Friedland and Richard Hecht show, an annual pilgrimage to the tomb of the prophet Moses (*maqam al-nabi Musa*) on the road from Jerusalem to Jericho contributed to the formation of a specifically Palestinian Islam.[12] The alleged tomb of Moses was developed by Muslims into a huge monument, in a number of phases stretching from the twelfth or thirteenth century to the end of the nineteenth century.[13] It was administered by the Husaini family in Jerusalem as a *waqf,* and a pilgrimage to this tomb was organized each year, beginning and ending in Jerusalem. During the period of British rule, the catchment area of the participants grew continually, in both geographical and societal terms. Increasingly, the speeches and banners also expressed political demands, and established a sense of communal identity among the Arabs in the villages and towns around Jerusalem. This was intensified in the twentieth century by the conflict with the growing Jewish community over the Wailing Wall. The remnants of the ancient Jewish temple formed the enclosure of the "noble sanctuary" of the Muslims. Only a few meters from the Wailing Wall lay a plot of land that was in the possession of Moroccan Muslims as a *waqf.* The more intensive the Jewish efforts to buy this plot of land or to exchange it for another, in order to have more space for those who prayed at the Wailing Wall, the more obstinate was the Palestinian resistance to this request, since they were afraid that the Jewish Temple would be rebuilt.[14]

Palestine became a British Mandate territory in 1920 after the dissolution of the Ottoman empire. Great Britain understood its task as both establishing a local self-administration of the Arabs and encouraging the creation of a home for the Jews. This not only accorded with power-political interests, but was also in keeping with the expectations of many British Evangelicals, who believed that in the end time Israel would be reestablished in the Holy Land.[15] The Mandate Authority thus conducted a double strategy. On the one hand, it recognized the Jewish Agency as the representative of the Jews; at the same time, it created the Supreme Muslim Council with Amin al-Husaini as president and mufti of Jerusalem. The numerous Islamic foundations and institutions in the country were put under his direction.

Islamist Militancy in Palestine

One pioneer and model for later Islamists was Izz al-Din al-Qassam, who was born in 1882 in Syria and moved to Palestine, where he became the imam of a mosque in Haifa and founded a Muslim youth organization on the analogy of the YMCA. He demanded that the young Muslims return to the Islamic order of things and use violence against the British and the Jews. With the slogan: "This is the jihad, victory or martyrdom [*istishhād*]!" he recruited several hundred fighters (*fidā'iyyīn*). He died in 1935 in a clash with a British patrol. As a martyr, he remained unforgotten; Islamists and nationalists equally praised the exemplary character of his willingness for sacrifice.

It is improbable that Izz al-Din al-Qassam was a formal member of the Egyptian Brethren; as yet, there were few points of contact between the Egyptian Muslim Brethren and Palestine. However, his message was in complete accord with the new type of Islamic community that Hasan al-Banna (1906–1949) had founded, namely, the Muslim Brethren.[16] Al-Banna came from a deeply religious family and belonged to a Sufi order (*tarīqa*). While studying at a teacher training college in Cairo, he was infuriated by the influence of Western culture on the city and horrified to see that even highly respected Islamic scholars at the al-Azhar University accepted this state of affairs without a protest. Driven by the desire to help the Islamic order of things regain recognition in the country, he went to work as a teacher in Ismailiya in the Canal Zone, where he sought followers among the workers and the lower civil servants, people who would help to renew Islam. He won over to his cause six Muslims who worked for the British. According to the foundation narrative, they solemnly declared that they agreed with him that the Muslims had been deprived of their dignity; since he alone knew the way to save the fatherland, the religion, and the Islamic community (*umma*), they would hand over to him the responsibility that they bore before God. They swore a vow to be "troops for the message of Islam" and to become brothers in the service of Islam, "Muslim Brethren" (*al-ikhwān al-muslimūn*).[17]

Al-Banna adopted vows, prayers, and daily Qur'an recitations from the Sufi orders, although he rejected the mystical religiosity that was otherwise their distinguishing mark. Unlike the orders, the Muslim Brethren were to be active in society, and their members were to be mostly laity. Al-Banna's interpretation of the situation of Islam in Egypt led him to regard legal scholars as helpful, but no longer as binding authorities. In his eyes, Egypt had lost its Islamic soul; in view of the universal disorientation and confusion in the country, the first priority was to rediscover the correct Islamic path.[18] Each individual had to begin with his own self and expel paganism and imperialism from his heart. The next step, following a directive in the Qur'an, was to bring others to do what was right and to omit what was reprehensible.[19] One who dies without having fought in this sense has died a "pagan" (*jāhiliyya*) death. In this way, jihad became the individual obligation of every Muslim in addition to the other five pillars of Islamic belief (the profession of faith, prayer, fasting in the month of Ramadan, the tithe for the poor, and the pilgrimage to Mecca).

Hasan al-Banna developed new plans of action for the path out of paganism, based on the genuinely Islamic idea that the believer has the task of rendering the truth into reality. Given the superiority of unbelief, however, this must inevitably be accommodated to the external circumstances: at present, the enforcement of an Islamic order (*al-nizām al-islāmī*) could occur only gradually and phase by phase. An initial phase of missionary work and propaganda must be followed by a second phase of the formation of Islamic milieus or Islamic enclaves. Finally, in a third phase, the state itself would become Islamic. This framing of the situation transformed Islamic traditions into scenarios that were sequentially related to one another: first the winning of adherents, then the creation of Islamic islands in the sea of unbelief, and finally the struggle for an Islamic political order.[20]

Islamizing Society and Developments in Gaza

In the course of the following years and decades, Muslim Brethren founded private mosques and associations in Egypt, which in turn supported clinics, schools for boys and for girls, handicraft businesses, and other societal institutions. This also happened in Gaza, which was administered by Egypt until 1967; generally speaking, the Muslim Brethren there shared the political fortunes of the Brethren in Egypt. After the Officers' Revolution in 1952, the Egyptian Brethren enjoyed their support for two years, but thereafter, prohibitions and persecution brought renewed difficulties for their activities. Israel's occupation of the Gaza Strip in 1967 improved the situation of the Muslim Brethren. Israel gave them a free hand, probably because it regarded them as an apolitical counterweight to the PLO. For their part, the Muslim Brethren concentrated on the

construction of a social Islam. The occupation by Israel brought one further improvement, namely, the end of the separation between the Muslim
Brethren in Gaza and the West Bank.

From the 1970s onwards, the driving force in the Islamization was
Sheikh Ahmad Yasin, who became a dominant figure among the Muslim Brethren and was regarded as the leader of the faithful (*amīr al-
mu'minīn*).[21] He initiated the formation of Islamic associations in refugee
camps, and founded in 1973 the Islamic Center (Mujamma' al-Islāmī) to
coordinate the work of the Muslim Brethren in Gaza. Israel legalized the
association in 1978, thereby establishing the legal precondition for the
success of the Muslim Brethren in civil society in Gaza. Committees for
faith, social service, health, sport, and conflict resolution were founded in
the Islamic Center. Kindergartens, schools, medical centers, sport clubs,
and vocational training centers for boys and girls were set up and operated
under the direction of these committees.[22] The Muslim Brethren got a
foothold in almost all the professional associations. In 1983, they gained
control of the Islamic University in Gaza, which had been founded in 1978
as a subsidiary of the al-Azhar University in Cairo.

These institutions derived most of their financing from *zakat* taxes
and donations. The Gulf states made large contributions, and Islamic relief
agencies throughout the world also helped.[23] The number of mosques grew
rapidly: from 200 to 600 in Gaza between 1967 and 1987, and from 400
to 750 in the West Bank in the same period, including a large number of
privately founded mosques (*ahlī*).[24] The Muslim Brothers were also able to
influence the administration of the *waqf* assets, which according to the assessment by Ze'ef Schiff and Ehud Ya'ari amounted to 10 percent of all the
property in Gaza, including private mosques, shops, small businesses, and
apartments.[25] It was possible for the Brethren to amass these assets and set
up these institutions because the administration of Gaza had been relatively
autonomous even in the Egyptian period, and it retained this status under
the Israeli occupying power, where an Israeli officer was responsible for the
legalization of the informal decision-making processes of the local authorities. Half of the Palestinian population was impoverished and lived on less
than $2 a day. In 1997, more than 22,000 families in Gaza and the West
Bank received support from this Center or from Hamas. The Brethren or
Hamas ran 40 percent of all the charities in Gaza and the West Bank.[26]

The Model: Islamic Cells of the Muslim Brethren in Egypt

In addition to the conception of phase-by-phase Islamization, al-Banna introduced another innovation that promoted the formation of Islamic enclaves, namely, a new membership organization. He set this up in 1943, in a situation of increasing repression by the state. Five members formed a "family" (*usra*, plural *usar*), which was headed by one of the members; four "families" formed a higher unity, the "clan" (*'ashīra*), which in turn was directed by one of the heads of the "families."[27] This form of organization went hand in hand with the expectation of a rebirth of Islamic identity. The members of a "family" were to treat one another like brothers and sisters, and to assume responsibility for one another. Accordingly, they were to meet once a week and practice the rituals of their faith together, to eat together, to take part in the Friday prayer, and to make financial contributions to a common fund. This community competed with the ties of family and relationship, which otherwise provided the orientation for the action of the individual in religious matters too. It was not necessary to have the consent of the head of the natural family before becoming a member, and this encouraged a religious individualism. When the Muslim Brethren gained a foothold in Palestine and Jordan, they brought their model of community formation; here, a "family" could have up to ten members.[28]

This societal form was approved by Islamic theoreticians, who regarded the present age as under the domination of a new godless paganism, the *jāhiliyya* (literally, "ignorance"). The most important figure here was the Egyptian Sayyid Qutb (1906–1966), who was initially enchanted by the West, but was then disappointed and became the spokesman of those who wanted to use violence to establish an Islamic order. He argued that the true enslavement of human beings begins whenever they submit to laws that they themselves have made. At present, this is how things were with Egyptian society, and the elites were guilty of apostasy. In this situation, if any convinced Muslims existed, they were obliged to form a movement (*haraka*) and break with the new paganism. Only an avant-garde of the righteous could save Islam. The scenario of a gradual, step-by-step rejection of paganism gave way to one of violent measures inspired by Qur'anic scripture: the apostates must be proclaimed pagans; fellowship with them must be renounced; and violent action must be taken against them. Jihad Islam abandoned the phase model of the Islamic Brethren and substituted a martial ethics of conviction. What was needed now was not patient waiting, but immediate action: the new Islamic beginning would be born in the intention and the convictions of Muslims.

Responding to this appeal in the 1970s, cells of students in Egypt opted out of the mainstream of the Muslim Brethren, calling themselves a "community" (*jamāʿa*) or "righteous struggle" (*jihād*). One should not, however, assume that all these groups were particularly faithful to tradition: Gilles Kepel has vividly described how the pressures of everyday life led such groups to abandon even obligatory Islamic norms governing the relationships between the sexes, causing great irritation to conservative Muslims. This means that they corresponded to the type of "cultural enclave" elaborated by Mary Douglas, where intense internal group pressure is linked to the pursuit of extraordinary values. Far from being identical, modern Islamism and Islamic traditionalism could clash violently.[29]

There was soon dramatic proof of this movement's new readiness to engage in violence. In 1981, Khalid Islambuli, an officer who was a member of a jihad group, had the opportunity to shoot President Anwar al-Sadat during a military parade, and he and co-conspirators were filmed doing so on October 6, 1981.[30] This attack unleashed a wave of repression and persecution of Islamists, and many left the country with the acquiescence, or even the support, of the Egyptian government. They then took part in the jihad against the Soviet Union in Afghanistan, with the result that forms of action and argumentation that had first been developed in Egypt made their way into Osama bin Laden's network.

The Islamist justification for the attack on Sadat is set out in a text composed by one of the conspirators, the electrical engineer Abd al-Salam Faraj (1954–1982),[31] which shows how jihad Islam had developed intellectually and organizationally since the execution of Sayyid Qutb in 1966. Struggling to establish an Islamic order had come to be seen as obligatory for true Muslim believers. The older generation had emphasized the patient Islamization of society and responsibility for the social Islamic institutions that were generated by this process, but Islamist spokesmen now demanded that priority be given to the violent struggle against their own unbelieving rulers.

"Islamic Jihad" in Palestine

Ziad Abu-Amr and Meir Hatina have shown the linkages between Palestinian students in Egypt and Egyptian jihad groups in the late 1970s. The Palestinian organization called Islamic Jihad concurred that the situation in which contemporary Islam found itself was not like that confronted by the Prophet in Mecca, where it had been possible to promote the faith without coercion, but like the one he had faced in Medina, where it had been necessary to defend the Islamic order against its enemies. Islamic Jihad too prized martyrdom, and gave priority to the armed struggle for an Islamic order rather than to the Muslim Brethren's strategies of a gradual Islamization. And its members, who took a vow, were organized in secret underground cells similar to the "families" of the Muslim Brethren.[32]

Ziad Abu-Amir gives the following description of the situation in which the new movement spread in Palestine at that period:

The Muslim Brotherhood, from the Islamic Jihad's point of view, concentrates on religious upbringing and education, in contrast to the nationalist factions of the PLO, which concentrate on struggle. The Muslim Brotherhood has chosen the "path of belief," and did not choose the "path of *jihad.*" The nationalists chose the "path of *jihad*" and have avoided the "path of belief." The uniqueness of the Islamic Jihad movement lies in forging a dialectical relationship between the path of *jihad* and the path of belief.[33]

A new generation of Palestinians was no longer willing to accept the "either/or" of secular political activism or religious quietism. Islamic traditions and models were drawn on to help interpret the situation of the Muslims in Palestine and to direct them to act correctly.

Students who returned from Egypt to Palestine were among the first to join Islamic Jihad. University graduates aged around thirty proved particularly receptive to its message, and they were joined by activists from Fatah, which had a larger number of Islamic activists than other liberation organizations in Palestine. The new group soon won adherents at the Islamic University in Gaza and in the mosques there. Between 1981 and 1983, Islamic Jihad also spread in the West Bank and East Jerusalem. New members were recruited through mosques (the "fortresses of Islam") and through the movement's own media. It entered the public scene thanks to student associations that took part in the elections for student parliaments. It is hard to say how many members it had; Meir Hatina reckons that there were between two and four thousand in Gaza in 1987. Like the Egyptian jihadists, they were not interested in founding and operating social institutions, since this definitely led to dependence on the state. For this reason, their numbers remained small.[34]

The first violent attacks took place in the period between 1983–1984 and 1987, in a phase of increasing tensions between Jewish settlers and Palestinians in the occupied territories. According to data supplied by the Israeli army, 656 disturbances of public order were recorded in the West Bank in 1977; in 1981, there were 1,556, and the number grew to 2,663 in 1984.[35] Ehud Sprinzak calculates that there were at least 3,000 instances of attacks by Arab youths on Israelis between 1981 and the beginning of the First Intifada in 1987.[36] It was in this societal milieu that the Islamic Jihad operated. In 1983, some of its members collaborated with Fatah in carrying out an attack on a talmudic teacher in Hebron. The escape of six Jihad members from the central prison in Gaza in May 1987 caused an especial furor, as did the killing of the commander of the Israeli military police in the Gaza Strip on August 2, 1987, and an armed clash with Israeli security forces on October 6, 1987. This last operation has a place of honor in the chronicles of Islamic Jihad, since it was allegedly the spark that kindled the intifada. Before this, however, the two founders of Islamic Jihad had already been eliminated. Israel condemned Fathi al-Shiqaqa in 1986 to four years in prison; he was expelled in 1988, and subsequently murdered in Cyprus by the Israeli secret service. Sheikh Abdulaziz ʿAuda was expelled from Palestine in November 1987. But the armed violence that they had promoted was soon to be adopted by the Muslim Brethren.

The First Intifada

Hamas was founded in connection with the First Intifada, or uprising of the Palestinians against the Israeli occupying power (1987–1991).[37] The external cause was a traffic accident: an Israeli truck crashed into a line of cars that were queuing at the border crossing of Eretz, and four Palestinians died. Palestinians from the neighboring refugee camp saw this collision as a deliberate act of revenge for an Israeli who had been stabbed earlier in the Gaza Strip. The protest of the enraged Palestinians expressed itself typically in actions of civil disobedience such as displaying forbidden Palestinian flags, shouting Palestinian slogans, and closing shops without giving prior notice. The First Intifada, the "war of the stones," declined in intensity from 1991 on, and finally ended with the signing of the Oslo Accords and the formation of the Palestinian National Authority in 1993.

When the Israeli army used force against the disobedient Palestinians and shot some of them, this provoked a wave of fury in Gaza and the West Bank, and the army increasingly lost control of the situation. The four nationalist fractions that were still operating in the occupied territories—Fatah, the Popular Front for the Liberation of Palestine, the Democratic Front, and the Communist Party—joined to form a United National Command (UNC). Events took the PLO umbrella organization, which had been forced to move to Tunis in 1982, by surprise, but it too got involved from afar in the formation of the UNC. Coordination of the uprising was made easier by the fact that over many years, in the absence of public institutions, numerous Palestinian self-help organizations had come into being. These were headed primarily by members of the younger generation, and this was not fortuitous, since the Israeli government, in the context of its settlement policy, had begun deposing local Palestinian politicians who sympathized with the PLO in 1981; and in the following year, it had completely expelled the PLO from the region. The ensuing gap was filled by student and youth organizations, whose high level of commitment kept the vital social institutions alive. It was also these organizations who gave the uprising its dynamic. The UNC attempted to influence them and direct their actions by means of leaflets.[38]

The uprising was preceded by a sequence of clashes between settlers and Palestinians in the period of the dramatic expansion of Jewish settlements in the occupied territories. If we look back at the initial situation in 1947, the wretched condition of the Palestinians becomes all too clear. The partition plan of 1947 had promised 47 percent of the land to the Palestinians; the Oslo Accord of 1993 granted them only 22 percent; and at the negotiations in Camp David in 2000, the only prospect held out to them was 80 percent of this 22 percent.[39] In addition, Israel's policies made the development of an autonomous Palestinian economy very difficult, precisely at a time when young Palestinians lost the possibilities of finding employment abroad—and the numbers of young people were growing rapidly.

The demands made in the second UNC leaflet of January 10, 1988, summarize the reasons for the Palestinians' rage. They demanded the return of the refugees, Palestinian self-determination and a state of their own, an end to martial law and the deportations, respect for their sanctuaries, the withdrawal of the Israeli army, a prohibition of shooting at young people, the dissolution of the governmental bodies set up by Israel, the holding of free elections, the release of all prisoners, the abolition of value-added tax, and a stop to the expropriations of cultivated land and to the construction of settlements.[40] The uprising was driven by fury at the Israeli occupation of the land and by dwindling hopes for the future.

In this emotionally charged situation, the head of the Islamic Center in Gaza, Sheikh Ahmad Yasin, took the initiative and consulted the most important members of his organization, including the physician Dr. Abdulaziz Rantisi and other Muslim Brethren. They decided that they would not leave the secular groups to coordinate the uprising on their own, since they too had long worked to bring this situation about. They founded their own organization, the Islamic Resistance Movement (Harakat al muqāwama al-Islāmiyya), abbreviated to Hamās (an Arabic word meaning "zeal"). The new organization presented itself on December 14 with its first communiqué; others followed.[41]

The Blessed Intifada of the *Murābitūn*

Initially, the Palestinians conducted the conflict with the instruments of civil disobedience, and the leaflets of the UNC only gradually called for the use of violence; but from the very start, Hamas interpreted the conflict in menacing terms of war and violence.[42] Their first communiqué already speaks of the Palestinian Muslims as "defenders of the border" (*murābitūn*), as the inhabitants of a border fortress (*ribāt*) who must defend Islamic territory against the external foes. Those shot by the Israeli army are martyrs on the path of God, and their death is an expression of the sacrificial spirit of these Palestinians, who loved eternal life more than their enemies loved earthly life. A people that does not fear death, does not die. The uprising is an unmistakable rejection of the Jewish occupation, of the expropriations of land, of the construction of settlements, and of subjugation to the Zionists; it stirs up the consciousness of those who are struggling for breath after a sick peace, after hollow international conferences, and after the traitorous agreement of Camp David. The intifada shows that Islam is the solution and the alternative. The settlers must be made to realize that the Palestinian people knows the path of sacrifice and martyrdom, and that it is generous in this regard.[43] The sixty-six acts of violence against Israelis in the first two years of the intifada, which were often carried out with knives, show how seriously this threat was meant.[44] The second communiqué, once again addressed to the *murābitūn*, speaks correspondingly of the "blessed intifada."

In August 1988, Hamas published its foundational Charter or Covenant. This was preceded by Jordan's renunciation of the West Bank, which cleared the path for a Palestinian state. At the same time, the tensions between nationalists and Islamists were increasing. In its charter, Hamas interpreted the intifada in Islamic language and asserted the claim to found an Islamic state.

In The Name Of The Most Merciful God!

"The Islamic world is on fire. Each of us should pour some water, no matter how little, to extinguish whatever one can without waiting for the others" (Sheikh Amjad al-Zahawi, of blessed memory).

Praise be unto God, to whom we resort for help, and whose forgiveness, guidance and support we seek. . . .

O People:

Out of the midst of troubles and the sea of suffering, out of the palpitations of faithful hearts and cleansed arms; out of the sense of duty, and in response to God's command, the call has gone out rallying people together and making them follow the ways of God, leading them to have determined will in order to fulfill their role in life, to overcome all obstacles, and surmount the difficulties on the way. Constant preparation has continued and so has the readiness to sacrifice life and all that is precious for the sake of God.

Thus it was that the nucleus (of the movement) was formed and started to pave its way through the tempestuous sea of hopes and expectations, of wishes and yearnings, of troubles and obstacles, of pain and challenges, both inside and outside.

When the idea was ripe, the seed grew and the plant struck root in the soil of reality, away from passing emotions, and hateful haste. The Islamic Resistance

Movement emerged to carry out its role through striving for the sake of its Creator, its arms intertwined with those of all the fighters for the liberation of Palestine. The spirits of its fighters meet with the spirits of all the fighters who have sacrificed their lives on the soil of Palestine, ever since it was conquered by the companions of the Prophet, God bless him and grant him salvation, and until this day.[45]

With these almost mythicizing words, the preamble gives the resistance movement a place in salvation history. The text goes on to say that the struggle against the Jews is great and difficult, and demands the utmost exertions. But the Qur'an gives hope and consolation: God and his messenger Muhammad will retain the upper hand. Hamas then presents itself as a wing of the Muslim Brethren (Art. 2) that will free the land from filth, infamy, and evil (Art. 3) and erect the banner of God on every corner of Palestine (Art. 6). The new movement then sets out its prehistory: it is a link in the chain of the jihad against the Zionist invasion and is continuous with the martyrdom of Izz al-Din al-Qassam in 1938, the war of 1948, and the actions of 1968.

This embedded Hamas's violence in a salvation-historical scenario. In Article 7, the charter appeals to a tradition about the Prophet that refers to the end of time. As a rule, Jews play no role in the traditional Islamic scenarios about the end of time; the only exception is the "stones and trees" tradition quoted here:

The Prophet, God bless him and grant him salvation, has said:

"The Day of Judgement will not come about until Moslems fight the Jews (killing the Jews), when the Jew will hide behind stones and trees. The stones and trees will say O Moslems, O Abdulla, there is a Jew behind me, come and kill him. Only the Gharkad tree [the boxthorn, Lycium] would not do that because it is one of the trees of the Jews." [al-Bukhari and Sahih Muslim bk. 041, no. 6985][46]

The Hamas charter then takes up the anti-Semitic conspiracy theory of the forged "Protocols of the Elders of Zion."[47] Art. 22 of the charter declares that the power of Jews lay behind the French Revolution, Communism, secret organizations such as the Freemasons, World War I, the Balfour Declaration, the League of Nations, World War II, and the United Nations. Other contemporary Islamic apocalypses have done the same; some of them seem to have used ideas drawn from Evangelical premillenialism, which says that the Antichrist will set up his bloody regime of terror in Israel in the Last Days.[48]

This interpretative pattern is presupposed in the graffiti, videos, and leaflets of Hamas that Anne Marie Oliver and Paul F. Steinberg have collected and published. Some demonize the Jews, in the style of Sura 5:60 of the Qur'an, as "sons of apes and pigs," paint a sadistic picture of the end they will meet, and positively revel in the fear that will seize the Jews' hearts when they see a "living" martyr. The forefinger raised to heaven, which symbolizes the uniqueness of God and of his Prophet, is celebrated as the finger on the trigger of a machine gun; one single drop of blood shed by a Muslim brings him redemption and a place in Paradise. The burial of a martyr is in reality his wedding.[49] Pictures show Hamas as the ship of redemption, with Sheikh Yasin and Hasan al-Banna hovering above it; on its sails are the words of the Hamas charter, "God is its target, the Prophet is its model, the Koran its constitution: Jihad is its path and death for the sake of God is the loftiest of its wishes."[50]

In this context, the Western media speak of anti-Semitism, but this conceptualization is somewhat misleading. Alexander Flores correctly points out that before the Middle East conflict there was no anti-Semitism in Islam such as there was in Europe.[51] It was only in the course of this conflict that Islamist authors adopted motifs of Western anti-Semitism, but not even this anti-Zionism was racist (as in Europe), although one must admit that the distinction between Zionists and Jews frequently disappeared in the course of the conflict. And in turn, it was this disappearance that strengthened the tendency of the religious Zionists to see in the Palestinians' hostility the manifestation of the anti-Semitism that they know all too well.

Palestine as the Foundational Land of the Prophet

According to the Hamas charter, the Islamic resistance movement came into being at a time in which the social reality of Islam was fading away. In place of the justice there should have been, injustice ruled: the Palestinians' native territory had been stolen from them and their land expropriated; violence had been used against women, children, and old people; houses had been destroyed; young people had been imprisoned (Art. 20). The aim of the struggle was to restore everything to its proper place.

(Art. 9) The Islamic Resistance Movement found itself at a time when Islam has disappeared from life. Thus rules shook, concepts were upset, values changed and evil people took control, oppression and darkness prevailed, cowards became like tigers: homelands were usurped, people were scattered and were caused to wander all over the world, the state of justice disappeared and the state of false-hood replaced it. Nothing remained in its right place. Thus, when Islam is absent from the arena, everything changes. From this state of affairs the incentives are drawn. As for the objectives: They are the fighting against the false, defeating it and vanquishing it so that justice could prevail, homelands be retrieved and from its mosques would the voice of the mu'azen emerge declaring the establishment of the state of Islam, so that people and things would return each to their right places and God is our helper. . . .

(Art. 10) As the Islamic Resistance Movement paves its way, it will back the op-pressed and support the wronged with all its might. It will spare no effort to bring about justice and defeat injustice, in word and deed, in this place and everywhere it can reach and have influence therein. . . .

(Art. 11) The Islamic Resistance Movement believes that the land of Palestine is an Islamic Waqf consecrated for future Moslem generations until Judgment Day. It, or any part of it, should not be squandered: it, or any part of it, should not be given up.

After the conquest of Palestine, Caliph Omar had resolved that the land should remain in the hands of its inhabitants, but that responsibility for the land should be entrusted as a *waqf* to the Muslims until the Last Judg-ment. When Hamas interpreted the situation in this way, it had recourse to a concept that acquired this pregnant meaning only in the conflict with Zionism.[52] The *waqf* institution is indeed ancient, but it is only in recent times that it has been ascribed to the whole of Palestine. In the 1930s, Is-lamic scholars spoke out against the sale of Palestinian land to Jews, and in 1935, the mufti of Jerusalem, Amin al-Husaini, issued a fatwa that declared Palestine to be a possession (*amana*) entrusted to the Muslims and de-nounced those who sold the land as apostates. On the analogy of the Jew-ish idea of a "redemption" of the soil, the Muslims demanded its "rescue."

This integration of an ancient Islamic legal instrument into the in-terpretation of the situation anchored Palestinian nationalism in Islam.

Article 12 states: "Nationalism [*wataniya*], from the point of view of the Islamic Resistance Movement, is part of the religious creed." Peaceful solutions to the conflict that renounce a part of the land are unacceptable. "There is no solution for the Palestinian question except through Jihad. Initiatives, proposals and international conferences are all a waste of time and vain endeavors" (Art. 13). The jihad for the liberation of Palestine is an obligation incumbent on every Muslim, even on women, who do not require the husband's permission for this. As soon as enemies conquer any Muslim territory, jihad is an individual obligation (Art. 15).

Hamas esteems and respects other Islamic movements, since everyone is entitled to an independent interpretation of Islam (*ijtihad*, Art. 23). The PLO is a close comrade, but it has committed the error of adopting the idea of the secular state, which must be rejected as a contradiction of religion. The Islamic character of Palestine is a part of the religion. If the PLO were to adopt Islam as its program, Hamas would be the fuel of its fire. A liberation of the land is conceivable only through the creation of an Islamic legal order, in which Jews and Christians too could live in tranquility and peace.

Martyr Operations / Suicide Attacks

In 1991, Hamas set up a department whose specific task was armed struggle. The military wing was named after Izz al-Din al-Qassam, thereby evoking the resistance of the 1930s.[53] The new brigade became notorious above all for its suicide attacks on civilians; but this practice, which broke international law, developed only gradually. Lebanon provided the model. Israel had unintentionally contributed to this development by expelling 415 Islamists, including Dr. Abdulaziz Rantisi, from the occupied territories in 1992. Lebanon refused to admit them, and they were stuck in no-man's-land for months on end, where members of Hezbollah looked after them and instructed them in the advantages of martyr operations or suicide attacks. Years later, Rantisi stated in a conversation with Mark Juergensmeyer that Hamas's first attacks were only on soldiers in the occupied territories, and that this had changed in 1994, after Baruch Goldstein massacred Muslims at prayer in the Cave of the Patriarchs in Hebron. Before this, only soldiers had been attacked; afterwards, civilians in Israel itself were also attacked.[54] It is possible to verify Rantisi's affirmation. Robert A. Pape has published tables of all the suicide attacks throughout the world between 1980 and 2003 and arranged them according to time, the kind of weapons used, the organization responsible, the goal, and the number of persons killed. His classification of this particularly objectionable form of violence shows two things: first, that (only) 50 percent of all the attacks of this kind were the work of Islamic groups, and second, that 95 percent of all attacks were carried out in organized campaigns within a limited space of time.[55]

The first Hamas campaign took place on April 6 and 13, 1994. Forty days after Goldstein's massacre in the Cave of the Patriarchs, a suicide attack was carried out against a bus in the town of Afula in northern Israel—a variant of the usual commemorative ceremonies for martyrs forty days after their death. A Hamas communiqué praised the perpetrator, Ra'id Zakarna, as a martyr. Following the instructions of Yahya Ayyash, the "engineer," he had packed a car with 157 kilograms of explosives and drove it directly into a number 348 bus, killing nine Israelis and wounding fifty-two, twenty of whom were so severely injured that—as the communiqué notes with sadistic satisfaction—they would have to live for the rest of their days with disfigured faces and amputated hands and feet.[56] One week later, a bus in Hadara in Israel was attacked; once again, some died and many were wounded. The perpetrators and their sympathizers completely overlook the fact that such an attack is a grave violation of the Fourth Geneva Convention. A 2002 Human Rights Watch report by Joe Stork titled *Erased in a Moment,* which denounces these suicide attacks as crimes against humanity and war crimes, recapitulates the legal rules governing armed conflicts.[57]

A second campaign began when the Israeli army attempted to use force to free a soldier who had been kidnapped by Hamas, and three Hamas guards (as well as the Israeli soldier) were killed. This was on October 9, 1994. Ten days later, Hamas took revenge in a suicide attack on a bus in Tel Aviv in which twenty-one Israelis and a Netherlander died. On November 2, an Israeli car bomb killed a leader of the Islamic Jihad in Gaza—this was avenged nine days later, when a suicide attacker rode his bicycle into an Israeli checkpoint and set off the explosives he was carrying, taking the lives of three soldiers and his own. After a further six attacks by the two organizations, this campaign closed with the last attack on August 21, 1995.

The next cycle began when the Israeli secret service killed Yahya Ayyash, the "engineer," with a bomb in his mobile telephone on January 5, 1996. This provoked a tremendous outrage, and 100,000 Palestinians attended his funeral. Four suicide attacks followed in February and March 1996. Another series of three attacks followed between March and September 1997.

The longest and most severe campaign, with a total of ninety-two attacks (according to the calculations by R. A. Pape), lasted from October 2000 to the end of December 2003. It was generated and sustained by the outrage provoked by Ariel Sharon, at that time leader of the Opposition, when he visited the Temple Mount. Accompanied by 4,000 heavily armed Israeli police officers and border policemen, he entered the Muslim precincts in order to display to the whole world (as he himself publicly declared) that the Temple Mount belonged exclusively and forever under Jewish sovereignty. The Second Intifada, which he thereby unleashed, was accompanied by a new campaign of martyr operations under the aegis of Hamas and Islamic Jihad. This time, this form of struggle was adopted by secular nationalist groups too. Fatah set up its own al-Aqsa Brigade, which operated in the same way. The Popular Front for the Liberation of Palestine also joined in. An incessant wave of suicide attacks were carried out on Israeli civilians in the heartland of Israel itself, each time prompting severe reprisals by Israel.[58]

Individual incidents outside such campaigns may already have occurred in Palestine at an earlier date. According to Ami Pedahzur, who has likewise investigated all the suicide attacks throughout the world and established a chronological sequence, the first attack by Hamas took place on November 2, 1993, that is, before Baruch Goldstein's massacre in Hebron; there were no deaths or injuries.[59] And according to Joseph Croitoru, a number of attacks of this kind were carried out by Palestinians as early as the 1970s.[60] However, the details are uncertain, and do not amount to a refutation of Pape's claim that the suicide attack is a weapon chosen by a community in a region that has been occupied by democratic states, and in which the people are too weak to mount a successful military resistance.[61] In such situations, a weapon of this kind can be meaningful. Opinion surveys among Palestinians confirm Pape's interpretation, since approval of such attacks on Israelis has grown since 1995. Pape's hypothesis is that this attitude among the public accounts for the growth in popularity of those liberation groups that practiced this form of struggle.[62] This would also explain why secular resistance groups too adopted it after 2000, in the Second Intifada. Pape concludes:

Hamas's discourse on martyrdom strongly reinforces the altruistic purpose of the group. Like Hezbollah, the main argument is that martyrdom is justified by its instrumental value in protecting the local community from a foreign occupation and not as an end in itself. Statements by the Hamas Political Bureau routinely follow the three-part logic that suicide operations are a response to occupation, mandated by the weakness in conventional force, and justified by Israel's vulnerability to coercive pressure.[63]

If it is correct to state that the suicide attack is not specifically Islamic, but is a weapon that people employ under the two conditions mentioned above, its diffusion in the Middle East may not be attributed to an intrinsically violent Islam. Rather, its evaluation must also bear in mind the occupation of Palestine by democratic Israel.[64]

The typical suicide attack is not an individual action, but is organized by a team that justifies the deed, determines its goal, and gives the perpetrator his instructions. The perpetrator often belongs to the middle classes; it is certainly not true that he is always a particularly uneducated believer. The more one knows about the campaigns, the action, and the profile of these perpetrators, the more clearly one sees that this action belongs to the category of suicide that Emile Durkheim called "altruistic"— a selfless death on behalf of a community. In this instance, the community is a faith community, and this means that special meanings are linked to dying and to death.[65]

Hamas's Relationship to Israel: Coexistence Within Conflict

Hamas's relationship to Israel is less clear-cut than this idealization of vengeance and violence might suggest. Although Hamas possessed institutions and structures that allowed it to mobilize its members and Muslims effectively against the occupying power, it also had interpretative patterns that allowed it to react flexibly to changing situations.[66] After the Oslo Accords, it could no longer avoid the question of participation in political elections. The members began to discuss this question and even to reflect on the possibilities of a truce (not a peace) with Israel. In 1992, in view of the expected Palestinian autonomy and the elections that would then be imminent, an internal Hamas document considered the various options: to boycott or prevent the elections, or to take part under another name or its own name. The movement tended to favor participation, since the Islamic movement had gained considerable prestige during the years of the intifada; it had won many followers and must not lose sight of its own fundamental interests. Hamas must not isolate itself politically, but must safeguard its popular basis by means of elections. At the same time, however, it must continue the jihad for the liberation of Palestine even in the time of autonomy, resisting the normalization of the status quo and any abandonment of Palestinian rights.[67] Two Israeli scholars have described this position as a "coexistence within conflict."[68]

When Hamas decided to take part in the elections in 2006, thus emphasizing coexistence rather than conflict, the governments of Israel and the United States saw this as the attempt by a terrorist organization to take over the Palestinian National Authority. The organization itself saw things very differently: the decision was the consequence of a new definition of the situation, which counseled a renunciation of violence. The social institutions that the Muslim Brethren and the Islamic Center ran, and that had become vitally necessary for many Palestinians, demanded an ethics of responsibility rather than a martial ethics of conviction.

The social network that the Muslim Brethren had created was a favorable breeding ground for the readiness of those who belonged to this network to defend it with violence against assaults from without or within. Nevertheless, precisely the same milieu made a certain flexibility in the struggle against Israel necessary. Both attitudes were rooted in the constraints imposed by the social work of Hamas. Unlike Islamic Jihad, which practiced a martial ethics of conviction, Hamas did not see the struggle exclusively from the perspective of a martial proof of the faith, but also as committed action on behalf of the common good (*maṣlaḥa*). This exposed them to a danger against which Abd al-Salam Faraj had warned in *The Neglected Duty*. He criticized Islamic institutions for contributing nothing to the formation of an Islamic state; on the contrary, they cemented a dependence of Muslims on the apostate state (§ 48). He also expressed a negative judgment about the formation of an Islamic party (§ 52) and about the adoption by Muslims of socially important professions such as doctor or engineer. No matter how numerous these were, they would only help consolidate a pagan state (§ 53).[69] Hamas, however, did not heed this warning. On this point, they remained a part of the Muslim Brethren.

The social network in which Hamas operated made caution and prudence necessary when conflicts arose with militarily superior Israel. The social Islam of Hamas had succeeded in intensively penetrating civil society, but this success confronted the Islamists with new tasks and compelled them to accept new rules, not only in Palestine, but throughout the world. Dietrich Reetz aptly summarizes the dynamic inherent in this civil-societal Islam when he writes that in most Islamic countries, the Islamists come under the heading of civil society because they exist in the "no-man's-land" between the individual household and the state— alongside the activists for human rights and for the environment, and the left-wing and democratic opposition. The Islamists increasingly see themselves as obliged to take up social, cultural, and political problems that the official state does not solve—either because it cannot or because it does not want to.[70]

The civil-societal institutionalization entailed limitations on action that the author of *The Neglected Duty* correctly recognizes; as a convinced jihadist, he completely rejects them. In the case of Hamas, we see this difference in the fact that its leaflets never preached only violence. They also preached patience, for example in the text: "Know that victory demands patience [*sabr*] and God is on the side of the righteous."[71] One and the same power of a social Islam both makes violence against the occupier possible and sets limits to violence. Hamas cannot imagine a genuine peace with Israel, but a truce (*hudna*) is conceivable.[72] This option, however, was dismissed as utterly absurd by the ruling politicians in Israel and the United States, although historical studies show that Islamic states certainly know an international law, and that there is a tradition of such treaties that guarantee security in the relationships with non-Islamic states.[73]

Even more striking is the case of the Egyptian Jama'a al-Islamiyya, which revised its strategy of violence in 1997 and made a truce with the institutions of the Egyptian state, which it had hitherto detested.[74] The reaction of the United States and Israel to the offer by Hamas shows the extent to which the cycle of violence has gained a firm place in the perception of the situation. But if these statesmen refuse in principle to study the way in which their political opponents interpret the situation, preferring instead to destroy them militarily as enemies of ordered human life in society, they themselves are acting in accordance with an ethics of conviction, not with an ethics of responsibility. They are perfectly well aware that this means that there is no chance of realizing the nonviolent options for action contained in Hamas's definition of the situation of its community.

CHAPTER 8

American Evangelicals Prepare
the Eschatological Battlefield in
Palestine

The culture of a country is a factor that influences its foreign policy, and it is time to take this connection more seriously with regard to
the religious history of a country too. The reversal in the American policy vis-à-vis Israel's settlement policy in the occupied territories, accompanied by the rejection of the justified claims of the Palestinians—who include Christians—cannot be satisfactorily explained without taking the
religious context into account. Here, we must bear in mind the special religious history of the United States, since even after the Enlightenment,
religious values and worldviews lost none of their power in American public life, and they influenced the process whereby the United States became
a nation.[1]

Since the end of the 1970s, changes have taken place in the relationship of Evangelical faith communities to politics similar to those that have
occurred in Judaism in Israel and in Islam in Palestine. In those cases,
we recall, the antagonism between a politics justified in secular terms,
on the one hand, and a distance taken by faith communities vis-à-vis
the political realm, on the other, gave way to a new union of the two.
Something similar happened in the United States, where the opposition
between liberal political involvement and fundamentalist quietism lost its

dominance and gave way to a new kind of religious activism on the part of fundamentalists.[2]

From the 1920s on, fundamentalist groups had withdrawn from the public political sphere and left politics to the parties. But as a reforming liberalism gained an increasing ascendancy from the mid 1950s to the mid 1970s and the neutrality of the state on moral questions began to gain acceptance, these groups felt summoned to put up resistance. The fundamentalists were particularly outraged by the Supreme Court's prohibition of prayer in public schools in 1962 and the partial liberalization of abortion in 1973; their reaction was shared by the Pentecostal movement, the charismatics, and the neo-Evangelicals. These "Evangelicals"—to use the collective term for this mostly white Protestant camp—saw these and other court decisions as undermining the morality of America and utterly unacceptable.[3] The Evangelicals differed from the "social gospel" of liberal Protestant churches by seeing the principal cause of societal disorders such as unwanted pregnancies, increasing numbers of divorces, prostitution, pornography, and dependence on alcohol and drugs, not in societal circumstances, but in the "unconverted" state of human beings. They fought for the United States as a Christian nation, a republic founded on the values of family and patriotism, with state institutions and laws that were meant to uphold this morality. If need be, a genuine American must rebel against legislation and an administration of justice that deviated from this. Evangelicals made their voice heard in the public arena by running radio and television stations and private schools. With their networks of parishes, schools, universities, judicial organizations, and media, they find approval by roughly a quarter of all American voters today.[4]

At the end of the 1970s, representatives of the political right wing joined the preacher Jerry Falwell and other pastors in founding the organization the Moral Majority. The electoral potential of the Evangelicals had become interesting. "Entrepreneurs of the movement" (to use Manfred Brocker's term) built up new and powerful organizations that drew on the already existing resources and networks to mobilize citizens against abortion, for the protection of the family, for the retention of laws prohibiting immoral conduct, and for a militarily strong United States. They made a decisive contribution to the election of Ronald Reagan in 1980, and he took up many of their views during his period in office, for example, when

he painted the scenario of a nuclear "Armageddon" or castigated the Soviet Union as the "evil empire." This, however, did not prevent him from
concluding disarmament treaties with Mikhail Gorbachev, on whose
forehead many Evangelicals thought they could see the mark of the Antichrist. As yet, Reagan's advisers were able to keep the neoconservatives,
who were then in the ascendant, at arm's length from the government.[5]

The Moral Majority collapsed as an organization in 1986–1987, but
its place was soon taken by successors such as the Christian Coalition. In
the 1990s, the New Christian Right, with a great number of organizations
and initiatives, became established as a political heavyweight and became
increasingly influential in the Republican Party.[6] This was paralleled by
the continuing ascendancy of the neoconservatives, who became leaders
of public opinion in the 1990s. After the end of the Cold War and the
disintegration of the Soviet Union, they proclaimed that the new task of
the United States was no longer only to advocate what was morally right,
but to enforce this militarily in the international arena. They saw the
Middle East as the principal arena for this struggle. They had a dismissive
attitude toward international organizations that preferred nonmilitary
solutions. The New Christian Right on its own could not determine the
outcome of elections, and the Republican Party with its neoconservatives
had no chance of winning without the Christian Right. In this situation,
the party's committees believed at the end of the 1990s that the governor
of Texas, George W. Bush, was the most promising presidential candidate, because he was well established in the Evangelical camp. After he
was elected president, neoconservatives were given key positions in the
new administration, and this brought a new orientation to Middle East
policies.

Already in 1996, neoconservatives acting for the American Enterprise
Institute had advised the Israeli Prime Minister, Benjamin Netanyahu, to
free himself from the fetters of the peace process. In their eyes, Israel was
threatened by a loss of the critical mass for the nation: one disturbing
symptom of this state of affairs was the fact that Israel was negotiating
with the Palestinians even about its own capital, Jerusalem. And the fact
that Israel reacted to terror only with acts of reprisal, rather than by pur-
suing the terrorist groups into the neighboring countries and eliminat-
ing them militarily, was a sign of weakness. Israel ought to make a clean

break with the policy of "land for peace." It must strengthen its economy through liberalization and take pride in its own strength, independently of the United States. This is expressed as follows in a speech by an imaginary new Israeli prime minister in a report authored by Richard Perle and others for the Institute for Advanced Strategic and Political Studies' "Study Group on a New Israeli Strategy Toward 2000":

Our claim to the land—to which we have clung in hope for 2000 years—is legitimate and noble. It is not *within our own power,* no matter how much we concede, *to make peace unilaterally.* Only the unconditional acceptance by Arabs of our rights, *especially* in their territorial dimension, *"peace for peace,"* is a solid basis for the future.[7]

Instead of an equal treatment of Israeli and Palestinian claims, the neoconservatives one-sidedly aligned themselves with Israel. This change was religiously justified. One can see in this policy a desecularization of government action,[8] bearing in mind Ernst-Wolfgang Böckenförde's thesis about the genesis of the state in Western Europe: "At the mention of secularization in the context of the emergence of the state, most people think of the . . . declaration of neutrality with regard to questions of religious truth."[9] The neoconservatives' strategy did not remain pure theory. In their foreign policy, successive U.S. administrations have abandoned neutrality vis-à-vis religious claims and sided with Israel's policy on the question of the occupied territories.

The Desecularization of American Foreign Policy

Without the Evangelical voters, this political program would have stood no chance of becoming reality. Religions had already been growing in power in the United States over a long period, but this development took many by surprise, even among those who studied religion in an academic context. As late as the 1960s, the words of Arnold Toynbee expressed a consensus: "All current religions—whether tribe-bound or missionary or 'lower' or 'higher'—have been losing their hold on the hearts and consciences and minds of their former adherents."[10] Peter L. Berger himself had declared in his 1967 diagnosis of religious communality that it lacked societal reality in the modern world.[11] It may indeed have seemed at that time that communal religion was one of the losers of the modern period, but things soon changed. Two American sociologists of religion, Roger Finke and Rodney Stark, have calculated on the basis of statistics of American Christian denominations across the whole period from 1776 to 1990 that the percentage of citizens in the United States who were members of a Christian congregation has grown constantly. In 1850, one-third of all Americans were members; in 1980, two-thirds belonged to congregations.[12] The trend continued after that date. Those who profited from this enormous growth were not liberal communities, but closed communities ("sects") that made high moral demands of the lifestyle of their members.[13] The two sociologists looked for the explanation in a hypothesis of economics, according to which large hierarchical organizations tend toward complacency, whereas small faith communities compete with other groups and must therefore continuously try to recruit new members. This means that the religious market is exploited in the best possible way, stimulating a diversification of religion. Secularization is not the consequence of a declining religious need, but of an unattractive offer on the market.[14]

In addition to this explanation, which has not gone uncontested,[15] another explanation looks to the specific type of community formation. In the United States, religions have taken on the form of congregations. This applies even to religions (such as Hinduism) that traditionally were not congregational. One survey has counted more than 300,000 local congregations. These share certain organizational characteristics. As congregations, they possess land and buildings; laypersons play the dominant role in the leadership of the congregation; the congregation elects its ministers; the congregation is dependent on private financial backers. Its activities are not restricted to worship or religious instruction, but also include charitable assistance and active involvement in civil society. The relocation of residential areas from the city center to the suburbs helped to spread this type of faith community: the lack of public institutions in the suburbs made religious communality particularly attractive there.[16] It is not by chance that it was American social scientists who focused on the subject of the social capital of faith communities and its impact on civil society. The welfare legislation of 1996 even made it possible for faith communities to receive financial means from the state to support their social work. A number of solid monographs have recently investigated

both quantitatively and qualitatively the modern formation of faith communities in the United States, confirming that this continues to expand
greatly,[17] whereas this is not the case in Europe (with the exception of
migrant groups).

This new evidence led to a critical examination of the secularization thesis. Looking back over the 1990s, it became clear that the thesis
of a decline in the importance of religion as a necessary accompaniment
of modernization was due to specific circumstances and experiences of
the 1950s and 1960s.[18] Earlier sociologists such as Max Weber and Emile
Durkheim did not maintain the thesis in this form, since both these authors of classic works assumed that religion would be transformed in the
modern period, not that it would disappear. Studies by Callum G. Brown
in Great Britain are interesting in this context. In the "long sixties" (from
the late 1950s to the mid 1970s), church attendance declined so drastically
that one can speak of a collapse of the Christian life-world. Historians and
sociologists came to accept secularization as a kind of master-narrative for
the entire history of religion in the West since the seventeenth century.[19]
Similar expectations existed in the United States at the same time, as Peter
L. Berger's words attest. In reality, however, the development in the 1960s
was not in the least symptomatic of a long-term global tendency.

Premillenialist Constructions of
Contemporary Politics

The singular historical viewpoint of American Evangelical congregations was another force driving their increased religiosity. Complex and
intensive researches have shed light on this aspect of Protestantism. They
show, first of all, that one must not let oneself be astray by the word "fundamentalism." The "fundamentalists" were indeed concerned to defend
the true faith through the dogmatization of "fundamental" Christian
doctrines. For example, the General Assembly of the Presbyterian Church
in 1910 declared the following five dogmas to be binding in their literal
sense: the infallibility of scripture, the birth of Jesus Christ from a virgin,
his atoning sacrifice, his bodily resurrection, and his power to work mira-
cles.[20] We must however draw a distinction between the acute controver-
sies that these dogmas provoked in the first two decades of the twentieth

century, leading to schisms above all in Baptist and Presbyterian congregations, and an older religious movement that had joined forces with this religious tendency. Here, I follow Ernest R. Sandeen, who clearly separates the controversy and the movement. The formulation of the right faith in the form of fundamental dogmas rested on the doctrine of the literal inspiration of the Bible, which the Presbyterian Princeton Theological Seminary upheld with particular emphasis (and indeed exaggeration) against liberal theology. The movement, on the other hand, was inspired by a view of salvation history: "It is millenarianism which gave life and shape to the Fundamentalist movement," Sandeen writes.[21] The book series *The Fundamentals,* which made the new faith known in the country between 1910 and 1915, was based on a conjunction of biblical literalism and millenarianism. When the World's Conference on Christian Fundamentals was formed in 1919, this alliance received an organizational form and the millenarians became fundamentalists.[22]

Premillenialism went back to John Nelson Darby (1800–1882), a Briton whose teachings swelled to become an ever mightier current in the United States from 1875 to the present day.[23] Darby taught that after Israel had rejected the Messiah, Jesus Christ, the further fulfillment of the biblical prophecies had been interrupted; Israel's salvation history was suspended for a period, during which the Church was the bearer of salvation history. In the present age, however, this period ("dispensation") was nearing its end. Very soon, the eschatological clock will begin striking again, and all the prophecies that are still pending will be fulfilled in a final phase of history. These include the reestablishing of the people of Israel in Palestine. Darby's teachings did not predict when this would take place: it could happen "at any moment."

Premillenialism did not owe its influence to any precise chronological predictions of the day and the hour of the coming of the Lord. The situation was different in the first decades of the nineteenth century, when many Christians believed William Miller's prediction that the age of salvation would dawn in 1844. After the inevitable "great disappointment," the adherents of Darby's premillenialism refused to tie themselves down to a precise chronology. This, however, did not lead to any relaxation of the tension between the false present-day order and the future kingdom of God, since it is precisely the possibility of a sudden and unforeseeable irruption of the eschaton that demands of the believers a continuous sanctification of their life and a permanent alertness, less they fail to notice the first indications that history is about to change.

This tension was intensified by a puzzling and much disputed detail that Darby had added to the apocalyptic scenario, namely, the doctrine of the "rapture" of the righteous or of the Church. The question of its provenance has not been completely cleared up. Before the period of sufferings begins, the elect will be caught up to the Lord, thus escaping the terror that will then ensue.[24] The textual basis for this belief was the First Letter of Paul to the Thessalonians.

For the Lord himself shall descend from heaven with a shout, with the voice of the archangel and with the trump of God: and the dead in Christ shall rise first. Then we which are alive and remain shall be caught up together with them in the clouds, to meet the Lord in the air; and so shall we ever be with the Lord. (1 Thess. 4:16–17)[25]

Darby taught that after the rapture, a terrible tribulation (Matt. 24:21) would begin for those left behind. This would last for seven years. In this period, the Antichrist would exercise his reign of terror over the world; the Jews would return to Palestine and rebuild the Temple, in accord with him. At the end, however, the Lord Jesus Christ would annihilate the Antichrist, together with the Gentiles and the Jews—if they remained obdurate—in the battle of Armageddon in Palestine. Jews who refused to abandon Judaism and become Christians would be destroyed because of their unbelief. After this, the thousand-year kingdom of God would begin.[26] This doctrine was called premillenialism because it taught that there would be a first appearance of Jesus Christ before the time of horror. It differs on this point from postmillenialism, which holds that he will appear only at the very end of time.[27]

This view of history transforms experiences of meaninglessness into a meaningful sequence and imposes on the contemporary power of evil a historical scheme.[28] Stephen D. O'Leary has used a rhetorical analysis to distill the discursive strategies and arguments from American millenarian writings and speeches,[29] which provide a particularly fruitful and informative object of study. At the heart of premillenialism is the diagnosis of the manifestations of evil and the symptoms of the approaching end here and now. This gives premillenialism a considerable potential for sensitivity in the diagnosis of contemporary history and the politics of the day. Premillenialism is a cultural "superpower" in the generation of situational definitions that guide concrete action. It is only through analyzing its rhetoric that one can understand a contradiction that has so often been noted, namely, that although premillenialism teaches a pessimistic view of history, it also generates political activism.

The Miracle of the Restoration of Israel

American fundamentalism's creed affirms what the Apostle Paul once entrusted to the community in Rome as a great mystery: "A hardening has come upon part of Israel, until the full number of the Gentiles come in, and so all Israel will be saved" (Rom. 11:25–27). Some of the Fathers of the Church, such as Augustine, believed that the biblical promises that had not yet been fulfilled no longer concerned the Jewish people in any way, but referred to the Church as the "true Israel," but English and American Puritans continued to understand the promises of salvation as speaking of the people of the Jews. They awaited a return of the Jews to Palestine as the final event of the beginning of the Last Days. Israel is a decisively important actor in the final act of human history.

When innumerable Jews were forced to flee from Russia in the second half of the nineteenth century, American Evangelicals submitted a petition in 1891 to U.S. President Benjamin Harrison and Secretary of State James Blaine in which they took the lead in pointing out the plight of these refugees and requested a solution—six years *before* the First Zionist Congress in Basle (1897). They wrote that the situation of the two million impoverished Jews who could find no permanent home in Europe was intolerable. Why not give them back Palestine, instead of bringing them to America? After all, God had once given it to them as their inalienable land. Jews had once again settled there, and the first signs of a new age of salvation could be discerned. The Blackstone Memorial of 1891 states:

Does not Palestine as rightfully belong to the Jews? It is said that rains are increasing and there are many evidences that the land is recovering its ancient fertility. If they could have autonomy in government the Jews of the world would rally to transport and establish their suffering brethren in their time-honored habitation. For over seventeen centuries they have patiently waited for such a privileged opportunity. They have not become agriculturists elsewhere because they believed they were mere sojourners in the various nations, and were yet to return to Palestine and till their own land. . . . We believe this is an appropriate time for all nations, and especially the Christian nations of Europe, to show kindness to Israel. A million of exiles, by their terrible suffering, are piteously appealing to our sympathy, justice, and humanity. Let us now restore to them the land of which they were so cruelly despoiled by our Roman ancestors.[30]

As an Evangelical petition, this document is astonishing: at a time when the nascent Zionism was propagating the national right of the Jews to a state of their own, the petitioners saw in the Jewish settling of Palestine the imminent end of the exile and the sign of a new age of salvation. The puzzle is solved when one considers the theological background of the initiator of the petition, William E. Blackstone.[31] He belonged to the same tradition as Darby and had declared in his book *Jesus Is Coming* (1881) that in a very short time, the fifth epoch of world history, which had ended with the crucifixion of Jesus, would be followed by the sixth and last epoch. All those prophecies that had not yet been fulfilled would now come to pass— including the restoration of Israel. This, however, would be followed by a terrible period of castigations and sufferings for Israel. The Antichrist would appear and establish himself as the ruler of the Jewish state. The terror would end only with the battle of Armageddon in Palestine (Rev. 16:16). Then the powers of evil would be destroyed and the thousand-year reign of Christ would begin (Rev. 20).

Blackstone's affirmations about Israel resemble those of Orthodox Jews who likewise regarded the restoration of Israel as a messianic act— though with the difference that they saw the settling of the Land before the days of the Messiah as apostasy. Only the adherents of religious Zionism would have been more to Blackstone's taste—but once again, with the difference that he would have demanded that they too convert to Jesus Christ. At a Jewish Zionist meeting in Los Angeles in 1918, he was bold enough to say that secular Zionists and assimilated Jews must expect to suffer the most dreadful terrors of the Last Days. He regarded a secular justification of Zionism as completely erroneous.[32] As a matter of fact, most American Jews at that time spoke against a Jewish state, since they tended rather to see the United States as their "Zion." Accordingly, there were few convinced Jewish Zionists in the United States; before World

War I, according to data obtained by Timothy Weber, of 1.5 million Jews only 20,000 were members of Zionist associations. He concludes from this that at that period, more American Evangelicals than American Jews were interested in a Jewish state in Palestine.[33]

The religious interpretation of the Zionist settlement had repercussions on the way in which the authors of the Blackstone Memorial understood their government. They saw the Americans as the descendants of the Romans—a view supported also by terms such as "Senate" and "Capitol" for the political institutions of the United States. They believed that God had envisaged for the United States a role similar to that of the Persian king Cyrus, who helped the Jews to return to Palestine from their Babylonian exile and who is therefore called the "anointed [*mashiach*] of the Lord" in Isaiah 45:1. Blackstone believed that he had also found a biblical prophecy that predicted in advance the special role of the United States. When the prophet Isaiah spoke of the "land of whirring wings" that would bring gifts to Zion (Isa. 18:1,7), he could only have meant the United States—as is indicated by the bald eagle on the Great Seal of the United States.[34]

Belief in prophecy is more central to the political culture of America than was long supposed; this has been demonstrated above all by the historian Paul S. Boyer in his thorough study of the modern American belief in prophecy. All the political events surrounding the foundation of a state of Israel kindled an apocalyptic fever in American Evangelicals: the Balfour Declaration of 1917, which held out to the Jews the prospect of Palestine as their homeland; the withdrawal of the British from Palestine and the partition plan of the United Nations in 1947; the proclamation of the state of Israel on May 14, 1948; the Suez War in 1957; the conquest of the Old City of Jerusalem by the Israeli army on June 8, 1967, and the occupation of Gaza and the West Bank in the course of the Six-Day War in 1967; and finally, the settling of the occupied territories. The conclusion that Boyer draws from his investigation of the belief in prophecy is similar to that drawn by O'Leary. Boyer too sees premillenialism as an instrument employed by believers to interpret their situation and to infer practical consequences for action. This applies to other parts of the premillenialist interpretative pattern too. The last chapter of Bernard McGinn's study of the history of the Antichrist is entitled: "Antichrist Our Contemporary."

Americans are obsessed with putting a name to the Antichrist.[35] They have repeatedly been convinced that some particularly cruel ruler was the Antichrist: Benito Mussolini, Adolf Hitler, Saddam Hussein, and most recently Osama bin Laden. When the first photographs were circulated after Mikhail Gorbachev's election as general secretary of the Communist Party of the Soviet Union, fundamentalists similarly believed that the red birthmark on his forehead was the sign of the Antichrist.[36]

"Specifics change; underlying thematic structures remain," P. S. Boyer aptly writes of American premillenialism.[37] The premillenialists saw fresh confirmation of their position in the period leading up to the Iraq War, when not a few Americans read the contemporary events through the filter of their belief in prophecy.[38] This was repeated during Israel's war against Lebanon in the summer of 2006.

Timothy Weber's investigation concentrates somewhat more on political activity. The "restoration" of Israel in Palestine in the course of the twentieth century also had repercussions on the attitude taken by the premillenialists to politics. "For the first time [they] believed that it was necessary to leave the bleachers and get onto the playing field to make sure the game ended according to the divine script," Weber observes.[39] The Evangelicals were no longer content with the role of onlookers: they wanted to be actors. Weber demonstrates this by means of a presentation of the military and political steps whereby the state of Israel came into being, identifying in each case the active part played by Protestant states and statesmen. And the exorbitant military and financial aid that the United States supplies to the state of Israel is due not only to the influence of a Jewish lobby, as has recently been asserted:[40] another reason lies in the wide diffusion of this Evangelical view of history.

The Popularization of the Premillenialists' View of History

The premillenialist conception of history has had an influence far beyond the fundamentalist faith communities. The precursor of a popularization of the eschatological scenario was Hal Lindsey, with his book *The Late Great Planet Earth* (1970).[41] Lindsey was born in 1929 and studied at Dallas Theological Seminary, a stronghold of dispensationalist premillenialism.[42] In the spring of 1968, as head of the organization Campus Crusade for Christ, he visited California universities and held a series of lectures on five consecutive evenings about the imminent End of the Ages. These became the core of his book about the "defunct" great planet Earth. He preached that the final epoch of the fulfillment of the biblical prophecies about the end of time was imminent: the infallible sign of this was the restoration of Israel in the Holy Land in 1948. The theater of war was being made ready. The time had come of which Jesus said:

From the fig tree learn its lesson: as soon as its branch becomes tender and puts out its leaves, you know that summer is near. So also, when you see all these things, you know that he is near, at the very gates. Truly, I say to you, this generation will not pass away until all these things take place. (Matt. 24:32–34)

Now that Israel has been restored, only one generation separates us from the beginning of the seven-year epoch of tribulation. In other words, this will begin in 1988 at the latest. Usually, premillenialists exercise caution in questions about the calculation of the end, but here Hal Lindsey throws caution to the winds. Almost imperceptibly, a prognosis once again accompanied the diagnosis.[43]

His interpretation of history goes on to say that the necessary precondition for the rebuilding of the Temple had been fulfilled with the 1967 war and the incorporation of the Old City of Jerusalem into the state of Israel. Besides this, the geopolitical alliances of the battle of Armageddon could already be discerned (chaps. 5–9). The threat to Israel from the Soviet Union in the north and Egypt in the south, as well as the return of the Roman empire in the form of the European Community, belonged to the Last Days. The next event would be the rapture of the righteous from the earth. People would be caught up all of a sudden from the cars in which they were traveling, or from a football match or from religious education class. Even heads of state would suddenly disappear, and the United Nations would promise its help to find them.

After the rapture, there would be a period of suffering. In World War III, Israel would be attacked from all sides. The Antichrist would promise to give peace to this world, and Israel would make a pact with him. Through a clever solution to the Middle East problem, the Antichrist would make good his promise and give the war-weary world peace. This would be followed by the coming of the Lord (chaps. 11–13). A nuclear war would destroy the world, and Jesus Christ would establish the kingdom of God.

In the run-up to the presidential election in 1980, Hal Lindsey published a new book.[44] He paints a gloomy picture of the various fates that threaten the United States: it may be taken over by the Communists, or it may be destroyed in a surprise nuclear attack by the Soviet Union, or it may become dependent on the ten states of the European Community. Nevertheless, he sees a glimmer of hope. A political program could save the United States—a program that cuts back the welfare state and bureaucracy, rejects disarmament treaties, and makes America a military superpower through rearmament. This is presented as a way to preserve the faith in the struggle against the powers of the Antichrist; in reality, it was the electoral program of the Republicans. However, the new president, Ronald Reagan, was not himself an Evangelical, nor did he come from the circle of the New Christian Right. As a Hollywood actor whose first marriage had ended in divorce, he was not their ideal candidate, but he positioned himself so skillfully that their choice soon fell on him. When the Soviet Union disintegrated, Lindsey wrote a book with Chuck Missler, *The Magog Factor,* in which he reallocated the role of the Evil One in the apocalyptic drama. Now it was the Islamists who took on the role of the Antichrist and his adherents.[45]

"Rapture" as the Plot of a Novel

Hal Lindsey's *The Late Great Planet Earth* was almost unimaginably successful: thirty-five million copies of this book were sold up to 1990, contributing to an enormous popularization of the premillenialist conception of history. But even this success was outdone by *Left Behind,* a series of novels by Tim LaHaye and Jerry Jenkins. Tim LaHaye, born in 1926, studied at the fundamentalist Bob Jones University and was one of the founders of the Moral Majority. He taught that the rapture would take place before the beginning of the time of tribulation. He wished to use novels to make this view popular, and he found a partner in the gifted author Jerry Jenkins. The first novel, *Left Behind: A Novel of the Earth's Last Days,* was published in 1995, and the sixteenth, *Kingdom Come,* appeared in April 2007. These books were not only sold in religious bookstores; they also found many purchasers in Barnes and Noble, Borders, and Wal-Mart stores. More than sixty million copies of some volumes were sold, far outdoing Hal Lindsey's bestseller. The publisher, Tyndale House, intensified the popularization of this view of present history through other product lines, such as comics, audio cassettes, web sites, computer games, videos, and DVDs.[46]

The plot of the series is based on a small correction to the theological concept of the rapture that has considerable dramatic potential. In Darby's teaching, those left behind have no possibility of escaping their fate, but this series gives those "left behind" the chance to escape damnation through conversion. This modification generates the basic plot of the entire series, which underlies the storyline in all the individual scenes.[47] Those who are left behind still have the chance to prove themselves in the faith. For the men, of course, this means fighting heroically and courageously against the Antichrist and his accomplices.

The protagonist of the story is Rayford Steele, a pilot who is en route from O'Hare Chicago to London Heathrow in his Boeing 747, when the passengers and crew suddenly discover that dozens of passengers have disappeared, leaving only their garments and their jewelry on their seats. Steele is ordered to fly back to O'Hare, where he finds a world in chaos. Airplanes without pilots have crashed everywhere in the world. When he gets home, his house and his bed are empty. His wife, a born-again Christian, has also been caught up. Rayford Steele and others now form a "Tribulation Force" in order to oppose the powers of evil. They fight against Nicolae Carpathia, the head of the United Nations, who is in reality the Antichrist—he makes peace treaties with Israel only because he wants to safeguard his own rule. However, the truth demands that during the seven years of his rule, there should be no peace, but only war.

This storyline is staged in such a way that it evokes a flood of projections and associations in the readers and beholders with regard to correct conduct: in a deliberate amalgamation of male and female attributes, we are told that women are devoted and self-assured, while men are dominant and humble. The true America is represented, not by the political institutions, but by the believers; the UN is an instrument of the Antichrist. As time goes by, the moral, religious, and economic decline picks up speed.

Peace treaties and rearmament pacts are the work of the Antichrist, as is also the protection of the environment.[48]

Immediately after its publication in 2002 in a first edition of allegedly 2.75 million copies, the volume *The Remnant* leapt to the top of the *New York Times* bestseller lists. Gershom Gorenberg, the author of the studies about the struggle for the Temple Mount in Jerusalem and the settling of the occupied territories mentioned earlier, has drawn attention to the anti-Judaism of the series.[49] Although the Jews of Israel are at the center of the story, the only choice they ultimately have is between converting to Jesus Christ and being annihilated. The exclusive concern of premillenialism in the past and the present has been the salvation of Christians, never the salvation of the Jews qua Jews.[50]

The success of this series brings something to light that otherwise escapes notice, namely, the matrix of an American popular culture that generates specific views of contemporary history and politics. Its basic structure is an all-pervasive dualism. Evil is not something that has its origin in one's own world: it comes from outside. Human beings are not simultaneously good *and* evil: they are *either* good *or* evil. The solution to the existence of evil is its violent elimination. At the end, the good wins the day. This basic structure, which developed over a long period in the United States, is well known from Hollywood films, comics, and science fiction.[51] *Left Behind* takes up a widespread popular fascination with one particular type of masculine violence and links this to premillenialism. The idealization of violence is transformed from a "religious semi-product" into a model of subjective religiosity.[52]

The plot of the novels clearly promotes not only an alignment of the United States with Israel and support for its reestablishment in the Holy Land, but also a distancing vis-à-vis the Palestinians and their resistance to the expropriation of their land and the deprivation of their rights by Israel. The 145,000 Christian Palestinians are never mentioned in these books—absolutely in keeping with political reality. For while American fundamentalists cultivate exceedingly friendly relations with religious Zionists, the Arab Christians with their justified claims must take a back seat (as Timothy Weber observes with a critical undertone).[53] Israel's acquisition of statehood is interpreted as a stage in salvation history, while the bitter opposition by the Palestinians is interpreted without any nu-ances as the expression of a metaphysical evil.

Scholars of the media are rightly very cautious about defining the influence that fictional works can have on human conduct. In this case, however, it seems possible to demonstrate that an influence does exist. The powerful networks of the Moral Majority or the New Christian Right introduced these patterns of interpretation into the world of politics, al-ready under Ronald Reagan and obviously to an even greater extent under George W. Bush. The positive evaluation of military strength, which most of the Evangelicals share with the neoconservatives in the think tanks and the administration, promotes an intensification of the Middle East con-flict. A typical representative of this way of thinking is the televangelist Jim Robinson, who was invited by President Reagan to say the opening prayer at the National Republican Convention in 1984. He is reported to have said on another occasion: "There'll be no peace until Jesus comes. Any preaching of peace prior to his return is heresy; it's against the word of God; it's Antichrist."[54]

CHAPTER 9

September 11, 2001: A Raid on the Path of God

Two months after the 9/11 attacks, Osama bin Laden told Saudi visitors how he and his companions had experienced that day. They were in Afghanistan, listening to an American short-wave radio. When they finally heard the news of the attacks, they intoned an *Allāhu akbar*. "Muhammad [Atta] from the Egyptian family was in charge," Bin Laden told them.[1]

The preparations for the attack had begun in 1998, when a group of Islamist students in Hamburg led by Atta listened receptively to bin Laden's summons to war. We do not have any precise information about a link between Atta and Egyptian Jihadists, but bin Laden was certainly justified in establishing a connection between 9/11 and the latter.

Jihadists in Afghanistan Become the Basis of a Worldwide Network

Bin Laden's organization goes back to the 1980s, when Muslims throughout the world were being recruited for military resistance to the occupation of Afghanistan by the Soviet Union. Two training camps in Peshawar in Pakistan were particularly active in recruiting young Muslims and training them as fighters: a "Bureau for Mujahedin Services," founded by the Palestinian Islamic scholar Abdallah Azzam, who belonged to the Muslim Brethren; and a guesthouse called the "House of the Helpers," where Osama bin Laden was the director.[2] Abdallah Azzam (1941–1989) and Osama bin Laden (born 1957) knew each other from the time when bin Laden studied economics and management at the University of Jeddah and the Islamic legal scholar Azzam taught Islamic theology there. Bin Laden's interests were not confined to his own academic discipline. He attended Azzam's lectures, as well as those of Mohammed Qutb, the brother of Sayyid Qutb, whom the Egyptian government had executed in 1967 because of his subversive writings. In Peshawar, where they met up again, a close collaboration developed between the two men. Azzam, the brilliant Palestinian scholar, put forward an Islamic justification for the struggle against the occupation of Afghanistan—a justification that went beyond that specific case. He argued that faith imposed on the individual an obligation to defend the territory of Islam when enemies invaded it. This obligation was incumbent first and foremost on the Muslims of the region that was attacked, but if they were too weak to mount an effective defense, the obligation widened gradually to include the entire Islamic community. Azzam's vision encompassed more than a liberation of Afghanistan: his hope was nourished by the ancient expectation that the black banners of the Mahdi, the Islamic Messiah, would come from the east, from Khorazan, bringing liberation to all the Muslims. The liberation of Jerusalem had priority over that of Kabul,[3] for then all those regions that had once been Islamic but had subsequently been conquered (or reconquered) by Christians, such as Palestine, Lebanon, Andalusia, and so on, would once again be Islamized. And no compromises were possible here. "Jihad and the rifle alone—that was the only option: no negotiations, no conferences, and no dialogues."[4]

According to this way of looking at things, genuine Islamic faith showed itself in the fight against the infidel occupying powers. One who hastens to aid brothers who are in need earns prestige in the eyes of both human beings and God; but one who abandons them forfeits both prestige and salvation. Azzam was no longer concerned only with the liberation of an Islamic country from foreign rule: the individual's own salvation too was at stake. One who took part in this struggle need not ask the consent of any authority, nor of his wife or his parents. The two contact points of Azzam and bin Laden in Peshawar became the meeting place for convinced Muslim fighters from many countries. The total number of foreign combatants in the war against the Red Army was probably somewhere between 10,000 and 20,000 men, although only a few hundred of them took part in actual fighting—a tiny figure in comparison to the roughly 250,000 Afghan mujahedin.[5]

Not all the fighters agreed with Azzam in seeing the expulsion of the unbelievers from Islamic territories as the highest priority. Egyptian Islamists, who had moved to Afghanistan not least because of the repression they experienced at home, believed that it was no less urgent to fight against their own, merely nominally Islamic governments. These men included former members of Egyptian Jihad who had been responsible for the attack on Sadat in 1980. Bin Laden had made the acquaintance of their emir (commandant), Aiman az-Zawahiri, in 1987.[6] When Abdallah Azzam was killed by a car bomb in 1989, Egyptian Jihadists took over the direction of his Services Bureau in Peshawar. It is difficult to say whether they were involved in some way in his death (as has often been suspected); all we can say with certainty is that Azzam did not share their view that weapons should be directed primarily against one's own government, and that he accordingly refused to give financial support to this particular struggle.[7] At any rate, when Egyptians took over the organization, this opened the door to a new justification of the struggle against the enemies of Islam.

Bin Laden's Declarations of War on the United States

After the Red Army withdrew from Afghanistan in 1989, bin Laden and his followers, numbering scarcely more than a dozen at that period, left Pakistan and moved first to Saudi Arabia, then to Sudan, and finally in 1996 to Afghanistan, where the Taliban had come to power in the same year. There he wrote a letter to "the brothers" throughout the world, and especially to those in the Arabian Peninsula,[8] in which he summoned all Muslims to the defensive jihad against the Americans in Arabia and against Israel in Palestine. He accused these enemies of being responsible for the death of Azzam. Bin Laden also accused the United States of aggression against the land of the two holy places, Mecca and Medina. In many countries, Muslims had suffered terrible things, since their blood was the cheapest blood anywhere in the world; but it was the absolute height of arrogance to invade the house of Islam (*dar al-Islam*). The two holy places of Islam were debased by the presence of Crusader troops. The establishment of American military bases in Saudi Arabia during the first Gulf War (1990–1991) was sacrilege, which all Muslims were called upon to expiate. In an allusion to the early Islamic traditions about the Mahdi, bin Laden writes that he is issuing this declaration from Khorazan.

Two years later, in 1998, a similar declaration was issued, this time by the "World Islamic Front for the Jihad against Jews and Crusaders." The summons to the jihad was signed not only by Osama bin Laden, but also by Aiman az-Zawahiri as the emir of Egyptian Jihad, Rifa'i Ahmad Taha on behalf of the Egyptian Jama'a al-Islamiyya,[9] and a Pakistani and a Bangladeshi on behalf of their groups.[10] This declaration, which is briefer and more concise than the text two years earlier, begins with the so-called "sword verse" (Sura 9:5): "Then, when the sacred months are drawn away, slay the idolaters wherever you find them, and take them, and confine them, and lie in wait for them at every place of ambush." The Arabian Peninsula is infested by the Crusaders, who are like locusts that devour its riches. This event has a salvation-historical significance.[11] The declaration mentions three circumstances as evidence of the conspiracy against Islam and of the threat facing the Muslims. The declaration explains them:

- the United States has occupied the most sacred places on the Arabian Peninsula in order to steal the natural resources, to humiliate the Muslims, and to use military means to oppress the Muslim peoples;

- the United States has inflicted grave damage on the Iraqi people, and continues to do so by means of the embargo, although this has already cost the lives of a million people;

- the United States is destroying Iraq and wants to break up all the other states in the region into defenseless mini-states, in order to guarantee Israel's superiority over the neighboring Arab states.

The political events mentioned here are understood as a declaration of war against God. The declaration, which is cast in the form of a legal instruction (*hukm*), affirms that the highest obligation of all the believers is now the defense of Islam:

To kill the Americans and their allies—civilian and military—is an individual duty incumbent upon every Muslim in all countries, in order to liberate the Al-

Aqsa Mosque and the Holy Mosque [in Jerusalem] from their grip, so that their armies leave all the territory of Islam, defeated, broken, and unable to threaten any Muslim.[12]

The scope of this declaration goes far beyond the duty of the believers to defend Islamic territories. It proclaims that the killing of Americans and their allies, whether soldiers or civilians, is a duty. The declaration also exhorts Muslims, in view of the inevitability of war, not to be attached to their lives—are they really going to prefer life in this world to life in the world to come? At stake is not only the common good of the Islamic community, but also the salvation of each individual.

The emirs of the Jihad groups who are speaking here wanted to take the war into the wider world after the liberation of Afghanistan. They saw the victory over the Soviet Union as a sign from God that it would be possible to defeat the other superpower too. However, they fail to mention that the fighters owed their victory over the Red Army above all to the hundreds of Stinger anti-aircraft missiles with which the United States had supplied them—and with which they had shot down 269 Soviet aircraft and helicopters.[13]

The justification of the struggle has become more a matter of principle. In addition to the collective endeavor to liberate Islamic territory from infidel aggressors, we now find a religious ethic that sees the struggle as a means to attain personal salvation. This is a further development of the idea of an Islamic *umma,* which is linked here primarily to a specific lifestyle, and only secondarily to one specific territory.

Martial Jihad as a Maxim of an Ethics of Conviction

The masterminds of this deterritorialization of the Islamic commandment were Egyptian Islamists. There were personal overlappings between them and the Arab Mujahedin (the "Arab Afghanis") who swore fidelity to Osama bin Laden and took part in the fight against the Soviet Union. The brother of Khalid al-Islambuli, one of those who killed Sadat, belonged to the innermost circle around Osama bin Laden. *The Neglected Duty,* which taught that jihad was an individual obligation of faith equal to the other "five pillars of Islam," had its origin in Egyptian Jihad.

Excerpts from this text were used in the training of Islamic fighters in Afghanistan,[14] but originally it was an "internal discussion paper" (to borrow Jansen's phrase) of the group that was responsible for the attack on President Anwar al-Sadat. It was written by Abd al-Salam Faraj, an electrical engineer (1954–1982), who was executed along with the perpetrators of the attack. It takes up point by point all the objections and doubts with regard to the absolute priority of the militant struggle vis-à-vis a nonviolent spreading of the faith.[15] It shows more clearly than any other Islamic text all the individual links in the argumentation that make it possible to draw a militant ethics of conviction out of the rich store of Islamic traditions, conceptions, and practices. And it shows all that must be reevaluated or rejected in this process as allegedly un-Islamic.

Faraj interpreted the situation of Islam in Egypt on the analogy of the Mongol rule in the thirteenth century. Although the Mongol ruler Ghazan converted to Islam, he did not make Islamic law absolutely binding in his empire. This led the mediaeval scholar Ibn Taymiyya to reject his rule as un-Islamic and to assert that opposition to Ghazan was an imperative.[16] Faraj took up this mediaeval interpretative pattern and declared that the contemporary rulers of Egypt were apostates who made common cause with the Crusaders and must be punished even more harshly than unbelievers (§§ 25–28).[17] In order to set up an Islamic state in Egypt, charitable associations are not suitable, since they make Muslims dependent on the apostates' state (§ 48); nor can knowledge and education (*'ilm*) achieve this. Only the jihad can set up an Islamic state (§§ 63–64). Islam was spread by violence (§ 71), and it follows that an Islamic state cannot be founded today through nonviolent propaganda (*da'wa*), but only through violence and against the will of the majority and of the unbelievers (§§ 54–59).

The difference in the Prophet's behavior first in Mecca and then in Medina plays a paradigmatic role in Faraj's definition of the contemporary situation of Egyptian Islam. Egypt today (he writes) does not resemble in any way the situation of Mecca in the days of the Prophet, where believers and unbelievers still lived together without violence (§ 83). Instead, it resembles the situation in Medina, where Islam was threatened by both external and internal foes, and needed therefore to be defended with violence. All the earlier statements in the Qur'an that reflect a peaceful coexistence between Muslims and those of a different religion are abrogated by the "sword verse" (Sura 9:5) and by the commandment to fight (Sura 2:216;

§§ 76–79). The fight is directed first and foremost, not against the distant enemy (Israel or the United States), but against the apostates in Faraj's own country. It is only when the Islamic order is enforced in Egypt that it will also spread throughout the world (§§ 68–70). Faraj holds that the tradition that says that the Prophet recommended the spiritual (greater) jihad as a continuation and substitute for the military (lesser) jihad is a falsification. The jihad against one's own soul, against Satan, and against the unbelievers and hypocrites are three aspects of one and the same religious practice (§§ 88–90). The violent establishing of an Islamic state is the execution of a divine commandment, and the believer is not responsible for the consequences that then ensue (§ 91).

Faraj formulates new practical rules that are meant to do justice to the contemporary situation. The fight is an individual duty; one need not ask one's parents and family for their consent (§ 87). However, the fight can be carried on only under the direction of a righteous leader who has proved his suitability through his religious practice. One may swear allegiance unto death to this leader, even in a period in which there is no caliph (§§ 95–97). The war against the unbelievers knows no limitations: deceit and falsehood are permitted in dealings with them, provided that no treaty has been made with them (§§ 107–109). One is even allowed to serve in secret in pagan armies (§ 118). Where necessary, an attack on the unbelievers may be carried out without previous warning (§ 119). Quotations from the traditional literature are adduced as proof that even Muslims who died in battle were not martyrs, if their intention was not genuinely pure—that is, if their principal motivation was the expectation of rich booty or even the acquisition of religious prestige (§§ 130–131). In this way, Faraj seeks to clear up every doubt concerning the consequences of the jihad obligation. One may not indeed deliberately kill innocent civilians, children and women of the pagans; but it can be accepted that this will in fact happen (§§ 121–122). On the battlefield, the fighter should prefer to die rather than to capitulate and be taken captive (§§ 127–129). The text closes with an exhortation to the leaders of the Islamist organizations (*jamāʿāt al-Muslimīn*) to charge every member to obey these rules (§§ 142–143).

This military ethic is generated by a salvation-historical interpretation according to which the Prophet predicted not only the conquest of

Constantinople, but also of Rome, which has still to happen (§§ 10–11), as well as the coming of the Mahdi who fills the world with justice—just as it is filled at present with injustice (§ 14). In this way, *The Neglected Duty* anchors the militant practice in a salvation-historical scenario.[18] It is only the interior disposition that counts: secondary intentions that the fighter links to the jihad destroy the redemptive effect of the action (§§ 130–133). This rigorous militant ethics of conviction parts company both with the morality of the present-day Islamic community and with the views of the legal scholars, who publicly opposed *The Neglected Duty* and endeavored to rebut its position by means of arguments.[19]

The fundamentally new idea of the militant Islam borne up by an inner conviction is formulated most clearly by Sayyid Qutb, whose writings the author of *The Neglected Duty* knew and quoted (§ 135). Sayyid Qutb regarded the culture of the Islamic countries as so comprehensively corrupted by paganism that all that remained as a dwelling and "territory" of Islam was the heart and its intention. This gloomy diagnosis was however accompanied by a hope nourished by the beginnings of Islam. Before Muhammad could establish the Qur'an as a legal system, it had to be anchored in human hearts: only thus was it possible for the community of Muslims to achieve autonomy vis-à-vis the overwhelming superior power of paganism. In the same way, the Islamic faith must first become once more a reality in living souls and in a vigorous community today, before it can become a political movement that puts an end to the overwhelming superior power of paganism.[20] This means that the exclusive community of the perfect and the pure is the sole source of "Islamicness." The traditional balance between the individual and the order of society, that many Islamic thinkers have celebrated, is destroyed today.[21] The only remaining criterion of the Islamicness of an action is the intention (*niyya*) of the individual actor.[22]

Al-Qaeda: Nodal Point of Worldwide Networks

Shortly before the withdrawal of the Soviet forces, bin Laden and his comrades in arms compiled a data base of all who had fought in Afghanistan against the USSR, so that the volunteers who were registered would provide a base for militant Islam in the future too. When Egyptian Jihad, under the leadership of the physician Aiman az-Zawahiri (born 1953), amalgamated with the followers of bin Laden, and members of the Egyptian Jamā'a al-Islāmiyya likewise joined them, bin Laden's "basis" began to take on the character of a social community. The Egyptian doctrine of the jihad, Saudi money, and the motivation of simple Muslims from the Arabian peninsula formed a powerful brew. Even after this, however, the name al-Qaeda, "the basis," remained more a description of a function than the name of a group.[23] Bin Laden employed it only when others used it in speaking with him, and even then, he employed it reluctantly. He and his followers referred to themselves as the "World Islamic Front for the Jihad against Jews and Crusaders."[24] Scholars have proposed the terms "militant Islamists with a link to Afghanistan" or "transnational militant Islamism"; some also use the term "Bin Laden Brotherhood." This variation in names is typical of the fluid borders of this social entity, which has caused problems for the Americans who have suffered under its attacks. In 1995, a report by the U.S. State Department spoke of transnational terrorists who were much harder to track down than the members of groups known by name. President Bill Clinton spoke of bin Laden's "network." It was only after bin Laden's declaration of war and the attacks on the embassies in Nairobi and Dar-es-Salaam and on the warship USS *Cole* in 1998 that the secret services and politicians disregarded the nebulous quality of the matter and declared al-Qaeda to be an international organization that must be militarily destroyed, together with the rogue states that support it. Fictions have the power to create new realities—and this is what happened in this instance. Governments that had long clashed with militant Islamic opposition groups in their own countries (e.g., Russia, India, China, the Philippines, Thailand, and Israel) felt that this opportunity was too good to miss and declared their opponents to be branches of al-Qaeda in the hope that the United States would support them in their fight.

Jason Burke has investigated the various kinds of membership in this network.[25] First, in the center, are bin Laden and his closest advisers. Second, in addition to the inner circle, there is the group of those who have sworn the oath of loyalty to bin Laden as their emir. A study by Peter L. Bergen contains new documents relevant to this oath. These were found in Bosnia, in a computer file called *tārīkh Usāma* (The History of Osama) containing letters, minutes, and other documents from the beginnings of al-Qaeda in 1988. The minutes of one of the meetings at which al-Qaeda was founded contain the formula of the oath with which a member solemnly swears to obey his superiors, so that God's Word is the highest authority.[26] According to another source, after the Soviet forces had left Afghanistan and bin Laden had formed a group of his own, the members swore an oath of personal loyalty (*bay'a*) to him.[27]

This sworn community was not hermetically closed, but was open to new adherents from anywhere in the world. A study of the biographies of 172 members of al-Qaeda has shown that in many instances, the initiative to join came from local groups who sought contact with bin Laden via men who had previously fought in Afghanistan:

> The process of joining the jihad . . . is more of a bottom-up than a top-down activity. A lot of Muslim young men want to join the jihad but do not know how. Joining the jihad is more akin to the process of applying to a highly selective college. Many try to get in but only few succeed. . . . I did not detect any active top-down organizational push to increase al Qaeda's membership. The pressure came from the bottom up. Prospective Mujahedin were eager to join the movement.[28]

Bin Laden's followers were recruited primarily from below, and more rarely from above. Factors encouraging young men to join included already-existing social relationships such as friendship, family ties, teacher-pupil relationships, or membership of a mosque, and so on.[29] In this context, Marc Sageman writes that real recruiters for al-Qaeda existed only in training camps of the Tablighi in Pakistan, and nowhere else, but other accounts call this into question. For example, Roland Jacquard has collected pieces of information that point to a deliberate recruitment in North Africa and Europe by bin Laden's closest associates.[30] There is some evidence to support the thesis of the organizational sociologist Renate Mayntz that al-Qaeda is based on a combination of traits of a hierarchical organization and vertical network structures. This hybrid form explains something that is typical of al-Qaeda, namely, that the lowest units are autonomous and at the same time subject to central control. Their members are isolated from one another, but they are guided in their activities by a common core idea, and are in contact with the innermost circle.[31] This confirms the rule that it is precisely the weak and informal relationships that construct especially strong and lasting networks.[32] In general, cells that act with a large measure of autonomy, supported by shared convictions and commitment, are

more successful than hierarchical structures of command. Bin Laden's socially heterogeneous followers are bound together by his religious prestige.
There are historical analogies to this in the history of Islamic North Africa,
where Ibn Khaldūn relates how fragmented and rival social relationships
were mobilized by a religious leader, whose great prestige allowed him to
direct them to a common goal. Concentrating social relationships and the
dynamics of various conflicts into a comprehensive solidarity (*'asabiyya*)
intensified the potential of such coalitions to acquire power, and constituted the basis for the formation of new dynasties. Clearly, bin Laden has
succeeded in a similar manner in becoming the nodal point of disparate
social unities and conflicts.[33]

A third kind of membership in al-Qaeda concerns groups that have
their roots in other countries and are associated with the "basis" in Afghanistan. They collaborate with it only occasionally. Sometimes this
is a collaboration on one specific project, limited in time; sometimes, it
involves only subgroups. Accordingly, Jason Burke speaks of a loose network of networks, comparing it to the network of the opponents of globalization. Since however bin Laden has considerable financial resources,
his organization sometimes also resembles an international business undertaking that finances local "entrepreneurs in violence" and gives them
logistical support. Most of the money comes, not from the private fortune
of bin Laden (estimates of which are often wildly exaggerated), but from
donations by about fourteen private Islamic organizations.[34]

Banks are not needed for financial transactions between parts of the
network, since the *hawala* system is also available. This consists of two
business partners in different countries who trust each other completely,
for example, because they are relatives. When one partner receives from a
depositor in one place (e.g., in Peshawar) a sum for a recipient in another
place (e.g., in London), the partner in London pays this sum to the intended recipient, and vice versa. A telephone call suffices, and the transaction is carried out. If the debit and credit amounts of the two partners do
not balance over time, they must be balanced in some other way. Thanks
to this *hawala* system, large sums can be transferred without involving
banks, and without leaving any documentary traces.[35]

The Hamburg Cell and the Preparations for 9/11

The planning of the 9/11 attacks began in 1998, when bin Laden with the other emirs declared war on the United States. He now planned raids on the early Islamic model. In his military defense of the emerging Islamic state in Medina against external enemies, the Prophet had recourse to the form of surprise attacks, or raids, practiced by the Bedouins, called *ghazwa* in Arabic. As early as August 7, 1998, in keeping with this pattern, the first bomb attacks were carried out against the U.S. embassies in Dar-es-Salaam and Nairobi in East Africa.

From the end of 1998, Islamist students with Arab origins shared a rented apartment in Marienstrasse 54 in the Harburg district of Hamburg. They gave their little community the eloquent name *dār al-ansār,* "House of the helpers"—the same name as bin Laden's guesthouse in Peshawar. In their minds, the three men who lived there, Muhammad Atta, Ramzi bin al-Shib, and Marwan al-Shehhi were living in the time of Medina, when the Prophet was in urgent need of helpers in order to achieve recognition and power for Islam. The jihad was at the center of their conversations, although it was as yet undecided whether this would be in Kosovo, Chechnya, Afghanistan, or Bosnia.[36] Ziad Jarreh had joined their group in 1997, but he did not himself move into the apartment with them. Other young Muslims moved in, while some moved out. In the course of two years, more than a dozen men were registered with the municipal authorities under this address, as Terry McDermott discovered in his researches into the Hamburg cell. Most of them had met in the al-Quds mosque in the center of Hamburg, where young Arab Muslims prayed together, listened to sermons, and attended or themselves gave courses in Islam. Their principal theme was the jihad as an obligation that most Muslims neglected to shoulder. Muhammad Haydar Zammer, a veteran of the Afghan war, had preached this doctrine in the al-Quds mosque, but it is not probable that he had intentionally recruited the students on the orders of al-Qaeda. This is suggested by the *9/11 Commission Report,* when it calls him a possible recruiter, but the *Report* itself indicates that his influence was apparently limited to questions of religious conviction.[37] Abu Musab, a Mauritanian whose real name was Mohamedou Ould Slahi, probably played a more important organizational role. He was an active member of al-Qaeda and lived in Duisburg; today, he is a prisoner in Guantánamo.

Ramzi bin al-Shib heard of him by chance and then visited him in Duisburg together with Ziad Jarreh and Marwan al-Shehhi. Slahi told his visitors, who wanted to go to Chechnya, how difficult it was to get there directly, and suggested instead that they should first train in Afghanistan before traveling further. They should get visas for Pakistan and then await further instructions from him.

In the fall of 1999, the four men left Hamburg for Pakistan, each taking a separate route in order not to attract attention. From Quetta in Pakistan, they went to an Afghan training camp near Kandahar, where they were brought to bin Laden. At that period, bin Laden and his closest advisers were contemplating an attack with airplanes in the United States, and the technically skilled Arab students from Hamburg, who spoke English, arrived just at the right moment. It was in the interests of both sides to have them swear the oath of loyalty to bin Laden and to be informed by him about the plan. In Kandahar, the first fighters had already been chosen to carry out the plan. These included the Saudis Khalid al-Mihdhar and Nawaf al-Hazmi, who entered the United States by way of California in January 2000.[38] An al-Qaeda propaganda film shows how other fighters were preparing themselves for the operation.[39] Ahmed al-Haznawi al-Ghamidi made a farewell video, subsequently transmitted by al-Jazeera, in which he declares that he and the others want to die as martyrs. The time of humiliation is past, and the power of the United States is based merely on propaganda; now, Americans are being killed on their own soil. As a "living martyr," he beseeches God to let the Islamic *umma* come to life again through "our" death.[40]

The flexibility of the organization is also demonstrated by the fact that the 9/11 attacks were carried out by nineteen perpetrators who came from completely different circles. Three of the four pilots (Muhammad Atta, Ziad Jarrah, and Marwan al-Shehhi) belonged to the Hamburg cell. After Ramzi bin al-Shib was refused permission to enter the United States from Yemen, he worked as coordinator between the Hamburg group and the chief of the al-Qaeda military committee, Khalid Sheikh Muhammad, and his representative, Atef. Hani Hanjour entered the United States as the fourth pilot. Two close personal associates of bin Laden, Khalid al-Mihdhar and Nawaf al-Hazmi, were on board American Airlines Flight 77, which was crashed into the Pentagon. Finally, there was another group of twelve men from Saudi Arabia who were known as the "muscles," since it was their task to restrain the crew and passengers in the hijacked planes.

In addition to their civil names, all nineteen perpetrators bore an additional name, a *kunya*. In the traditional Islamic bestowal of names, such an additional name could be given to a person in the course of his life, for example, when he became a father ("Abu") and thus bore the name of his son. The *kunyas* of the perpetrators of 9/11 are names of exemplary fighters or steadfast believers from the history of Islam. The source does not state when they adopted these names; this may have been when they obligated themselves (as documented by the video) to die as martyrs. In that case, the *kunyas* would have been their names as "living martyrs."[41]

The Spiritual Manual for the 9/11 *ghazwa*

The participants in the attacks were given a manual to take with them. The FBI found a copy in Muhammad Atta's bag, which had not been loaded onto the plane in Boston; another copy was found in the car that Nawaf al-Hazmi had parked at Dulles Airport in Washington, DC, and the FBI also found fragments of the text in the ruins of the plane that crashed in Pennsylvania. The FBI placed the Arabic text on the Internet on September 28, 2001, with details of where it had been found.[42]

It is clear that the author was not an educated Islamic clergyman. This, at any rate, is indicated by his remark when he recommends the recitation of the Qur'an: "Know that the best way of recitation is reciting the Noble Qur'an according to a consensus of the scholars, *as far as I know*" (1/6); similar phrases are found at 3/1 and 3/14. Only one who is not wholly certain of his own scholarship would speak in this manner. This is not uncommon, since in Islam it is often the laymen who preach; only the knowledge of the legal tradition is professionalized. All this would fit Muhammad Atta, the emir of the 9/11 attacks, were it not for information that argues against this.

Yosri Fouda, a journalist working for the Arabic al-Jazeera news network, met Ramzi bin al-Shib under conspiratorial conditions in Karachi in 2002 for a detailed interview in which bin al-Shib described how the attacks were prepared. Bin al-Shib also showed Fouda a suitcase with "souvenirs" from his time in Hamburg, including a pamphlet depicting flight maneuvers, which had belonged to Muhammad Atta. Fouda discovered handwritten notes on this pamphlet, but these looked different from the more beautiful handwriting of the "Manual for a Hijack" (the name he gave to the *Spiritual Manual*, which he knew from the Internet). Bin al-Shib told him that the manuscript that was in Atta's possession had not in fact been composed and written out by Atta, but by Abdul Aziz al-Omari,[43] who had been greatly admired by the others because of his knowledge of Islam and his beautiful handwriting.[44] Al-Omari too left a video, made in Kandahar before he traveled to the United States on June 29, 2001, in which he states that what he will do is fully deliberate. The *9/11 Commission Report* contains information about al-Omari which accords well with the hypothesis that he was the author of the *Spiritual Manual*. After graduating with distinction from high school and taking his degree at the Islamic Imam Muhammad ibn Saud University, he served as prayer leader in a mosque in Saudi Arabia and studied under the radical Saudi clergyman Sulaiman al-Alwan, whose mosque in the province of Qassim was known to other clerics as the "terrorist factory."[45]

It is certain that all the nineteen men who took part in the attacks knew what was intended. In the *Spiritual Manual*, the words "airport" and "airplane" are not written out, but are abbreviated, doubtless for reasons of caution—lest a copy fall into the wrong hands. But the participants were not all equally informed of all the details of the plan. A remark by bin Laden himself suggests that only the four pilots and his own close associates were fully informed.[46] Nevertheless, all knew that they were setting out on a mission that—if it succeeded—would end in their certain death.

Mutual Pledge to Die and Renewal of Intention

The *Spiritual Manual* prescribes a prelude to the violent attack in the form of a mutual pledge to die and renewal of intention. In the history of the formation of Islamic communities, *bay'a* designates the solemn act with which believers are confirmed in their loyalty to a legitimate leader, their emir.[47] Associations of men (*futuwwa*) had long been founded according to this principle. The Egyptian Muslim Brethren too knew this practice and were united by means of an "oath of allegiance." But an oath of allegiance unto death, which was sworn here, is a different matter. In

The Neglected Duty, Faraj took up the question whether an oath of allegiance unto death could be made to anyone other than the Prophet. He answered in the affirmative: such an oath is owed to every legitimate leader in a jihad (§§ 95–97);[48] in the present case, to bin Laden.

The brotherhood is formed in order to "renew the intention" (*niyya*). "Intention" is a fundamental category in Islamic law. An act of worship without *niyya* is invalid, just as a *niyya* without action is invalid.[49] Both Sayyid Qutb and his brother Mohammed (one of bin Laden's teachers in Jidda) held the view that the identity of Muslims could no longer consist of their external actions, but only in their intention (*niyya*).[50] The *Spiritual Manual* speaks of Ali, Muhammad's nephew and son-in-law, in the Battle of the Trench (627 CE), as an instance of exemplary preparation for an act of martial violence. The choice of this particular model sheds an eloquent light on the aim of the author of the *Manual*:

Do not take vengeance for yourself, but make your strike and everything else for the sake of God. Take for example Ali ibn Abi Talib. When he once fought against an unbeliever, the unbeliever spat on him. Ali then let his sword pause and did not strike him. Only afterwards, he struck him. After the battle, one of the companions asked him why he had done so, why he had not struck the unbeliever, and first left and only later struck him. Ali answered: "When he spat on me, I feared I would strike him in vengeance. Therefore I held my sword," or how he said. When he had called the intention to mind, he turned to him and struck and killed him. All this means, that the human being should prepare his soul in a very short time, and then all he does is for the sake of God. (3/13–15)

The insult to Ali demands punishment; but it is the inner preparation that determines whether this is merely a personal revenge, or genuinely a military act carried out in the name of God.

The *Manual* says nothing about the injustice that the World Islamic Front adduced in 1998 as the reason for the declaration of war on the United States, although we know that Muhammad Atta was personally indignant at this.[51] The deed must speak entirely for itself. The goals of the attacks were the arrogant seats of power of contemporary "paganism": Wall Street's capital, residing in the World Trade Center, the military power that dwelt in the Pentagon, and (the goal of the fourth plane, which crashed in Pennsylvania) the political power of the United States, which was located in the Capitol.[52] The perpetrators are executing the divine sentence pronounced by God on these powers of contemporary paganism. At the same time, each fighter becomes a martyr through his death. Since the only criterion for the admission of a martyr to paradise is his intention at the moment of his death, the perpetrators felt no hesitation of any kind about leading an un-Islamic lifestyle before the attacks, with the conscious aim of misleading their enemies.[53] Martyrdom wipes out all one's earlier sins.[54]

Spiritual techniques accompanied the militant action, as we see in the subdivision of the attack into three phases, in a manner similar to the subdivision in *The Neglected Duty,* where the true jihad consists of three different endeavors, which are aspects of one and the same action: the jihad against one's own soul, against Satan, and against the unbelievers and hypocrites (§§ 88–89). The tripartite division of the action in the *Spiritual Manual* presupposes a similar view, namely, that the jihad is an endeavor that must be directed against one's own soul, against Satan, and against the unbelievers, if it is to be pleasing to God.

The First Phase of the Raid: Attaining Purity

The renewal of the intention begins on the night before the attack, when the men purify their bodies and prepare themselves for the action step by step, through recitations, prayers, meditations, and ritual ablutions. The Arabic word for "recitation," *dhikr,* which is used frequently in the *Manual,* never means only "reciting a text." It always also means "remembering" and "representation." The recitation brings one to participate today in the supernatural power of the Prophet.

The fighters are to recite Suras 8 and 9 and to reflect on what they mean (1/3). The Prophet himself commanded that these Suras should be recited before the raid (*ghazwa*), with the result that they captured much booty. The choice of the Suras 8, "The Spoils," and 9, "The Repentance," is significant, since both come from the period when Muhammad left Mecca and founded a state in Medina, and then went to war against Mecca. Muhammad the persecuted Prophet became Muhammad the warlord and founder of a state. The principal example that provided orientation for the perpetrators' action was the Battle of the Trench in 627 CE, which was fought against both external and internal enemies.[55] In the years before this, Muhammad had had peaceful relations with the unbelievers in

Mecca, but this changed in Medina, and the "sword verse" documents this new attitude:

Then, when the sacred months are drawn away, slay the idolaters wherever you find them, and take them, and confine them, and lie in wait for them at every place of ambush. But if they repent, and perform the prayer, and pay the alms, then let them go their way: God is All-forgiving, All-compassionate. (Sura 9:5)

The change from toleration of the unbelievers to violence against them is a central theme of Islamic theology. Some Muslim scholars hold that the "sword verse" has replaced other revelations that sound a different note. They appeal for support to Sura 2:106, which admits such a possibility: "And for whatever verse We abrogate or cast into oblivion, We bring a better or the like of it." In *The Neglected Duty* (§§ 76–79), Faraj appeals to scholars in support of his affirmation that the "sword verse" has abrogated no less than 114 other verses in 54 Suras that presuppose a peaceful coexistence with unbelievers, replacing these with the requirement: "Prescribed for you is fighting, though it be hateful to you" (Sura 2:216). Other scholars disagree with such an interpretation of Sura 2:106 and have called into question the whole principle of the abrogation (Arabic *naskh*) of revelations made to the Prophet.[56] In his rebuttal of *The Neglected Duty*, the Egyptian mufti Sheikh Jadd al-Haqq simply quoted the second part of the "sword verse" in order to dismiss the martial interpretation: "But if they repent, and perform the prayer, and pay the alms, then let them go their way: God is All-forgiving, All-compassionate."[57]

The recitation of the martial Suras is followed by meditations (1/4):

Reminding oneself of unconditional obedience that night, as you will encounter decisive situations that require 100 percent unconditional obedience. Pull yourself together, make yourself understand, convince yourself and incite yourself to this action.

This is how the perpetrator is to overcome his natural self, which wants to go on living.[58] He is to remain awake in the night and to pray that he may later remain "undetected" (1/5). He must then break strictly with the world:

Purify your heart and cleanse it from stains and forget or ignore that thing named "World." The time for playing is over, and the true appointment has come. How much of our lifetime here did we waste! Why don't we use these hours profitably by offering acts pleasing to God and pious deeds? (1/7)

It is vital now to liberate the intention from all those emotions that are foreign to it. In his mind, the fighter should tell himself that his wedding day is approaching and that any difficulties that may occur are tests by God, designed to give him a higher rank. If God truly so desires, even a little band is capable of beating an entire army. All this, however, presupposes that the fighter recites prayers together with his brethren, without forgetting all the practical details. The morning prayer in the fellowship of the brethren (*jamāʿa*) at the end of the night puts the seal on their purity. The angels will pray that he be forgiven, as long as he is ritually pure; they will pray for him (1/15).

The Second Phase, in the Airport: Having No Fear of the Satanic Western Civilization

In the airport, which is under the rule of the pagan powers, the believing Muslim needs one thing above all else, namely, protection, and he obtains this through recitation and prayer.

Wherever you go and whatever you do, always perform the prayers. God grants his pious servants protection, facilitation, success, strengthening, assistance, and everything else. (2/15)

Thanks to his recitation and prayer, the angels protect the fighter, although he himself does not notice this (2/2). He has nothing to fear from the technology of the airport; one who nevertheless is afraid of this is in reality a friend of Satan (2/6–7).

Those who are enchanted by Western civilization are people who have drunk their love and reverence with cold water. They feared their [own] weak fragile devices. "Therefore do not fear them; but fear you Me, if you are believers" [Sura 3:175]. Fear is a great act of worship. The followers of God and the believers offer it only to the One and only God in whose hand are all things. Be sure that God will frustrate the guile of the unbelievers. (2/8).

This is the only passage in the entire document that names the jihadists' enemy by name: Western civilization in general. One cannot exclude the possibility of an allusion to Samuel Huntington's assertion about the ir-reconcilable conflict between the Western and the Islamic cultures,[59] but this theory is amplified by means of a spiritual aspect: Western civilization inspires terror in people, and only the Muslim fighter is a match for this. Others do not perceive what he is doing when he speaks the first part of the creed in the airport building: *lā ilāha illā llāhu*, "There is no God but God." These words are heavier than heaven and earth together, and make the fighter miraculously unassailable (2/9–11). This is why he remains un-recognized, despite the terrifying superior power of paganism: it is God who protects him by hiding him from his foes.

The theology of the overcoming of the fear of Western superiority is connected to one specific diagnosis of the present day. In an age in which weakness has taken root in the hearts of the faithful and Islam is threatened with extinction, an avant-garde of Muslims rises up and dem-onstrates a superhuman fearlessness.[60] This theology of the overcoming of fear likewise finds expression in statements by bin Laden. The 1996 letter in which he issued the summons to the jihad begins with quotations from the Qur'an that make the fear of God the very heart of the Islamic faith. This interpretation of the situation of the fighter is accompanied by an affirmation about his identity, which remains hidden from outsiders. In the kingdom of Satan, the soldier of the Highest Power remains unrecog-nized. In a world of falsehood, his true identity must be concealed. But the practice on its own does not suffice to guarantee success. Only God can make this practice successful (2/3; cf. 1/5).[61]

Behind all this lies the fundamental maxim of jihad Islam, namely, that the external world is so thoroughly corrupted by unbelief that the only remaining dwelling place of Islam is the heart and its intention. This complete dismissal of external realities also explains why the fighters could adopt a Western lifestyle, shaving off their beards and drinking alcohol. It is no longer possible for a harmonious relationship to exist between the external visible world and the invisible world of faith.

The Third Phase, on Board the Plane: Attack and Martyrdom

There now follows the third part of the action: the attack. God's warrior enters the plane unrecognized; here too, the first step is secret recitations and prayers. The theme of martyrdom takes center-stage. Despite all their willingness to die, martyrdom is not their personal achievement: "Ask God to grant you martyrdom" (3/7).[62] When the moment of decision comes, the young Muslim springs up like a hero who does not wish to return to human life, and cries: *Allāhu akbar!* ("God is the greatest!"), filling the hearts of the unbelievers with fear. The unknown soldier of the Highest Power discloses his true identity and does what Sura 8:12 commands: "Smite above the necks, and smite every finger of them!" He knows that Paradise and the virgins of Paradise await him. The experience of salvation is depicted in metaphors of sexual fulfillment.[63] If God grants him the favor of sacrificing someone with his knife, he is to do this for his father and his mother. Since the practice of the Prophet included plundering the enemies, this too is to be done on the plane, provided it does not hamper the operation. "The benefit of the action has priority, and (in general), the (interest of the) group has to be given priority over following the custom [*sunna*]" (3/12). Some enemies are to be taken captive and killed. If everything goes according to plan, each one is to pat his brother from the apartment on the back (3/17), and it would be good if one could recite the following verse from the Qur'an: "Count not those who were slain in God's way as dead" (Sura 3:169). A small amount of booty should be taken, even if this is only a cup or a glass of water.

When the true promise and the zero hour approach, tear your suit and open your chest, welcoming death on the path of God. Always mind God, either by ending with the ritual prayer, if this is possible, starting it seconds before the target, or let your last words be: "There is no God but God, and Muhammad is his Prophet." After that, God willing, the meeting in the highest paradise will follow through God's mercy. (3/21–23)

When he puts this framework around the violent deed, the author of the *Spiritual Manual* is imitating early Islamic battles, even down to actions that are out of place, such as the plundering of the foes. The success of the operation depends on the correct recitations of Suras and on the very precise enactment of the attack: it is these that guarantee the purity of the intention.

This practice has a prehistory. From the early period on, war for the cause of God was a Muslim obligation. The believer had to be ready for military service when the state ordered wars against pagans. In addition to this, however, a "stricter" religious view held that the war against the pagans was the place where faith really proved its worth. The true Muslim voluntarily gives proof of his faith in the war against the pagans. When the Prophet says that the monasticism of his community is the jihad,[64] this is not only polemic against Christianity, but also makes a positive link between the ascetic rejection of the world and the militant ethos. The same link is found in classic Islamic sources, as Albrecht Noth has shown. The fighter prepares himself for the war with the aid of ascetic abstinence. A Christian who was taken captive by Muslims described what he had experienced there: they were "knights-at-arms by day and monks by night." The fighters were encouraged to speak the formulae of the praise of God, to recite from the Qur'an, to utter prayers, to fast, and to declare the praises of God (*dhikr*) before going into battle.[65] The model here was to be found in the Prophet's raids (*ghazwa*) when he enforced the Islamic order of things from Medina, especially the Battle of the Trench in 627 CE, which oriented the fighters of 9/11 too.[66] These raids integrated both spiritual and military practices. Albrecht Noth's research led him to the conclusion "that in Islam the struggle against the unbelievers was regarded and proclaimed as a possibility of 'worship.'"[67]

The Cultivation of a Fighter Ethos in the Diaspora

The religious rejection of the world generates its own practices. The means whereby believers hope to attain "otherworldly" salvation have a psychological effect, thereby creating "innerworldly" states of affairs. This difference was the basis on which Max Weber constructed the whole of his sociology of religion: "Psychologically considered, man in quest of salvation has been primarily preoccupied by attitudes of the here and now."[68] The world renouncer experiences his opposition to the world not as a flight from the world but as a victory over its temptations. "The ascetic who rejects the world sustains at least the negative inner relationship with it which is presupposed in the struggle against it," Weber observes.[69]

A "negative inner relationship with the world" finds an echo among Muslims today, especially in the diaspora. Where there is no societal and cultural integration into the host countries and Muslims are marginalized, the identity of the godless enemy changes: it is no longer the corrupt regime in their countries of origin, but Western culture. This means that new practices arise. In Middle Eastern countries, the goal of Islamism was a re-Islamization of society and state; in the diaspora, what Olivier Roy catchily calls "neo-Islamism" developed in the form of an Islamic lifestyle.[70] An institutionalized religion turns into a personal religiosity. In this process, the imagined Islamic community (the *umma*) loses its geographic tie to a territory and becomes a global "faith community" based essentially on lifestyle.

The assimilation of Islam to types of Western religiosity does not however reduce the tensions with Western culture, since the geographical boundaries are replaced by mental boundaries that are defended no less rigorously. The detachment of Islam from its tie to statehood and territoriality promotes an individualization that gives birth to new forms of communality. This is why there is an intimate link between the enormous expansion of new Islamic communality and the spread of a posttraditional individualized Islam. But it remains unclear whether the driving forces necessarily inspire a martial ethics of conviction, or whether they could equally well give rise to a societal ethics of responsibility.[71]

It is worth looking at the biographies of the perpetrators of 9/11 more closely. A person's motives for committing suicide are not the same as the significance his death has for others, and that depends on transmitted patterns. We must examine each individual's motives separately, and these can vary greatly.[72] Terry McDermott has begun this investigation in the case of three perpetrators from the Hamburg cell—Muhammad Atta, Marwan al-Shehhi, and Ziad Jarrah—and their organizer, Ramzi bin al-Shib, and has assembled all the biographical information that he was able to find in Germany. He wanted to know who the people capable of committing such a monstrous act were; and he was deeply disturbed by what he discovered: "The men of September 11, were, regrettably, I think, fairly ordinary men." They were young Muslims who had become believers in the diaspora—believers untroubled by even the slightest doubt about their faith. And he sees this as one cause: "It is this certainty, not the belief itself, that causes the problems."[73] Olivier Roy envisages the same state of affairs when he speaks of a detachment of the Muslims' identity not only from the political order, but also from culture.[74] In a study of the Muslim diaspora in Germany, Stephen Holmes reaches a similar conclusion: despite their education, young Muslims feel alienated both from their countries of origin and from German society. As migrants who are able to live a "purer" Islam than the "hypocrites" in their lands of origin, they cultivate their rage and frustration in religious coteries.[75] They strike up their jihad songs even at weddings—as the perpetrators of 9/11 did.[76]

The understanding of martyrdom has taken new paths in the diaspora. The Iranian Shi'a, Hezbollah, and Hamas have declared freely chosen death by one's own weapon in the resistance struggle against Israel and other occupying powers to be an exemplary religious action. In this case, the action remains dependent on the authorized and comprehensible judgments that the faith community makes with regard to the seriousness of the threat. Through the al-Qaeda network, however, another type of martyr has come into existence. This type detaches the militant ethic from the situation in which the territory of the community is under threat and links it to a personal rejection of Western civilization. The suicide attack becomes a means to liberate oneself of one's entanglements in a culture that both fascinates and repels the perpetrator. September 11, 2001, was the date on which this new category of martyrs made its first appearance in the West.[77]

CHAPTER 10

The U.S. War on Terror: War
Without Limits or Borders

In his book *Bush at War,* Bob Woodward describes the speed with which one particular interpretation of the attacks of September 11, 2001, became established in the U.S. administration. In his very first reactions, George W. Bush spoke only of "terrorist attacks," but soon he was declaring: "We're at war."[1] In line with neoconservative thinking, the 9/11 attack was interpreted as a military challenge that had to be answered with an attack on states that sheltered terrorists. In addition, there was also a religious interpretation. In an address to his fellow Americans on September 16, George W. Bush warned them: "This crusade, this war on terrorism, is going to take a while." The word "crusade" seems to have slipped out unintentionally; at any rate, Bush later used much more cautious language. But the impression remained, especially in the Islamic world, that the United States was engaged in a crusade. This impression was strengthened by an American tradition of political rhetoric that bears the traces of civil religion and of mission.[2]

The American Concept of Terrorism

The concept of terrorism elaborated in Israel's fight to crush the resistance of the Palestinians quickly became established in the United States. George P. Shultz, U.S. secretary of state from 1983 to 1989, took part in the second conference on terrorism that Benjamin Netanyahu organized in Washington in 1983. The participants rejected the idea that one man's terrorist is another man's freedom fighter. In his address, entitled "The Challenge to the Democracies," Shultz explicitly welcomed the fact that thanks to the endeavors of the Jonathan Institute the "free world" was now at last getting to grips with the problem of terrorism. With rare exceptions, it was the goal of terrorists to impose their will on others by spreading fear. Terrorism was a form of political violence directed against "us," against the democracies, against "our" fundamental values, and against "our" fundamental strategic interests. Shultz appealed here to the words of Senator Henry Jackson in 1979 at the first conference:

The idea that one person's "terrorist" is another's "freedom fighter" cannot be sanctioned. Freedom fighters or revolutionaries don't blow up buses containing non-combatants; terrorist murderers do. Freedom fighters don't set out to capture and slaughter school-children; terrorist murderers do. Freedom fighters don't assassinate innocent businessmen, or hijack and hold hostage innocent men, women, and children; terrorist murderers do. It is a disgrace that democracies would allow the treasured word "freedom" to be associated with acts of terrorists.[3]

Taking his lead from Jackson, Shultz reaffirmed that the terrorist does not fight in order to convince others of the rightness of his cause: he fights in order to kill innocent people. Once one has grasped this, it is not difficult to distinguish terrorists from freedom fighters.

This definition parts company with an understanding of terror that had arisen in Europe. Bruce Hoffman, an American expert on terror, recalls the view of Maximilien Robespierre that terror is nothing other than immediate, ungenerous, and unrelenting justice, and that it therefore constitutes an expression of *virtue*.[4] Unlike the criminal (on this view), the terrorist is not acting for egoistic personal motives; he is a "criminal" with a good conscience. In his interpretation of today's violent fundamentalism, Shmuel N. Eisenstadt takes Jacobinism as his paradigm.[5] The one who breaks the law is impelled not by too little morality but by too much.

In the period at which the Jonathan Institute held its conferences, the U.S. Department of State committed itself to the definition of terrorism that had been proposed at these conferences:

The term "terrorism" means premeditated, politically motivated violence perpetrated against noncombatant* [interpreted to include unarmed or off-duty military personnel] targets by subnational groups or clandestine agents, usually intended to influence an audience.[6]

This definition outlines the praxis of combating the enemy. First, it splits off into two parts the ambivalent concept of the exemplary freedom fighter who also incurs guilt through the perpetration of violence. On the one hand, there is a justified resistance that is not terrorist; on the other hand, there is a terror that despises human life and cannot in any way claim justification.[7] As in the *Left Behind* series, a fighter can only be one *or* the other. Second, agents of terror can only be subnational or subversive groups. A state becomes a "rogue state" only when it offers shelter to such groups—otherwise, states are not agents of terror. All the reports drawn up by the Department of State about terror activities in the following years are based on this categorization. When Palestinian or Lebanese Shi'ite militias shot at Israeli settlements, these were acts of terror; when the state of Israel shot at Palestinian or Shi'ite villages, that was justified defense. When Israel supported Christian Lebanese militias, it was entitled to do so; when Syria supported the Hezbollah militia, it showed thereby that it was a state that cared nothing for the rule of law. The recognition or rejection of Israel (as the occupying power) becomes the criterion of the legitimacy or illegitimacy of a group in legal terms. In the Middle East conflict, we see once again what James R. Lewis noted in the American debates about cults: conflicts about the legitimacy or illegitimacy of a group are fights about how it ought to be classified. Third, we should note that the definition of the Department of State broadens the category of civilians to include the military, as the footnote indicated by the asterisk explains:

(*) For purposes of this definition, the term "noncombatant" is interpreted to include, in addition to civilians, military personnel who at the time of the incident are unarmed or not on duty. . . . We also consider as acts of terrorism attacks on military installations or on armed military personnel when a state of military hostilities does not exist at the site, such as bombings against US bases in Europe, the Philippines, or elsewhere.

This means that an attack by freedom fighters on military establishments of an occupying power is classified as an act of terror.

This new view gave rise to a suggestive political rhetoric, and this too demands a closer look. As soon as one speaks of "terrorists," the audience loses all interest in learning about the reasons why the "terrorists" are acting in this way. One thus deflects attention from the possibility that one's own politics may have contributed something to the genesis of their fury and their resistance. One suggests that it is meaningless to negotiate with such people. One detaches the act of violence from its reasons. And so the only appropriate reaction is counterviolence. The semantics of the designation "terrorist" confront us with an almost metaphysical concept that admits of only one solution, namely, its elimination. Terrorists are moral nihilists who stand outside the legal order and must be annihilated.[8]

If however we switch from the semantics to the practical applications, inconsistencies appear. For example, let us look at the instances adduced by George P. Shultz in support of his assertion that it is crystal-clear who is a resistance fighter—and thus not a terrorist:

Once we understand terrorism's goals and methods, it is not hard to tell, as we look around the world, who are the terrorists and who are the freedom fighters. The resistance fighters in Afghanistan do not destroy villages or kill the helpless. The Contras in Nicaragua do not blow up school buses or hold mass executions of civilians.[9]

However, the Contras, who were supported by the United States, did in fact kill some 3,000 civilians in Nicaragua in the 1980s, and those who fought against the Soviet forces in Afghanistan were likewise guilty of atrocities. Not only are Shultz's two examples thus seen, when looked at more closely, to be badly chosen, but his rhetoric of terrorism is imbued with the quotidian friend/foe formula of U.S. politics. When it is employed, the term "terrorist" becomes quasi-automatically identical with the political foes of the day. Accordingly, an official decision was required ex cathedra in Washington to say what was a terror organization and what was not. This led to inconsistencies.

When the United States held talks with the PLO about a solution to the Middle East conflict, for example, members of the House of Representatives wanted to know how this was compatible with the classification of the PLO as a terror organization, and it was frequently asked whether an attack by the PLO on an Israeli unit was an act of terror. No, replied the deputy secretary of state, not according to our definition; but he then conceded that attacks on military targets could also be acts of terrorism—it depended on the circumstances. When he was asked what these circumstances might be, he replied that it was inappropriate to describe them more precisely.[10]

"The Call of History": A Global War of Uncertain Duration

The image that the U.S. administration had of the enemy and of itself in this struggle is expressed with particular clarity in President George W. Bush's State of the Union speech on January 28, 2003.[11] At that date, the war against the government of the Taliban in Afghanistan appeared to be over, and the war against Saddam Hussein's regime in Iraq had not yet begun. The text was drafted by Michael Gerson, a theologian from the Evangelical camp who was Bush's speechwriter and an influential adviser up to 2006.[12] In his drafts, Gerson used Bush's own language, and the president read through the speeches before delivering them. The 2003 State of the Union address thus reproduces the president's thinking.

After discussing the need to stimulate the U.S. economy, affordable medical care for all Americans, independent supplies of energy, and the care of the poor and the sick, Bush turned to the "war on terror," saying: "There's never a day when I do not learn of another threat, or receive reports of operations in progress, or give an order in this global war against a scattered network of killers."[13] Bizarrely, the terrorists he describes have no homeland and no creed. "We fight against people who have no country, no ideology; they're motivated by hate."[14] Their sole aims are unbounded cruelty and murder.[15] Although the justifications offered in Osama bin Laden's declaration of war—the presence of American troops in Saudi Arabia, the embargo on Iraq, and the deliberate weakening of the states in the region to strengthen Israel—were well known, Bush did not allude, even fleetingly, to anything that might explain the actions of these perpetrators. These complaints are not mentioned. Instead, he simply picked up the gauntlet:

The threat is new; America's duty is familiar. Throughout the 20th century, small groups of men seized control of great nations, built armies and arsenals, and set out to dominate the weak and intimidate the world. In each case, their ambitions of cruelty and murder had no limit. In each case, the ambitions of Hitlerism, militarism, and Communism were defeated by the will of free peoples, by the strength of great alliances, and by the might of the United States of America. . . . [The] call of history has come to the right country.[16]

The political differences between the currents of National Socialism or Communism or violent Islam are leveled down in favor of a metaphysical category. The enemy is global, and is the embodiment of evil. The fight against him is the order of the day, and it must be waged on a worldwide front.

Bush's address picks up popular ideas that have wandered through American culture in various guises for a long time.[17] Innocent persons are rescued by a hero—Captain America, Rambo, Terminator, or even (as in the film *Independence Day*) the president himself. He employs the same categories to interpret the situation of the American nation:

We're asking [all free nations] to join us, and many are doing so. Yet the course of this nation does not depend on the decisions of others. Whatever action is required, whenever action is necessary, I will defend the freedom and security of the American people. . . . [18]

We sacrifice for the liberty of strangers. . . . The liberty we prize is not America's gift to the world, it is God's gift to humanity.[19]

With the help of an Evangelical adviser, the president of the United States thus put a premillenialist framework around the Islamist attacks on 9/11, thereby also adumbrating a model for political and military action. Bruce Lincoln has pointed out that the framing of the situation and the script for action are symmetrical to the conception of bin Laden: the difference is that in bin Laden's speeches, it is the Americans who are the metaphysical evil.[20]

This rhetoric did not fail to influence the action of the U.S. administration. The official document that formulated U.S. "National Security Strategy" in September 2002 likewise contains no information about the nature, the goals, and the strategy of the enemy. It makes the lapidary claim: "The United States of America is fighting a war against terrorists of global reach. The enemy is not a single political regime or person or religion or ideology. The enemy is terrorism—premeditated, politically motivated violence perpetrated against innocents."[21] Any reasons and justifications that the perpetrators and their comrades-in-arms might possibly have for their actions are ignored; we hear nothing about what their interests and aims are. Such an enemy, who can be everywhere and nowhere, demands the employment of all available means, for only so is there at least a possibility of protecting oneself from immeasurable harm.

The U.S. administration did not take seriously or discuss indications that the perpetrators saw the attack of 9/11 as a trap.[22] They had dropped a piece of bait that the United States had bitten; an attack that cost al-Qaeda only $500,000 dollars had enticed the United States into a war that had already cost it $500 billion. Bin Laden made this calculation in a speech on the eve of the presidential election in 2004, thus incidentally assisting the reelection of his enemy.[23] The costs of the war in Iraq are now reckoned at $2 trillion.

The war that the United States is waging on terror is a global war of uncertain duration, and this must be so, as we can infer from a statement by Secretary of Defense Donald Rumsfeld at a press conference in June 2002:

All of us in this business read intelligence information. And we read it daily and we think about it and it becomes, in our minds, essentially what exists. And that's wrong. It is not what exists. . . . I found that . . . there are very important pieces of intelligence information that countries . . . did not know; [they did not know] some significant event for two years after it happened, for four years after it happened, for six years after it happened, in some cases 11 and 12 and 13 years after it happened. Now what is the message there? The message is: there are known "knowns." There are things we know that we know. There are known unknowns. That is to say there are things that we now know we don't know. But there are also unknown unknowns. There are things we don't know we don't know.[24]

If one knows nothing at all about the existence of a danger, the statesman will do well to behave accordingly. Rumsfeld—who (one may recall) was taken by surprise in his office when the Pentagon was attacked on September 11, 2001—used this logic to justify the war against Iraq. He told the Senate Armed Services Committee that the United States had not acted because dramatic new evidence of Iraq's weapons of mass destruction had been found: it had acted, because the available indications were seen in a new light, through the prism of the events of 9/11.[25] On another occasion, he declared that the lack of evidence was no proof that such evidence was in fact lacking.[26] Deputy Secretary of State Paul Wolfowitz made similar statements: the fact that the FBI and the CIA had failed to prove the link could not mean that this link did not in fact exist.[27] The perceived threat was enough; an analysis of the de facto threat was unnecessary.

In the first days of the war against Iraq in April 2003, the U.S. administration placed full-page advertisements in the country's newspapers, invoking this perceived threat:

You've probably wondered, "Is there anything we can do to protect ourselves from the threat of terrorism?" Here's your answer. There is no reason to feel helpless in the face of terrorist threats against the United States. You can get information, take action and be prepared. Step one—make an emergency kit . . . Step two—make a family communications plan—Step three—be informed.

Attention should be paid to the following details:

Emergency Supply Kit: Start with three days worth of non-perishable food and water. You may need to shelter at home for a couple of days. Roads and stores may be closed—electricity may be turned off—your water supply might be interrupted. Add flashlights and a battery-powered radio to hear the latest instructions from local authorities. Don't forget extra batteries, a blanket, a first aid kit and medicines, and a manual can opener. Stash away duct tape and pre-measured plastic sheeting for future use. Experts tell us that a safe room inside your house or apartment can help protect you from airborne contaminants for approximately five hours—that could be just enough time for a chemical agent to blow away. Family Communication Plan: Make certain that everyone knows how to get in touch, and knows what the emergency plan is for different types of attacks. Every state, every community, every school and every workplace should have an emergency plan. Find out what that plan is and who is in charge. If your school or employer does not have a plan, volunteer to be part of a group to create one. Choose a meeting place, maybe a friend or relative's house, that's well *away* from your neighborhood. Keep your gas tank half-full. And always make sure you have a set of emergency and contact numbers posted by the phone. Be Informed and Aware: Log onto www.ready.gov or call 1–800–BE-READY. In the event of an emergency, listen to local authorities for instructions.[28]

The Department of Homeland Security here not only gives practical advice. It also communicates a quite different message, which jars on people's nerves: the enemy is in your immediate vicinity, even if you do not know him or see him. The only correct action is to take account of every eventuality. Since every link between the policies of the United States and the attacks is excluded, it is necessary to drum into U.S. citizens the awareness that the 9/11 attacks were aimed at innocent civilians—not at the centers of American power.

Attack on the Social Capital of Islamic Networks

The president reacted to the attacks with an Executive Order (No. 13224) that froze the assets of terrorist persons or groups and forbade donations to persons or groups that practiced terrorism, threatened to practice it, or supported it. This presidential decree was issued on September 23, 2001. It was not the first of its kind: in January 1995, Bill Clinton had frozen the assets of organizations that wanted to derail the peace process in the Middle East, and had forbidden transactions or donations in favor of these groups. An appendix to his Executive Order (No. 12947) lists twelve organizations affected by these provisions, including Hezbollah and Hamas, but also two Jewish organizations (Kach and Kahane Chai).

An appendix to the decree issued by George W. Bush after the 9/11 attacks lists twenty-seven natural and juridical persons associated with al-Qaeda. The Executive Order envisaged that the list would be expanded by the State Department and the Department of the Treasury. Subsequently, more and more persons and groups were added, although a connection to al-Qaeda was not always discernible. This applies above all to the organizations that supported Hamas and Hezbollah. Since donations to these movements, which organized the resistance to the Israeli occupying power in Lebanon and in Palestine, were now regarded as hostile acts in the war on terror, the Middle East conflict too became a part of this war on terror.

In 2003, the State Department's list comprised thirty-six organizations. The case of "terror organization" no. 22 shows that the list of these organizations was also subject to considerations of the politics of the day. After invading Iraq in 2003, the United States made a truce with an Iranian opposition group, the Mujahedin-e Khalq, which for years had been making preparations there to overthrow the regime in Iran by violence. This group was allowed to keep its weapons and use them against any intruders from Iran. First, however, the group had to be removed from the terror list—and this was done.[29]

It is worth taking a look at the list of persons and organizations drawn up by the Department of the Treasury. A new department in this ministry, the Foreign Terrorist Asset Tracking Center, was given the task of tracking down the flows of money with which terrorist groups were financed, and of halting all such transactions.[30] The list became ever longer; today, it runs to more than 100 pages of very small print.

After an attack by Hamas in August 2003, the president and the Department of the Treasury added to the list five Palestinian relief agencies that supported Hamas. In connection with this, an information sheet distributed to the press claimed that Hamas received more than $10 million in donations and that the "charitable" aspect was merely a smoke screen:

HAMAS raises tens of millions of dollars per year throughout the world using charitable fundraising as cover. While HAMAS may provide money for legitimate charitable work, this work is a primary recruiting tool for the organization's militant causes. HAMAS relies on donations from Palestinian expatriates around the world and private benefactors located in moderate Arab states, Western Europe and North America. HAMAS uses a web of charities to facilitate funding and to funnel money. Charitable donations to non-governmental organizations are commingled, moved between charities in ways that hide the money trail, and then often diverted or siphoned to support terrorism.[31]

The Hamas leaders themselves admitted that the military wing is subservient to the political wing: "We cannot separate the wing from the body. If we do so, the body will not be able to fly." This is the justification offered by Sheikh Ahmad Yasin in a press release by Reuters on May 12, 1998. Although in reality the resistance movement Hamas is both a social agency and a militia, the U.S. administration makes it a one-sidedly violent organization, with the consequence that all donations to Hamas are liable to prosecution. This affects all the Islamic relief agencies that collect donations in the United States and other countries for needy Palestinians, and distribute these in Palestine through the Brotherhood.

The criminalization of Islamic relief agencies brings the war deep into impoverished Islamic milieus and poses a threat to the very existence of Muslim families. The glimpse that Zaki Chehab gives us of this war, which is waged parallel to the war in Iraq, is particularly valuable, since the Western public is scarcely aware of it. Chehab shows the impact that the freezing of the assets of the Holy Land Foundation for Relief and Development in the United States had on the eleven members of Ahmed Abu al-Kheir's family in Nablus. In 2000, the relief agencies had collected more than $13 million in donations and had distributed this sum in Palestine through Hamas. The family of Ahmed Abu al-Kheir, who had been unable to work as a result of a traffic accident, received a small monthly sum of between $55 and $85; this was paid by the local *zakat* committee in Nablus. Hundreds of poor Palestinian families, orphans, handicapped persons, and students received support in this way. Thanks to the prohibition, this aid dried up. The Bush administration justified its prohibition by saying that the financial means of the organization went to Hamas, and that Hamas used the money to support schools where children were encouraged to become suicide attackers; besides this, Hamas had used these funds to recruit suicide attackers, by assuring their families of financial support. According to the head of the *zakat* committee in Nablus, however, these funds do not in any way benefit Hamas qua organization; they are distributed according to the principles that govern the distribution of the *zakat* funds in general.[32] We must not underestimate the hostility and hatred that *this* war causes. But as yet, there has been no critical evaluation of goods between the justified aim of drying up the funds of al-Qaeda, on the one hand, and the violent reactions provoked by such a comprehensive threat to Islamic families, on the other.

Martial Law Is Suspended in the Case of Captured Jihadists

In February 2002, President Bush signed an internal memorandum that drew consequences for martial law from the above-mentioned concept of terrorism.

Humane Treatment of Taliban and al Qaeda Detainees

2. Pursuant to my authority as commander in chief and chief executive of the United States, and relying on the opinion of the Department of Justice dated January 22, 2002, and on the legal opinion rendered by the attorney general in his letter of February 1, 2002, I hereby determine as follows:

   a. . . . none of the provisions of Geneva apply to our conflict with al Qaeda in Afghanistan or elsewhere throughout the world because, among other reasons, al Qaeda is not a High Contracting Party to Geneva. . . .

    d. . . . I determine that the Taliban detainees are unlawful combatants and, therefore, do not qualify as prisoners of war under Article 4 of Geneva. I note that, because Geneva does not apply to our conflict with al Qaeda, al Qaeda detainees also do not qualify as prisoners of war.

3. Of course, our values as a nation, values that we share with many nations in the world, call for us to treat detainees humanely, including those who are not legally entitled to such treatment. . . .

5. I hereby reaffirm the order previously issued by the secretary of defense to the United States Armed Forces requiring that the detainees be treated humanely and, to the extent appropriate and consistent with military necessity, in a manner consistent with the principles of Geneva.[33]

Without this command, the practices in the prisons of Abu Ghraib and Guantánamo would scarcely have been possible. Seymour M. Hersh has collated the debates in the U.S. administration about torture at Guantánamo. The intention of these debates was to widen the "room for maneuver" in interrogations, in keeping with the military necessities. The unanimous opinion was that not every form of ill treatment by American interrogation teams would cause so much pain and suffering that it would fall under the prohibition of torture.[34]

    Paradoxically, one factor in the watering-down of the prohibition of torture was a manual for U.S. Marines, who were required to attend a course about how to behave while on active service in Iraq. This manual, entitled *Semper Sensitive,* sought to inculcate a sensitivity to the special characteristics of the Iraqi culture. Under the rubric "Respect," it listed actions that could violate the feelings of Iraqis:

Do not shame or humiliate a man in public. Shaming a man will cause him and his family to be anti-Coalition.

The most important qualifier for all shame is for a third party to witness the act. If you just do something likely to cause shame, remove the person from the view of others.

Shame is given by placing hoods over a detainee's head. Avoid this practice.

Placing a detainee on the ground or putting a foot on him implies you are God. This is one of the worst things we can do.

Arabs consider the following things unclean:

Feet or soles of feet.

Using the bathroom around others. Unlike Marines, who are used to open-air toi-
lets, Arab men will not shower/use the bathroom together.

Bodily fluids (because of this they love tissue paper).[35]

The interrogation teams in Abu Ghraib turned upside-down the practical
rules for conduct that were meant to help members of the military win the
trust of Arabs. The cameras that were used to photograph their treatment
were meant to make it unmistakably clear to the detainees that their humiliation did not end when the treatment ended: on the contrary, it always
remains available, and the prisoners can do nothing to change this situation. The photographs were conceived as a "shame multiplier."[36]

A letter written to Senator John McCain (R-Ariz.) by a U.S. officer
fighting in Iraq sheds light on the problem from another aspect.[37] Captain
Ian Fishback of the 82nd Airborne Division wrote that after witnessing
the mistreatment of Iraqi prisoners, he had asked his superiors and other
authorities to clarify what exactly the rules were for a legal and humane
treatment of the detainees under interrogations in Iraq, and what was not
permitted. Seventeen months later, he had still not received an answer:

Instead of resolving my concerns, the approach for clarification process leaves me
deeply troubled. Despite my efforts, I have been unable to get clear, consistent answers from my leadership about what constitutes lawful and humane treatment of
detainees. I am certain that this confusion contributed to a wide range of abuses
including death threats, beatings, broken bones, murder, exposure to elements,
extreme forced physical exertion, hostage-taking, stripping, sleep deprivation and
degrading treatment. I and troops under my command witnessed some of these
abuses both in Afghanistan and Iraq.

Congress reacted with a law prohibiting such mistreatment, but the president watered this down by means of a "signing statement" when he signed
it, declaring that he would judge the new limitations on the methods of
interrogation in the light of his empowerment to safeguard national security. If necessary, he would suspend them.

In retrospect, there was certainly no compelling necessity to declare
the war on terror and to attack the regimes that had genuinely or allegedly given shelter to al-Qaeda (namely, Afghanistan and Iraq), without a
mandate from the United Nations. Nor was it necessary to withhold from

the detainees the protection of the Geneva Convention. The process of coming to terms with 9/11 would have taken another course if the acts of terror had been prosecuted internationally as criminal acts—an alternative that in fact existed.[38] But there was no place for such a procedure in the premillenialist framework of the 9/11 attack, although many instruments that would have been needed were available.[39] In a public trial, the culprits would be able to bring charges of their own against the West, and these allegedly hate-filled monsters might be transformed into angry young Muslim men capable of offering justifications for their crimes.

CHAPTER II

Concluding Remarks:
Wars of Religion in the
Age of Globalization

Every day, news reports reach us from the Middle East that recall a poem written by Andreas Gryphius in 1636, in the age of the wars of religion:

The church is overthrown; our mighty men are slain;
The town hall lies in dust; our towers burn;
Virgins are raped; and everywhere we turn
Are fire, plague, death to pierce us—heart and brain.[1]

It is not by chance that such historical memories are evoked: in his study of the "new" wars, Herfried Münkler has demonstrated the similarities to the Thirty Years' War.[2] Just as at that time, so today the war parties include private militias; just as at that time, so today religions are seldom the real cause of the fire, but they have often had the effect of accelerating the blaze; just as at that time, so today it is only in the course of the war that faith communities have engaged in violent acts. This means that one must be cautious about defining too simply the causal relationship between the military course of a conflict and the explosion of religious violence: the chief culprit can neither be identified as cults, fundamentalism, or terrorism, on the one hand, nor political oppression or disfranchisement, on the other. The violence is not caused solely either by a faith community or by the circumstances of social conflict. Acts of violence are generated by the interplay between the two sides. It is only when this diagnosis has been made that one can reflect on the appropriate therapies.

Violent Religious Language and Actions

If one wishes to understand (and thereby to explain) religious violence, one must draw a distinction between two conceptions of "understanding," namely, understanding the motives of an actor and understanding the significance of an action. If one wishes to understand the motives of an actor, one must discover the circumstances and motivations of this individual that impel him or her to act. If one wishes to understand the significance of an action, one must discover what model provides orientation for an action, and how far this orientation is acknowledged or disputed by other persons. In the investigation of violent religious actions carried out by a community, the only way to make progress is to pay closer attention to how the significance of an action is understood. It is indeed true that one must not omit to look for the causes of violence in the personal motives of those involved: the murder of members of one's family, imprisonment, torture, humiliations, and experiences of injustice form motives without which there would be no perpetrators.[3] But although anger and revenge should not be disregarded as the motivating force in the radicalization of the perpetrators, on their own they do not constitute a sufficient condition for the praxis of religious violence. As a number of relevant studies show, there was all too often no difference between the perpetrators and other members of their group.[4] The only difference was that the perpetrators dared to do something that others only imagined doing. The individual situations of people's lives are indeed one factor in the willingness to follow a summons to violence, but they do not provide a sufficient basis for understanding and explaining this willingness. This is why we must investigate the discourses about violent religious actions in religious communities.

The Thomas Theorem as an
Investigative Instrument

If it is correct to affirm that the link between religion and violence is neither impossible nor necessary, we must concentrate our investigation on those situations in which this link arises. One explanatory model for this connection is the Thomas theorem: "If men define situations as real, they are real in their consequences."[5] This formulation affirms that the definition of a situation is not inevitably generated by objective accompanying circumstances, but that actors impose the definition on these circumstances. And when they then act accordingly, this imposition has real effects. In sociology, this theorem explains the discrepancies that can so often be observed between people's attitudes and their de facto conduct. In the case of violent religious actions, this theorem can be employed in order to measure more precisely the ambivalence of religions. Religions are potent principles for the establishing of societal bonds; at the same time, however, they are potent principles for the destruction of such bonds. Although this ambivalence is determinative of the history of religions, it usually receives too little attention in the analysis of religion. Researchers seldom investigate precisely those cases that concern the destructive aspect of religions—and when this does happen, the intention is often merely to withdraw such a case from the competence of religious studies and assign it to other academic disciplines. However, the cases we have analyzed show that perpetrators of violence also find orientation in religious scenarios and exemplary models. With the help of the Thomas theorem, it is possible to clarify how and why this happens.

The conflicts in the course of which religious communities resorted to violence were neither from the outset nor per se religious. The conflict between parents and the authorities and the Peoples Temple; between the police and the FBI and the Adventists in Waco; between the Shah's regime and the Shi'ite activists; between the religious communities in the Lebanese civil war; between the Israelis and the Palestinians in the occupied territories; between the jihadists and the United States—all these are conflicts rooted in opposing legal, societal, political, and military interests, and they can also be described in a corresponding terminology. But we should not draw the conclusion that this proves that religion is being manipulated and used for purposes that are intrinsically alien to it. Actors who advocate religious interpretations of a conflict alter the course of this conflict. Max Weber's view that religion is a category of the subjective expectation of salvation on the part of the actors, and that it can be directed to various kinds of innerworldly actions, helps to clarify this state of affairs. Religion need not be the cause of a conflict, but it can be one possible interpretation of the conflict. Our task is then to use the Thomas theorem in order to recognize that a religious interpretation is being imposed on a situation of conflict, and to grasp the consequences of this.[6]

On the Performance of Violent Religious Actions

This book has shown us religious communities that employ violent religious language to describe their situation. This is something we have repeatedly observed: in the Peoples Temple and the Adventists in Waco; in the Shiʿites in Iran and Lebanon; in Jewish religious settlers; in the resistance movement of the Muslim Brethren; in the praxis of American premillenialists; and in global jihadists. In each instance, the situation of one's own religious community is defined with the help of traditional eschatological scripts. In keeping with this, believers were told that they must find orientation for their action in scripts about how to acquire salvation and in exemplary fighters for the faith. But what reality is in fact being elaborated by the religious language here? In order to ascertain this, it is helpful to compare religious and secular language.

Let us do an intellectual experiment. It is one thing when the Peoples Temple or the Adventists in Waco engage in a legal conflict with opponents and with local authorities about questions of guardianship or the observation of laws regarding weapons. It is quite another matter when they understand these same conflicts as assaults on the community of the elect by the destructive powers of this world, or by the Babylon of the Last Days, and put up the appropriate resistance. The framing of the conflicts in a religious language generates a corresponding way of acting, thereby creating a reality all of its own. The conflict offers the chance to prove one's faith and unleashes energies born of the believers' commitment.

Similarly, the power of religious language to establish reality can be seen in the Middle East conflict and in the rival claims to the occupied territories. It makes a difference whether Israelis speak of "occupied territories" or of "Eretz Yizrael." The justification of territorial claims in terms of the return or "ascent" to Jerusalem is not the same thing as the justification of these claims in simple terms of immigration. The same applies to the Palestinians: if they speak of "Palestine" or of an Islamic foundational land (*waqf*); if they speak of the national anti-imperialist liberation movement or of the Islamic resistance movement, whose *murābitūn* are defending the land. The actors are putting a different framework around the conflict, thereby creating a different competence with regard to action and giving the conflict a different course.

American Protestants are a further participant in the conflict, and they too have offered a religious interpretation of the Middle East conflict. This is the historical image of premillenialism, which spread gradually in the United States and has exercised influence on foreign policy particularly since the election of Ronald Reagan. These Protestants believe that after the foundation of Israel in 1948, the biblical prophecies that still await their fulfillment will very soon be realized, and they demand that their government (like the Persian ruler Cyrus of old) should aid the Jews in their repatriation from exile and in the reestablishment of an independent Israel in the whole of Palestine, although this Israel will either convert to Christ or be destroyed in the Last Days. Numerous contacts with religious Zionists in Israel are a part of the religious praxis of these Protestants, who however give little or no support to Christian Palestinians.

When they attacked the United States in September 2001, jihadists were interpreting the Middle East conflict in Islamic concepts, but they did so in a radically different manner from the mainstream of the Muslim Brethren. The power of the United States and of Israel has made Islam so rotten and corrupt that no external institution is now able to represent it credibly; it is only the pure intentions of the last surviving upright believers that can form the core of a new community of the elect. And this is what they demonstrate by means of martyr operations.

One should not attempt to define religion as the immutable transmission of faith. Nietzsche observed correctly that "Only that which has no history is definable."[7] A concept of religion that includes violence must take account of the difference between faith traditions and the relationship of believers to the world. Religion does not possess validity independently of the believers' relationship to the world,[8] which in turn must not be restricted to the religious interpretation. Since the conflicts are not per se and a priori religious, the violent actions always possess an *instrumental and tactical* character for the believers. Beside this, they communicate the message that the believers have suffered injustice. In this sense, they are *communicative.*

When the violence is oriented to scripts for action or to models, however, the action takes on a further significance: the violent praxis of a fighter for the faith becomes the action of a zealous God. This type of action is different from the other two, because it gives the violent action an immediate meaning: the action bears the meaning in itself. In his essay on religious languages of violence, Bernd Weisbrod speaks here of a *performative* meaning.[9] Such a meaning does not serve a calculable goal, a prudent tactic, or a readily comprehensible message. It presents the action as the carrying out of the divine will. All at once, this meaning translates an existing secular conflict into an act in the history of salvation.

The religious language of the actors introduces new motivations for action and new courses of the conflict into the existing clashes of interests. This applies above all to the nation-state. As long as the secular law of the modern nation-state with its promise of the liberty, equality, and fraternity of all the citizens is able to safeguard the internal freedom of a political entity even in the case of conflicts, the religious language of violence will not find a ready audience. Where people lose their confidence that the nation state can truly achieve these goals, however, religious communality can unexpectedly become its rival.[10] And when alternative communities are demonized, and the believers experience this as a situation of threat, membership in a religious community can be transformed from something about which one has scarcely reflected into the assured trust that this community is the ultimate haven of rescue and salvation. The hostile forces are promoted to eschatological agents of evil, apostates become the fifth column of Satan, and fighters for the faith become saints.

New Forms of Religious Communality
and Acts of Violence

In order to understand the forms taken by religious acts of violence today, we must begin by looking at the contemporary forms of religious communality. In addition to the familiar societal forms of synagogue, church, and mosque, regional, national, or transnational networks have come into being, and these constitute a specific public societal form of religion. Existing legal forms permit laypersons to found religious associations independently of state privileges—but also independently of traditional religious authorities. In these religious networks, problems of the day are discussed, as well as the urgent concerns, humiliating experiences, and intense expectations of the members of one particular religion; and all this is linked to the beliefs and practices of their faith. Such networks have spread above all in regions where the welfare state is weak or nonexistent, the order of society collapses in crises and wars, and a continuing expansion of the market economy leads to an individualization of existential risks. Where neither the state nor traditional loyalties offer the individual a safety net in situations of distress, waning loyalties based on family, neighborhood, local region, tribe, language, or nation are absorbed into the religious social capital of an ethic of brotherliness, which becomes a motor in the creation of societal institutions.

In the past, the performance of religious actions was embedded in existing loyalties. Today, however, acknowledged religious authorities proclaim loudly that it is up to the individual to decide and then to do what is correct in religious terms. This can be seen with particular clarity in the case of the intention to kill or to die for a community. When people decide to act in this way, it is the faith community that must approve of this action, and that must share in the responsibility for its consequences. This is the source of the incentive to idealize the martyr and to form institutions that guarantee solidarity. The new forms of the practice of violent religiosity are thus both innovative *ad intra* and hierarchical *ad extra*: on the one hand, they are detached from the traditional modalities and restrictions related to the practice of religion, but on the other hand, they need to be legitimated by the faith community and by its authorities. This explains the paradox that the individualization of religions can be accompanied by an increase in the power of faith communities.

On the Validity of Salvation-Historical Interpretative Frameworks and Scenarios for Action in the Modern Period

Even in modern society, religious interpretations of meaning with their roots in conceptions of salvation history do not simply belong to the past. As recently as thirty years ago, such interpretations were regarded as definitively obsolete. "Only when intelligent and educated men ceased to take prophecy seriously were the Middle Ages truly at an end," Marjorie Reeves writes, to which Peter Burke adds: "It was almost as natural for educated men to scoff at prophecies in 1800 as it had been for them to take prophecies seriously three hundred years before."[11]

In the twenty years after Burke wrote these words, a significant change occurred in the scholarly evaluation of this question. "We need to see men like Joachim of Fiore [ca. 1130–1202] and Hal Lindsay [b. 1929] on the same level plane, and to recognize the persistent existence of a tradition of messianic revolution in the West, stretching from the Middle Ages until our own time,"[12] David Katz and Richard Popkin write in conclusion to their study of the history of the idea of a messianic turning point in time. One can no longer speak of a disappearance of belief in prophecy in the modern period (not even among educated persons). Such a view is obviously more realistic than Burke's. It is true that militant anticipations of the kingdom of God had been discredited in the aftermath of the European wars of religion in the sixteenth and seventeenth centuries, but the almost blind trust in the power of reason itself called forth a new renaissance of the old expectations, since many regarded the bloody end of the French Revolution as compelling evidence that human beings could never succeed on the basis of their own reason in bringing about a better state of affairs.[13] An additional motive power in modern salvation-historical expectations was industrialization and the changes in living conditions that this entailed. Between 1790 and 1850, England witnessed an explosive spread of Nonconformist sects with burning eschatological hopes.[14] The historian E. P. Thompson identified what he called a "chiliasm of despair" as one of the driving forces;[15] another was the performance strength of the communality of the faith communities that were founded. Under the conditions of industrial society, where the individual could no longer rely on the traditional loyalties of family, relatives, or neighborhood, and where all the risks fell on his or her own shoulders, the religious ethics of brotherhood became immensely attractive. In nineteenth-century England and Germany, religious eschatological expectations became more intensive, especially in the industrialized regions. The wretched living conditions in industrial society at that time paved the way for apocalyptic communities—but also for the Communist movement. Both of these seemed able to bestow a meaning on the intolerable living conditions, either as one step in the direction of the divine "judgment of the world" or as one step in the direction of the socialist "world revolution."[16]

As Lucian Hölscher has brilliantly shown, these two interpretative frameworks, the salvation-historical and the secular-progressive, had been competing for a long time before this. From the eighteenth century on, with the rise of the sciences and the increasing ability to explain and control natural processes, the future had moved more and more into the realm of the manageable. These new technical and scientific possibilities did not lead to the disappearance of belief in salvation history, but to the "doubling of the concept of the future." The expectation of a coming—*adventus*—of the Lord continued to exist alongside scientific and social planning of a better future.[17] The starting point for sketching out the future, in the sense of scientific and social progress, was the present day; the starting point for sketching out the future, in the sense of salvation history, was the end, namely, the day of judgment.

Even in the twentieth century, expectations of salvation sometimes became attached to social movements. This poses a difficulty from the perspective of a clear separation between the religious and the political. It is more easily understood if we recall the insight of Max Weber that every kind of everyday action can be given a religious "framework." As an expectation of salvation, religion can attach itself to purposive-rational and value-rational everyday action, and from this perspective we must agree with those who hold the conventional separation of politics and religion, or government and salvation, to be unfruitful.[18] The relationships between secular political currents and religious currents today are in fact varied and close, and there is no difficulty in forging alliances between the new civil forms of religious networks and political parties with their programs. This has happened in Israel with the religious settler movement and the right-wing Likud Party; and Hezbollah in Lebanon and Hamas in Palestine exemplify the processes whereby a religious organization can become a political party.

Time as a Process of Creation

In order to reconstruct the genesis of salvation-historical scenarios for action, one should not take one's starting point in "sacred" time as a rebellion against historical time, as Mircea Eliade did. Rather, one must look squarely at "time" itself.[19] Stephen Hawking's bestseller *A Brief History of Time,* first published in 1988, shows very well what natural scientists and philosophers have found so fascinating in the "riddle of time" since the beginning of the twentieth century,[20] namely, that it is not a universal entity, and that the proper time of moving systems is different in relation to one another. The revolutionizing of the concept of time—the "new time" in the scientific sense—also removes a number of constraints that the model of a universal time had imposed on cultural studies. This had already been recognized by Henri Bergson (1859–1941), when he complained that the customary expressions for time were often borrowed from spatial language. Duration was cut up into fixed points of time, which in turn were linked causally as past, present, and future states. Scarcely any philosopher had looked for positive qualities in time. New metaphors and models were needed: "The more we study the nature of time, the more we shall comprehend that duration means invention, the creation of forms, the continual elaboration of the absolutely new,"[21] Bergson writes; time involves an unceasing creation of reality, generating actions that are not determined. It is the *élan vital,* a process of creation. Bergson's conception of time helps make sense of the fact of the activation of religious scenarios for action, and he himself gives a memorable example of this. When he opened the newspaper *Le Matin* on August 4, 1914, and read the headline: "Germany declares war on France," he had "the sudden feeling of an invisible *presence.* It was as if a legendary figure stepped out of the book that tells his story and placed himself comfortably in the room. In reality, of course, I had no encounter with the complete person. All that was present of him was what was necessary to have a certain effect. The figure had waited for his hour to strike, and unhurriedly sat down in his place."[22]

The cases we have studied display this elusive presence of something belonging to the distant past. An Adventist faith community, besieged by the FBI, behaves as if it were living in the Last Days; in Iran and Lebanon, the battles of Karbalā (680 CE) are fought out afresh; Israel interprets the military victory over the neighboring Arab states and the settling of the regions that once belonged to the Holy Land as the beginning of the redemption of Israel and the world; under the state of siege, at the very moment when they have lost most of the land assigned to them by the United Nations in 1947, the Palestinians claim the whole of Palestine as the foundational land entrusted to them by the Prophet; American Evangelicals interpret Israel's victory as its salvation-historical restoration, and hence as the arena of the upcoming struggle against the Antichrist; jihadists carry out an attack on the U.S. centers of power, like the attacks carried out by Muhammad and his adherents in the period when Islam became established as the order of the state in Medina and had to be defended. In all these cases, a situation of threat to the community is interpreted in salvation-historical conceptions, and people gain confidence from this interpretation.

Salvation-Historical Scenarios of Religious Violence

All eight cases described above grew out of the course of a longer-term conflict. A clash over alternative values, the failure of a modernization, a civil war, and a territorial conflict formed fields of conflict in which faith communities became public actors and abandoned their traditionally passive attitude to the world.

The American cases of Jonestown in 1978 and Waco in 1993 show how faith communities under attack mobilize particular patterns of action. Both communities broke with the morality that is dominant in American society, and turned their members into enclaves bound together by alternative values. The members of the community associated their hope of salvation so closely with the existence of their community that under the increasing pressure of persecution, the only remaining choice seemed to be between capitulation to the destructive powers of this world or else dying for the sake of the truth. And from the perspective of the law enforcement unit, a negotiated solution was completely unthinkable. The meaning that the term "cult" had in their eyes made such an idea appear utterly absurd.

The 1978–1979 Iranian revolution was simultaneously the rise of the concept of an Islamic "fundamentalism." This term, which had been in use (mostly in a pejorative sense) in the United States since the 1920s, was applied by the English-language media to events in Iran at the end of the 1970s in order to bestow a name on something incomprehensible. In Iran, the Shiʿite faith community had been prompted by the collapse of a Western model of modernization to revise its ethic: the patient endurance of tyranny and injustice was no longer to be the model, but rather the active struggle against these powers. Ancient theological hesitations and reservations about a self-inflicted death in the struggle against the foes of the Imam were dropped: now, consciously chosen death in the fight against the godless was to confer the prestige of martyrdom.

In Lebanon, it was the inability of the state to build up civil institutions and offer military protection in areas of Shiʿite settlement that led the Shiʿites, under the leadership of their imam, Musa al-Sadr, to slough off the obligation to suffer injustice passively. In 1978, their imam suddenly and inexplicably disappeared. The shock that this caused, and the political victory of their coreligionists in Iran at almost the same time, turned the Shiʿites into an active community who drove the foreign occupiers out of Lebanon by means of spectacular suicide attacks. As the "party of God" (Hezbollah), they drew strength from their salvation-historical expectations, not only for the armed struggle against the infidel occupiers of the country, but also for the construction of a comprehensive Islamic social system. When the Lebanese civil war ended in 1989, Hezbollah became a national political party. Since the state of war between Lebanon and Israel continued, however, both Israel and the United States regarded the "party of God" as a terrorist fighting organization and attempted through a war in the summer of 2006 to liberate Lebanon from this "cancer." All that resulted was an increase in Hezbollah's strength.

The Middle East Conflict in the Prism of Salvation History

From the mid 1970s on, salvation-historical expectations have determined the political developments in the Middle East conflict, which—to a greater degree than other conflicts in the world—effectively established religious interpretations of the situation and concepts for action in the public political sphere. Religious Zionists interpreted the military conquest of East Jerusalem, the West Bank, and the Gaza Strip in 1967 as a war of redemption; American Evangelicals saw this as the beginning of the eschatological restoration of Israel; and Muslim Palestinians were unwilling to accept the loss of the foundational land they believed Muhammad to have entrusted to them until the Last Judgment. These interpretations led to corresponding actions. Religious Zionists, initially without the support of the government and later with this support, began to take possession of biblical land and to establish Jewish settlements on it. Plans even included blowing up the Islamic Dome of the Rock. In addition to the conflict with the Palestinians, there was a conflict among the Jews themselves, some of whom supported the return of land in exchange for a peaceful solution.

The Muslim Brethren mobilized Palestinians as *murābitūn* for a defense of the Islamic territory against Israel. When the construction of Jewish settlements continued unabated even after the Oslo Accords, and the Opposition leader Ariel Sharon and an armed escort entered the Temple Mount, which was administered by Muslims, in 2003, in order to lay the Jewish claim to this area as publicly as possible, this provoked the Second Intifada. The desecration of the "Noble Sanctuary" was understood by Muslims as the feared humiliation of the Islamic community predicted to occur in the Last Days. The prestige of the community was to be restored by means of martyr operations against Israeli soldiers and civilians.

The salvation-historical interpretation of the Middle East conflict did not halt at the shores of the United States. Here, as long ago as the end of the nineteenth century, Evangelical fundamentalists had taught that all the biblical prophecies that as yet were unfulfilled were addressed to the Jewish people—not to the Church. They followed the gradual restoration of Israel in the twentieth century with great fascination and saw it as evidence that the Last Days were drawing near. Evangelicals saw it as their task, too, using the means available to them, to influence American politics and to hasten on the restoration of Israel in the Holy Land.

Ethics of Responsibility and Ethics of Conviction as Options for Action

Since the beginning of the 1980s, an ethics of conviction that assumes that Sunni Islam in the Arab countries is completely corrupt has spread among Islamists. Founding Islamic institutions such as schools or hospitals leads merely to a further dependence on the infidel state. Only a small group of faithful men who have remained pure in their intention are able to take vengeance and restore Muslim dignity. This type of jihad was manifested in the attacks on September 11, 2001, on the centers of economic, military, and political power in the United States. Since martyrdom is granted only to those whose intention is pure, the men had in a first step to prepare themselves for the attack by means of recitations, prayers, and rituals. They took the second step in the airport, protecting themselves against the satanic power of Western civilization by means of prayers and recitations. Finally, they were to die with "Allāhu akbar!" on their lips. It was the intention at the moment of dying that decided the individual's salvation.

Speeches, military actions, and decrees of U.S. President George W. Bush interpreted the response to the attack on the United States as a struggle against the same evil that had once manifested itself in Bolshevism and Nazism. Jihadist captives thus had no right to be treated in accordance with the Geneva Convention, nor to a public trial that would give them the possibility of justifying their actions. The only option for action was war; negotiated solutions with the terrorists, or with states that gave them support, were unthinkable.

How Can the Cycle of Religious Violence Be Interrupted?

It is improbable that the faith communities will relinquish their roles as actors in civil society and withdraw from the fields of conflict at any time soon. For the foreseeable future, we can discount ultra-Othodox rejection of the Jewish state, a rise of social Islamization as opposed to militancy, or a depoliticization of Evangelical fundamentalism. Nevertheless, it is not correct to hold that a salvation-historical interpretation invariably intensifies conflict and is therefore a bad thing. The new forms of activated religion contain more options for action than the options that are enacted in violence. For example, the experience of Waco taught American law enforcement that in order to avoid the danger of an unintended escalation, one must begin by learning how a refractory faith community interprets the situation. All the cases described in this book could be looked at anew in this way, for as the analyses have shown, in none of these instances is the violence an inevitable result of the kind and the course of the conflict, nor of the type of faith community that is involved. Let me mention three points at which courses of action leading to religious violence might be short-circuited:

First, it is obvious that the conditions of a democracy favor a mobilization of religious networks for electoral purposes. Politicians seek the support of religious groups and thereby give religious worldviews a share in determining the way they speak and act. And this means that religious interpretations of situations and preferred options for action acquire public status and can serve to legitimate what the state does. In view of these circumstances, it is too optimistic to believe that a strong democratic state would automatically act as a brake, preventing such a development. Transreligious initiatives in civil society and international institutions are more likely to strengthen the rule of law and resecularize a state. David Shulman reports in his book *Dark Hope* on a common Palestinian-Israeli peace initiative called Ta'ayush. He concludes: "In the midst of it all, there will be the lonely few, on both sides, who refuse to be enemies, who will take any risk for the other's sake and for the sake of peace."[23]

Second, terminology is employed with regard to faith communities that come into conflict with government authorities or with the legal system that makes it seem absurd to negotiate with them in order to resolve conflicts. This vocabulary speaks of "cults," "fundamentalism," or "terror groups," thus denying them any genuinely religious character and excluding them as negotiating partners. This attitude has its roots in the Bible.

When Yahweh your God shall bring you into the land where you go to possess it, and shall cast out many nations . . . greater and mightier than you; and when Yahweh your God shall deliver them up before you, and you shall strike them; then you shall utterly destroy them: you shall make no covenant with them, nor show mercy to them. (Deut. 7:1–2)

The history of Judaism shows, however that this kind of language of violence has never in fact determined the practice of the Jewish faith community. On the contrary, the history of Judaism shows how treaties could be made with Gentiles. When Hamas offers a truce today, this option ought not to be dismissed with scorn. Recent German history is a good example of how it is possible to reach accords below the level of peace treaties that exclude recourse to weapons. It is when those who hold power in a state seek to eliminate faith communities militarily that the cycle of violence begins.

Third, it needs to be recognized that a faith community engaged in social work is more prone to reflect on negative consequences of violent action for their people than a group of young men who are fiercely determined to fight without such responsibility. Making this distinction is likely to have a particularly decisive impact, since it would surely allow for excluding Islamic relief agencies that distribute the alms tax and donations to Muslims in Palestine via the Muslim Brethren (and hence via members of Hamas) from the war on terror. Islam too is familiar with treaties with non-Muslims.

Notes

1. Bishop Hans-Jochen Jaschke, "Gottes heiligen Namen aufrichten," *Hamburger Abendblatt*, September 15, 2001, quoted in *Religion und Terror*, ed. Lutterbach and Manemann, 27–29.

2. For a working definition of religion as a self-positioning of human persons that transcends the world, see Kippenberg and Stuckrad, *Einführung in die Religionswissenschaft*, 13–14.

3. Smith, *Imagining Religion*, 104.

4. Henryk Broder in *Der Spiegel*, no. 38 (September 15, 2001): 168, 170.

5. Sofsky, *Zeiten des Schreckens*, 174. The Islamic scholar Navid Kermani, *Dynamit des Geistes*, 32–35, agrees with Sofsky in finding the lack of a claim of responsibility decisive for understanding 9/11 and argues that the ideology behind the attack is a variant of nihilism, an essentially Western phenomenon, reflecting the perpetrators' backgrounds in the West. Comparisons with Islamic groups such as Hamas do not help; rather, we must look to the Japanese Aum sect and other cults that believe they are engaged in a Manichaean struggle against evil.

6. Sofsky, *Zeiten des Schreckens*, 177–178.

7. Joas, *Kriege und Werte*, 64–67.

8. "The onlooker is aroused by the violence itself. It disgusts, causes fear, entices, and delights. The spasms and cries of the victim unleash a brief shock, a moment of nausea, of fear for one's own life" (Sofsky, *Traktat über die Gewalt*, 107). And see Weisbrod, "Sozialgeschichte und Gewalterfahrung," 118.

9. For the complete text of Ahmed al-Haznawi's speech, see *Anti-American Terrorism and the Middle East*, ed. Rubin and Rubin, 276. And see also http://en.wikipedia.org/wiki/Ahmed_al-Haznawi (accessed May 29, 2010).

10. *9/11 Handbook*, ed. Kippenberg and Seidensticker.

11. Waldmann, *Terrorismus*, 12–13.

12. On the linguistic character of violent actions, see also Weisbrod, "Religious Languages of Violence"; on the concept of performance used in the discipline of cultural studies, see Wirth in *Performanz*, ed. id., 34–42. Unlike the "performance" understood by linguistic studies as the execution of speech acts,

"performance" as understood by cultural studies refers to the staging of actions and the material embodiment of messages.

13. Krech, "Sacrifice and Holy War," presents a comprehensive overview of the research.

14. Girard, *Violence et le Sacré*. Burkert, *Homo necans. Interpretationen altgriechischer Opferriten und Mythen*, 341.

15. Girard presented a summary of his theses at a conference in the United States on "Generative Scapegoating," in which Walter Burkert and Jonathan Z. Smith also took part.

16. The two explanatory models are antitheses, which complement each other, according to Burkert, *Anthropologie des religiösen Opfers*, 35–36.

17. Greeley, *Religion in Europe at the End of the Second Millennium*, 78.

18. Assmann, *Moses der Ägypter*. On the status quo of research into monotheism by scientists of religion, see Lang, "Monotheismus."

19. "By 'cosmotheism' I mean an understanding of the world based on the translation of the divinity of the cosmos. This understanding experiences this divinity primarily, and naturally, as a plurality, but always bears in mind the unity of the cosmos too, and finally is able to move this unity into the center as the dominating principle" (Assmann, *Monotheismus und Kosmotheismus*, 26n62).

20. Assmann, *Mosaische Unterscheidung*, 36.

21. Assmann, *Monotheismus und die Sprache der Gewalt*, 21.

22. Ibid., 57.

23. See Schwartz, *Curse of Cain*.

24. Ibid., 4–13.

25. Stark, *One True God*, 115–172.

26. See Schwartz, "Holy Terror."

27. This is the important viewpoint of Zenger, "Was ist der Preis des Monotheismus?"

28. Kippenberg, "Entlassung aus Schuldknechtschaft."

29. On the course of events in the Maccabean uprising, see the brief and critical account by Schäfer, *Geschichte der Juden in der Antike*, 62–77.

30. There is an explicit biblical foundation for this, namely, God's covenant with Noah. After the Flood, God made a covenant with all peoples (Gen. 9:1–17). On this, see *Wege zur Toleranz*, ed. Schmidinger, 23–26.

31. The classic study of this subject is Peterson, "Monotheismus als politisches Problem."

32. Schäfer, "Geschichte und Gedächtnisgeschichte," 22.

33. According to Assmann, *Mosaische Unterscheidung*, 83–86, when the Mosaic distinction was first translated into practice by Israel, the Jewish people provoked the hatred of other peoples. The anti-Semitism of classical antiquity was

only the reverse side of the religious self-exclusion of the Jews, and was therefore in reality anti-monotheism.

34. Nirenberg, *Communities of Violence*, 3–17.

35. The thesis of the "persecuting society" derives from Moore, *Formation of a Persecuting Society*. For critical comments, see *Beyond the Persecuting Society*, ed. Laursen and Nederman, who in their preface (p. 5) point to a mostly tacit link to the evaluation of secularization: the thesis serves to shore up the assertion that only secularization succeeded in generating tolerance. The reverse viewpoint also exists, with the same point of reference: the idealization of the unified culture of the Middle Ages gave expression to a feeling of unease with regard to the secularized modern period and its inner strife. On this, see Oexle, "Das Mittelalter und das Unbehagen an der Moderne."

36. Borgolte, "Wie Europa seine Vielfalt fand." This essay is a summary of comprehensive studies by Borgolte on this theme: see id., *Europa entdeckt seine Vielfalt* and *Christen, Juden, Musulmanen*.

37. Angenendt, *Toleranz und Gewalt*, 92–95; on this, see also *Erfindung des inneren Menschen*, ed. Assmann.

38. Kakar, *Colors of Violence*, 166–167; see also Ashutosh Varshney, *Ethnic Conflict and Civic Life*.

39. Juergensmeyer, *Terror in the Mind of God*, 112–116.

40. Max Weber, *Economy and Society*, ed. Roth and Wittich, 399–400.

41. Hans G. Kippenberg, "Einleitung," in Max Weber, *Religiöse Gemeinschaften*, 38–44; see also Kippenberg, "Religionsentwicklung," in *Max Weber's "Religionssystematik,"* ed. id. and Martin Riesebrodt, 77–99.

42. Helmuth Plessner responded to the antithesis between *Gesellschaft* and *Gemeinschaft* proposed by Tönnies by demanding that the conception of *Gemeinschaft* should not be limited dualistically to natural (as opposed to social) forms: it is essential to include the aspects of differentiation, civilization, juridification, and publicity. See Plessner, "Grenzen der Gemeinschaft" (1924).

43. Lichtblau, " 'Vergemeinschaftung' und 'Vergesellschaftung' bei Max Weber"; Kippenberg, "Religiöse Gemeinschaften."

44. Jaspers, *Max Weber*, 46 and 44.

45. Joas, *Die Kreativität des Handelns*, 235.

46. Esser, "Die Definition der Situation"; id., *Soziologie*.

47. LaPiere, "Attitudes vs. Actions."

48. Esser, *Soziologie*, 1: 59–63, relates the experiment, with references to the relevant secondary literature.

49. Thomas and Thomas, *Child in America*, 572; Esser, *Situationslogik und Handeln*, 63. And see also Merton, "Thomas Theorem."

50. Esser, "Rationalität der Werte." For discussion of Esser's integration of the theory of value into the theory of action see Stachura, "Logik der Situ-

ationsdefinition und Logik der Handlungsselektion" and "Handlung und Rationalität."

CHAPTER 2

1. Hobbes, *Leviathan*.
2. Schmitt, *Begriff des Politischen*, 79–95.
3. Pufendorf, *Über die Pflicht des Menschen*, 56–58.
4. Rousseau, *Émile*, trans. Bloom, 286.
5. Rousseau, *Émile*, trans. Foxley, 379.
6. Berger, *Sacred Canopy*, 134. And see also Joas, *Braucht der Mensch Religion?* 32–49.
7. See Finke and Stark, *Churching of America*; Martin, *Tongues of Fire* and *Pentecostalism*.
8. Jenkins, *God's Continent*, 116, speaks of 7,000 foundations; see the survey for the different European countries in Allievi, *Conflicts over Mosques in Europe*, 23.
9. Kippenberg, *Vorderasiatische Erlösungsreligionen*, 119–138.
10. Weinfeld, *Organizational Pattern*.
11. See Kippenberg, "'Nach dem Vorbild eines öffentlichen Gemeinwesens'"; *Voluntary Associations in the Graeco-Roman World*, ed. Kloppenborg and Wilson; *Religiöse Vereine in der römischen Antike*, ed. Egelhaaf-Gaiser and Schäfer.
12. Rajak, "Was There a Roman Charter for the Jews?"; id., "Jewish Rights in the Greek Cities Under Roman Rule"; Noethlichs, *Judentum und der Römische Staat*, 34–36 (on the formation of associations in the cities); id., *Juden im christlichen Imperium Romanum*, 58–71.
13. Quigley, *Case for Palestine*, 17–19; 118–119.
14. Kippenberg, "Christliche Gemeinden im Römischen Reich."
15. On contemporary "financial worship" and those helped by Islamic NGOs, see Benthall and Bellion-Jourdan, *Charitable Crescent*, 7–28.
16. The fundamental study of this societal model is Scott, "Patronage or Exploitation?"
17. Ismael and Ismael, "Cultural Perspectives."
18. See, e.g., *Poverty and Charity in Middle Eastern Contexts*, ed. Bonner et al., pt. 3.
19. Eickelman and Piscator, *Muslim Politics*, 35–36.
20. Singerman, "Networked World."
21. Sullivan, *Private Voluntary Organizations in Egypt*; id. and Abed-Kotob, *Islam in Contemporary Egypt*.
22. There is an extensive secondary literature on the application of the concept of the "public sphere" to Islamic societies: see, e.g., *New Media in the Mus-*

lim World, ed. Eickelman and Anderson; *Public Islam and the Common Good,* ed. Salvatore and Eickelman, 3–27; and *Public Sphere,* ed. Hoexter et al.

23. Cattan, "Law of Waqf" (a presentation of the classical situation); on the revival of *waqf* in the twentieth century, see, e.g., Benthall and Bellion-Jourdan, *Charitable Crescent,* 29–84.

24. Hoexter, "'Waqf' and the Public Sphere"; Hartung, "Fromme Stiftung."

25. Schmidt, *Option für die Armen?* 333–356.

26. Sen, *Ökonomie für den Menschen,* 32.

27. From a philosophical perspective, Menke, "Innere Natur und soziale Normativität," treats the theme of self-realization similarly, making "subjective abilities" central.

28. Schuppert, "Skala der Rechtsformen für Religion," 21.

29. Casanova, "Public Religions."

30. *Desecularization of the World,* ed. Berger, 9.

31. Davie, *Europe,* 19–20.

32. Putnam, *Making Democracy Work,* 130; on Putnam as a representative of communitarianism, see Reese-Schäfer, *Kommunitarismus,* 103–110.

33. Putnam, *Making Democracy Work,* 179.

34. Tocqueville, *Democracy in America,* chap. 23.

35. Putnam, "Bowling Alone: America's Declining Social Capital," 64–66.

36. On this, see Lemann, "Kicking in Groups."

37. See Putnam, *Bowling Alone: The Collapse and Revival of American Community,* 65–79 ("Religious Participation"), 67 and 69 quoted. Faith communities raise enormous sums of money for welfare—Putnam estimates between $15 and 20 billion annually—and carry out various social activities (67–68). Graf, "'In God We Trust,'" correctly notes a tension between Putnam's thesis of decline and his euphoric description of North American religious culture.

38. On the American welfare legislation and its "charitable choice" regulation, see Nagel, *Charitable Choice.*

39. See *Democracies in Flux,* ed. Putnam. In the introduction to this volume, written together with Kristin A. Goss, Putnam states that the term "social capital" is first found in 1916 and was independently coined anew a further six times.

40. Coleman, *Foundations of Social Theory,* 300–321; see also his earlier study, "Social Capital in the Creation of Human Capital."

41. Coleman, *Foundations of Social Theory,* 321.

42. Granovetter, "Strength of Weak Ties"; and see also Beckert, "Soziologische Netzwerkanalyse."

43. Esser, *Soziologie,* 4: 256–260.

44. Lepsius, "Institutionenanalyse und Institutionenpolitik."

45. Portes and Landolt, "Downside of Social Capital," 18–21.

46. *Public Islam and the Common Good,* ed. Salvatore and Eickelman, 151–152 (comparison of Casanova's position with A. McIntyre's skeptical view).

47. Putnam, *Democracies in Flux.* The criticism of the idealization of "community" in Plessner, "Grenzen der Gemeinschaft" (1924), still remains valid today.

48. Varshney, *Ethnic Conflict and Civic Life.*

49. Douglas, "Grid and Group."

50. Sivan, "Enclave Culture."

51. Lepsius, "Parteiensystem und Sozialstruktur."

52. Riesebrodt, *Passion,* 29.

53. Ismail, "Popular Movements Dimension of Contemporary Militant Islamism"; id., "Religious 'Orthodoxy' as Public Morality."

54. Clifford, "Diasporas."

55. See Veer, "Transnational Religion" (2001); *Nation and Religion,* ed. id. and Lehmann, 3–13; Asad, "Religion, Nation-State, Secularism"; *Transnational Religion and Fading States,* ed. Rudolph and Piscatori. On security problems with regard to Islam, see Eickelmann, "Trans-State Islam and Security."

56. This is set out with extreme precision by Lepsius, "Eigenart und Potenzial des Weber-Paradigmas."

57. Max Weber, *Economy and Society,* ed. Roth and Wittich, 362.

58. Ibid., 363.

59. For more details, see Kippenberg, "Religious Communities."

60. Max Weber, *Economy and Society,* ed. Roth and Wittich, 452; id., *Wirtschaft und Gesellschaft,* vol. 2: *Religiöse Gemeinschaften,* 195.

61. Max Weber, *Economy and Society,* ed. Roth and Wittich, 580.

62. Max Weber, *Religiöse Gemeinschaften,* 373–374. Max Weber, *Economy and Society,* ed. Roth and Wittich, 581–583. The phrase "communism of love" was coined by Ernst Troeltsch.

63. Max Weber, *Economy and Society,* ed. Roth and Wittich, 576.

64. Max Weber, *Wirtschaftsethik der Weltreligionen,* 485–487; *From Max Weber,* ed. and trans. Gerth and Mills, 328–330.

65. Yokota, "Mit welcher Eigendynamik entwickeln sich Religionen?"; Tyrell, "Intellektuellenreligiosität, 'Sinn'-Semantik, Brüderlichkeitsethik"; id., "Die christliche Brüderlichkeitsethik."

66. Max Weber, *Wirtschaftsethik der Weltreligionen,* 497; id., *From Max Weber,* ed. and trans. Gerth and Mills, 339.

67. Schluchter, "Gesinnungsethik und Verantwortungsethik," 198. A similar conclusion is drawn by Tyrell, "Antagonismus der Werte."

68. Arendt, *Macht und Gewalt,* 45.

CHAPTER 3

1. See esp. Chidester, *Salvation and Suicide*; Hall, *Gone from the Promised Land*; *People's Temple and Black Religion*, ed. Moore et al. For methodology, see Hall, Schuyler, and Trinh, *Apocalypse Observed*, 15–43.

2. See Chidester, *Salvation and Suicide*, 51–78.

3. See Hall, *Gone from the Promised Land*, 77–105.

4. See ibid., 184–190.

5. Shupe and Bromley, "Evolution of Modern American Anticult Ideology."

6. "When a sect breaks away from a church, it takes with it the label 'religion.' But cults are not born with the religious label attached" (Stark and Bainbridge, *Future of Religion*, 34).

7. Melton, "Anti-Cultists in the United States." Robert Jay Lifton, who has worked as a psychologist in the anti-cult movement, identifies the essential elements of a cult as follows: totalitarian practices or forms of brainwashing; the veneration of a guru or leader; the combination of a spiritual search on the part of those below and exploitation (usually economic and/or sexual) on the part of those above (Lifton, *Destroying the World to Save It: Aum Shinrikyo, Apocalyptic Violence, and the New Global Terrorism*, 11n). As the title of his book shows, Lifton offers this as an explanation of terrorism itself.

8. J. Gordon Melton recounts the rise and fall of this theory in *Gehirnwäsche und Sekten*, ed. id. and Introvigne, 9–36.

9. Wessinger, *How the Millennium Comes Violently*, 51–52.

10. Moore, "American as Cherry Pie."

11. See the studies of this question in *Politics of Religious Apostasy*, ed. Bromley.

12. Chidester, *Salvation and Suicide*, 40–41.

13. Jeremiah Gutman was the author of this report (excerpts in Chidester, *Salvation and Suicide*, 30).

14. Chidester, *Salvation and Suicide*, 24–46.

15. Melton, "Einleitung: Gehirnwäsche und Sekten," 25. In the Molko Brief in 1987, the American Psychological Association declared the theory of coercive persuasion with regard to new religious movements to be unscientific and dissociated itself from members who had witnessed as experts in favor of it in court cases. The APA report can be found in *Gehirnwäsche und Sekten*, ed. Melton and Introvigne, 235–275.

16. Tabor and Gallagher, *Why Waco?* 100–103; Wright, "Construction and Escalation of a Cult Threat," in *Armageddon in Waco*, ed. id., 88–90.

17. Tabor and Gallagher, *Why Waco?* 63–76.

18. Robbins and Anthony, "Cults, Porn, and Hate."

19. Tabor and Gallagher, *Why Waco?* 64–65.

20. Newport, *Branch Davidians*, 278–324.

21. Festinger, Riecken, and Schachter, *When Prophecy Fails*, 12–23.

22. On their history, see Newport, *Branch Davidians;* Tabor and Gallagher, *Why Waco?* 33–39; Bromley and Silver, "Branch Davidians."

23. This is the view of Newport, "Heavenly Millennium."

24. Tabor and Gallagher, *Why Waco?* 80–93. Bromley, "Social Construction," 31–35, sees in the "whistleblower" a specific social form of leaving a community.

25. Hall, "Public Narratives and the Apocalyptic Sect," 212–228 (conjectures by the opponents and the action force about the impending collective suicide).

26. Tabor and Gallagher, *Why Waco?* 132–135.

27. The classic work on this subject is Mead, *Lively Experiment.*

28. For vivid overviews of the cycles, see Jenkins, *Mystics and Messiahs*, 13, 35, 126.

29. Tabor and Gallagher, *Why Waco?* 15–16 (copy of the letter). For an unfinished text by Koresh, saved from the fire by a survivor, see ibid., 189–203.

30. On the events, see Michel and Herbeck, *American Terrorist*; for a brief analysis centering on religion, see Juergensmeyer, *Terror im Namen Gottes*, 54–62.

31. Macdonald, *Turner Diaries* (1978). This is still in print. Its jacket states: "The book contains racist propaganda. The FBI said it was the blueprint for the Oklahoma City bombing. Many would like it banned. It is being published to alert and warn America."

32. Sullivan, " 'No longer the Messiah'," 228.

33. Ammermann, "Waco, Federal Law Enforcement, and Scholars of Religion."

34. Tabor and Gallagher, *Why Waco?* 1–12.

35. Catherine Wessinger, who took part in these events as an adviser, gives a detailed account in *How the Millennium Comes Violently*, 158–219.

36. Ibid., 202.

37. Rosenfeld. "Justus Freemen Standoff," 331.

38. Jean E. Rosenfeld, "Implications for Law Enforcement," 351.

39. Hall, *Gone from the Promised Land*, 296. Similar conclusions are drawn in *New Religious Movements*, ed. Moore and McGhee; *Armageddon in Waco*, ed. Wright; and *Politics of Religious Apostasy*, ed. Bromley.

40. Wessinger, "How the Millennium Comes Violently," 4.

CHAPTER 4

1. Taheri, *Spirit of Allah*, chap. 12; Fischer, *Iran*, 195–196.

2. Quoted by Azarine, "Frauen in der islamischen Bewegung," 126.

3. Bani, *Fatima statt Farah*, 85.

4. Ibid., 86–87.

5. For an account of the development of these celebrations, see Halm, *Shi'a Islam*, part 2.

6. Alavi, "Peasant Classes and Primordial Loyalties."
7. Aubin, "Le Chi'isme et la nationalité persane," 480.
8. DellaValle, *Reisebeschreibung in unterschiedliche Teile der Welt*, pt. 2, 70.
9. Kippenberg, "Jeder Tag Ashura, jedes Grab Kerbala," 220–236.
10. Turner, *Ritual Process*. On Turner, see Bräunlein, "Victor Witter Turner (1920–1983)."
11. The classic representative of this position is Gluckman, "Rituale der Rebellen in Süd-Ost-Afrika."
12. Turner, *Ritual Process*, 83.
13. Monchi-Zadeh, *Ta'ziya*, 193.
14. Generet, *Martyre d'Ali Akbar*, 30–31, frequently.
15. Ibid., 52–53.
16. Ibid., 56–57.
17. Ibid., 70–71.
18. Ibid., 78–79.
19. Whereas in European feudalism, the rivalries of client groups were subject to the institution of the contract, "oriental feudalism" gave the rivalries a free run (Vieille, *Féodalité*, 296).
20. At the end of the fourteenth century, in his *Muqaddimah*, the North African philosopher Ibn Khaldūn summarized the most important hadiths concerning the expectation of the Mahdi, examined their credibility, and concluded that they were not genuine. He attributed the political uprisings in North Africa inspired by this expectation to the social solidarity (*'asabiyya*) of expanding kinship groups (Ibn Kaldūn, *Muqaddimah*, trans. Rosenthal, 2: 156–200).
21. Keddie, *Religion and Rebellion in Iran*; Algar, *Religion and State in Iran*, 214.
22. Akhavi, *Religion and Politics in Contemporary Iran*, 32–59.
23. Lambton, *Landlord and Peasant in Persia*; Planck, "Teilbau im Iran"; Katouzian, "Land Reform in Iran."
24. Kazemi, *Poverty and Revolution in Iran*; for an overview of the land reform, see Keddie, *Roots of Revolution*, 160–182; for data on migration within the country, see Arjomand, *Turban for the Crown*, appendix, 216–217, with evaluation, 106–108.
25. Arjomand, *Turban for the Crown*, 91–94, with the relevant data.
26. The different currents in the Shi'a clergy are dealt with by Abrahamian, *Iran*, 473–479. On Khomeini's concept of a rule by the jurists, see Sachedina, *Just Ruler*, which explains the distinction between *velaya* and *saltana* as follows: whereas the sultan compels obedience, the one who possesses *velaya* can only demand obedience, not compel it (33).
27. Freamon, "Martyrdom, Suicide, and the Islamic Law of War."
28. For an explanation of the terms and concepts, see Halm, *Schia*, 134.
29. Kohlberg, "Some Imami-Shi'i Views on Taqiyya," 396 with n. 10.

30. Goldziher, "Das Prinzip der takijja im Islam," 65.

31. Meyer, "Anlass und Anwendungsbereich der taqiyya," 267.

32. Sachedina, "Treatise on the Occultation of the Twelfth Imamite Imam," 109–124 (on the argument from reason, see 113ff.); id., *Islamic Messianism,* 103–104.

33. Akhavi, *Religion and Politics in Contemporary Iran,* 112–113 (lectures by Bazargan on this subject) and 164–166 (on Khomeini).

34. Abrahamian, *Radical Islam,* 92–104.

35. Ahmad, *Occidentosis.* On this work and its author, see Hanson, "'Westoxication' of Iran," and Rahnema, *Islamic Utopian,* 190–192.

36. On Shariati's attitude to Frantz Fanon (and to Jean-Paul Sartre), see Rahnema, *Islamic Utopian,* 126–128.

37. Shariati was inspired by Louis Massignon, George Gurvitch, and Jacques Berque during his studies in Paris, according to Rahnema, *Islamic Utopian,* 119–126.

38. Ibid., 314–315; *Umbruch im Iran,* ed. Tilgner, 38.

39. Beeman, "Images of the Great Satan"; id., *"Great Satan" versus the "Mad Mullahs."*

40. Bateson, "'This Figure of Tinsel,'" 125–134.

41. On the paramilitary social group of the *basij,* from which most of the mobilized soldiers came, see Khosrokhavar, *L'islamisme et la mort,* 171–221. By the end of the war, it is said that 300,000 Iranians had died and 500,000 were war-disabled.

42. Davis, *Martyrs,* 45–66. She remarks quite correctly that shame would have been a more fitting reaction.

43. Kermani, "Märtyrertum als Topos politischer Selbstdarstellung in Iran."

44. Sahebjam, *"Ich habe keine Tränen mehr,"* 134–136.

45. Ibid., 9–11.

46. Reuter, *Mein Leben ist eine Waffe,* 59–60.

47. Durkheim, *Suicide,* 217–240.

48. Croitoru, *Märtyrer als Waffe,* 82–83.

49. Seidensticker, "Der religiöse und historische Hintergrund des Selbstmordattentates im Islam."

50. Khomeini, quoted in Schmucker, "Iranische Märtyrertestamente," 189.

51. Ibid., 220–222.

52. Ibid., 222–223.

53. Khosrokhavar, *L'islamisme et la mort,* 95–169; id.. *Suicide Bombers,* 41–48, 48–52, and 48–52.

54. Juergensmeyer, "Antifundamentalism."

55. *Strong Religion,* ed. Almond et al., 17.

56. Waldmann, "Wie religiös ist der 'religiöse Fundamentalismus'?" agrees (103).

57. *Strong Religion,* ed. Almond et al., 235. Similarly, Scheffler, "Islamischer Fundamentalismus und Gewalt," observes that the path taken by fundamentalist groups into violence was not inevitable, but was driven by several processes.

58. Appleby, *Ambivalence of the Sacred,* 81–120; on exceptional situations, see 88–89. Waldmann, "Zeitliche Dimension des Terrorismus," concurs: "Außergewöhnliche Zeiten erfordern extreme Maßnahmen" (164–171).

59. Eisenstadt, *Fundamentalism, Sectarianism, and Revolution,* 68.

60. Brocker, "Politisierte Religion."

61. Sick, *All Fall Down,* 164.

62. Thomas, *Religion and the Decline of Magic,* 652–669; see esp. 658, 662.

CHAPTER 5

1. Kramer, "Oracle of Hizbullah," 101; Sankari, *Fadlallah,* 176–181.

2. Rosiny, *Islamismus bei den Schiiten im Libanon,* 68–71; *tawā'if* is the linguistic designation for a "part" of the whole. On this, see Scheffler, "Religion, Violence and the Civilizing Process."

3. Schulze, *Geschichte der Islamischen Welt im 20. Jahrhundert,* 317–318 (list of the seventeen individual wars).

4. Picard, "La violence milicienne et sa légitimation religieuse."

5. Saadeh, "Basic Issues Concerning the Personal Status Laws in Lebanon."

6. Khalaf, "Radicalization of Communal Loyalties," 290; id.. *Civil and Uncivil Violence in Lebanon,* 270–272.

7. On Musa al-Sadr, see Ajami, *Vanished Imam;* Norton, *Amal and the Shi'a,* 39–58.

8. Norton, *Amal and the Shi'a,* 40–42.

9. Source material for this interpretation will be found in Nasr, "Mobilisation communautaire et symbolique religieuse."

10. Milani, *Making of Iran's Islamic Revolution,* 89.

11. There is an English translation of the Amal charter in Norton, *Amal and the Shi'a,* 144–166.

12. Ibid., 147, 151–152.

13. On this, see Rosiny, "Der *jihad.*" For a different view, see the pointedly military interpretation of the concept of "jihad" in Cook, *Understanding Jihad.*

14. Norton, *Amal and the Shi'a,* 52–56.

15. On the splinterings, see Rosiny, *Islamismus bei den Schiiten im Libanon,* 126–129; Sankari, *Fadlallah,* 196–199.

16. Similarly, Sura 58:22 states that those who believe in God and in the Last Day show no love to those who oppose God and his Messenger, "though they were their fathers, or their sons, or their brothers, or their clan. Those—He has

written faith upon their hearts, and He has confirmed them with a Spirit from Himself. . . . Those are God's party; why, surely God's party."

17. See Kramer, "Oracle of Hizbullah"; Sankari, *Fadlallah.*

18. Rosiny, *Islamismus bei den Schiiten im Libanon,* 132, gives a vivid portrayal of the Shiʻa hierarchy. Aziz, "Fadlallah and the Remaking of the Marjaʻiya," discusses Fadlallah's position in this hierarchy and his subordination to Ayatollah Khu'i. See also the detailed account in Sankari, *Fadlallah.*

19. This is the terminology used in Rosiny, "Religiöse Freigabe und Begrenzung der Gewalt."

20. In October 1982, an Israeli military convoy wanted to force a path through the Shiʻa city of Nabatiyya just when the ʻAshura celebrations were taking place. In ignorance of the situation, they used weapons against the "rebellious" masses and shot innocent persons.

21. Delafon, *Beyrouth,* 54–55. On the suicide commandos of 1983, see Rieck, *Die Schiiten im Kampf um den Libanon,* 489–500.

22. Waldmann, *Terrorismus,* 61–68.

23. English translation in Norton, *Amal and the Shiʻa,* 167–187.

24. Rosiny, *Islamismus bei den Schiiten im Libanon;* on Raghib Harb, 149–153.

25. Norton, *Amal and the Shiʻa,* 172.

26. However, Israel set up a 25-kilometer-wide buffer zone in southern Lebanon, covering an area of 1,100 square kilometers, which it occupied until 2000.

27. Kramer, "Hezbollah's Vision of the West," 38.

28. Pape, *Dying to Win,* 253–254.

29. The specific circumstances of the attacks remained unclear to many observers of the war in Lebanon in the 1980s. The overwhelming majority were military operations which were carried out on the orders of the Syrian army. According to Merari, "Readiness to Kill and to Die," only seven of thirty-one registered bomb attacks had an Islamist background. All the others were ordinary military operations.

30. Alagha, "Hizbollah and Martyrdom," 57; Rosiny, "Religiöse Freigabe und Begrenzung der Gewalt"; Qassem, *Hizbollah,* 85; Norton, *Hezbollah,* 80.

31. Rosenthal, "On Suicide in Islam"; on the conflict with the prohibition of suicide, see Seidensticker, "Transformation des christlichen Märtyrerbegriffs im Islam," 143–144, 148.

32. Freamon, "Martyrdom, Suicide, and the Islamic Law of War," 320–326.

33. Quoted by Kramer, "Hizbullah," 549.

34. Kramer, "Moral Logic of Hizballah," 146; this is also discussed by Rosiny, *Islamismus bei den Schiiten im Libanon,* 234; on Fadlallah's position with regard to military suicide operations, see Sankari, *Fadlallah,* 205–208.

35. Kramer, "Moral Logic of Hizballah," 147.

36. Kramer, "Oracle of Hizbullah," 112, on Khomeini's fatwa.

37. Kramer, "Sacrifice and Fratricide in Shiite Lebanon," 40.

38. Rosiny, *Islamismus bei den Schiiten im Libanon,* 257.

39. Jansen, *Neglected Duty,* 200.

40. Kramer, "Moral Logic of Hizballah," 137.

41. Information in Kramer, *Hezbollah's Vision of the West,* 37–39.

42. Kramer, "Moral Logic of Hizballah," 148.

43. For a vivid account, see Norton, *Hezbollah,* 107–112.

44. Hamzeh, *In the Path of Hizbullah,* 52; Danawi, *Hizbullah's Pulse,* 29.

45. Danawi, *Hizbullah's Pulse,* 66.

46. See further on Hezbollah's social institutions, ibid.; Rosiny, *Islamismus bei den Schiiten im Libanon,* 132–136; Jaber, *Hezbollah,* 145–168; Harik, *Hezbollah,* 81–94; Qassem, *Hizbullah,* 83–87; Hamzeh, *In the Path of Hizbullah,* 48–66.

47. For more information about the policy of "opening up" (*infitah*), see Harik, *Changing Face of Terrorism,* 73–79.

48. Danawi, *Hizbullah's Pulse,* 31.

49. Freamon, "Martyrdom, Suicide, and the Islamic Law of War," 358–359; Croitoru, *Märtyrer als Waffe,* 199.

50. Davies, *Martyrs,* 14–15, sees despair as the main motive force behind the spread of the martyr phenomenon in the Middle East. Stern, *Terror in the Name of God,* more persuasively arranges the data from two perspectives, (a) grievances that give rise to holy war and (b) holy war organizations; these are linked by the transmutation of the experience of injustice and humiliation into notions of salvation and divine election.

51. Jaber, *Hezbollah,* 1–6.

52. Davis, *Martyrs,* 67–84.

53. Scheffler, "Religion, Violence and the Civilizing Process," compares this outcome with that in Europe after the wars of religion in the seventeenth century, where—unlike in Lebanon—there was a deconfessionalization and detheologization of politics.

54. Rosiny, *Islamismus bei den Schiiten im Libanon,* 293–296.

55. Khalaf, "Radicalization of Communal Loyalties," 288. Khalaf cites Hanf, "Ethnurgy."

56. Khalaf, *Civil and Uncivil Violence in Lebanon,* 38–61.

57. Stephan Rosiny in *Orientjournal,* Fall 2001, 11.

58. This was how the Israeli government justified the war (Norton, *Hezbollah,* 139–140).

CHAPTER 6

1. Alexander the Great believed that conquest "with the spear" gave him the absolute right to rule territories; see Schmitthenner, "Über eine Formverände-

rung der Monarchie seit Alexander d. Gr."; Mehl, "*Doriktetos chōra.*" On violence in the foundational myths of European nations and of the United States, see *Der Krieg in den Gründungsmythen europäischer Nationen und der USA*, ed. Buschmann and Langewiesche, esp. Gladigow, "Gewalt in Gründungsmythen," 23–38.

2. *Völkerrecht,* ed. Vitzthum et al., 26.

3. *Documents on the Laws of War,* ed. Roberts and Guelff, 318.

4. Caradon, *U.N. Security Council Resolution 242.*

5. Benvenisti, *Intimate Enemies,* 34. The chapter entitled "City of Strife" (1–51) gives a vivid portrayal of the tensions in a city that had been united forcibly, where, for example, budgets place East Jerusalem at a significant disadvantage.

6. Benvenisti, *West Bank Data Project;* id., *1986 Report.*

7. Benvenisti, *West Bank Data Project,* 51–52; id., *Intimate Enemies,* 61, 65–66. "The Khartoum Resolutions; September, 1, 1967," http://avalon.law.yale.edu/20th_century/khartoum.asp (accessed July 22, 2010).

8. Benvenisti, *West Bank Data Project,* 52–55. Jewish traditions give varying accounts of the extent of the biblical land. The land of Israel could be the "promised" land of Canaan of which the patriarchal narratives speak, but it could also designate the area actually settled by Israel, or the land as defined by Halakha. It has its greatest extent in Genesis 15:18–21, where God promises Abraham to give his descendants the land between the Nile and the Euphrates. In Jewish tradition, the land is holy, since God is its owner. This means that it cannot be sold (Lev. 25:23). In this sense, "the land of Israel" is a "geotheological" concept. On this, see Krämer, *Geschichte Palästinas,* 15–21; 31–34; 36–39.

9. These figures are found in Gorenberg, *Accidental Empire,* 358.

10. Quigley, *Case for Palestine,* 176.

11. See for this legal opinion the web site of the Foundation for Middle East Peace, "Statements on American Policy Toward Settlements by U.S. Government Officials1968–2009," www.fmep.org/analysis/analysis/israeli-settlements-in-the-occupied-territories (accessed July 22, 2010).

12. *New York Times,* February 3, 1981.

13. Gold, "From 'Occupied Territories' to 'Disputed Territories.'"

14. See, e.g., www.fmep.org/analysis/analysis/israeli-settlements-in-the-occupied-territories (accessed July 22, 2010) under April 14, 2004.

15. Letter from U.S. President George W. Bush to Prime Minister Ariel Sharon, April 14, 2004, www.mfa.gov.il/MFA/Peace+Process/Reference+Documents/Exchange+of+letters+Sharon-Bush+14-Apr-2004.htm (accessed July 22, 2010): "The goal of two independent states . . . remains a key to resolving this conflict. . . . It seems clear that an agreed, just, fair and realistic framework for a solution to the Palestinian refugee issue as part of any final status agreement will need to be found through the establishment of a Palestinian state, and settling of

Palestinian refugees there, rather than in Israel." "As part of a final peace settlement, Israel must have secure and recognized borders, which should emerge from negotiations between the parties in accordance with UNSC Resolutions 242 and 338. In light of new realities on the ground, including already existing major Israeli population centers, it is unrealistic to expect that the outcome of final status negotiations will be a full and complete return to the armistice lines of 1949. It is realistic to expect that any final status agreement will only be achieved on the basis of mutually agreed changes that reflect these realities."

16. *Kirche und Synagoge,* ed. Rengstorf and von Kortzfleisch, 2: 680–681.

17. See Ravitzky, *Messianism, Zionism, and Jewish Radicalism,* esp. " 'Forcing the End'. Radical Anti-Zionism," 40–78; on the three vows, 22–26 and Appendix, 211–234.

18. On the view that the inbreaking of the messianic age can be imagined only as an unforeseeable catastrophe, see Scholem, *Über einige Grundbegriffe des Judentums,* 130 and 133.

19. On the history of this movement, see Heilman and Friedman, "Religious Fundamentalism and Religious Jews"; Heilman, *Defenders of the Faith.*

20. Ravitzky, *Messianism, Zionism, and Jewish Radicalism,* 145–180.

21. Heilman, *Defenders of the Faith,* 12.

22. Ravitzky, *Messianism, Zionism, and Jewish Radicalism,* 75.

23. Marty and Appleby, *The Story and the Power,* 110–112; Daniel Pipes, "Neturei Karta, Paid Agent of Israel's Enemies" (September 25, 2004), www.danielpipes.org/blog/331 (accessed May 30, 2010).

24. See www.baalshemtov.com/story08.php?type=4 (accessed May 30, 2010).

25. Scholem, *Major Trends in Jewish Mysticism,* sees mysticism as a means of neutralizing messianism and protecting it from its destructive consequences.

26. Dan, "Rav Kooks Stellung im zeitgenössischen jüdischen Denken."

27. Abraham Isaak Kook, "Die Tora des Auslandes und die Tora des Landes Israel." Hertzberg, *Zionist Idea,* 416–431, presents a selection from this book with an introduction.

28. See Yair Sheleg, "The National-Religious Camp's Flagship Yeshiva," www.haaretz.com/print-edition/news/the-national-religious-camp-s-flagship-yeshiva-1.240827 (accessed July 22, 2010).

29. Zvi Yehuda Kook, *Torat Eretz Yisrael,* 339; Aran, "The Father, the Son, and the Holy Land"; Gorenberg, *Accidental Empire,* 21–23.

30. Heilman, "Guides of the Faithful."

31. Ravitzky, "Messianism of Success."

32. Gorenberg, *Accidental Empire,* 129–162; see also Aran, "Jewish Zionist Fundamentalism." Aran presents eyewitness accounts of the early phase of the settler movement. During his sociology studies at the Hebrew University, he was active as driver, weapon-bearer, and bodyguard of leaders of the religious settler

movement; at the same time, he had a sociological interest in these events. See also for an account of the early period, Sprinzak, "Gush Emunim."

33. Gorenberg, *Accidental Empire*, 274.

34. Ibid., 336.

35. Ibid., 371.

36. Aran, "Gospel of the Gush"; Rosenman, "Apocalyptic Ideology"; Sprinzak, *Ascendance of Israel's Radical Right*, 110–127.

37. Quigley, *Case for Palestine*, 17–19; 118–119.

38. On Amana, see Benvenisti, *West Bank Data Project*, 39–43; Sprinzak, *Ascendance of Israel's Radical Right*, 127–129.

39. Car bumper stickers proclaiming: "Yesha is here" picked up the abbreviation for the territories of Judea, Samaria, and Gaza (*'azza* in Hebrew) and played on the two meanings: "These territories are a part of the state of Israel" and "The redemption is close at hand" (Heilman, "Guides of the Faithful," 344).

40. On the legal status of the settlements, see Benvenisti, *West Bank Data Project*, 39–43; Sprinzak, *Ascendance of Israel's Radical Right*, 129–130.

41. Benvenisti, *Intimate Enemies*, 59–60; for a detailed presentation of how this system was put in place, see id., *West Bank Data Project*, 37–39.

42. Benvenisti, *West Bank Data Project*, 49–63, describes the various types of Jewish settlements and their diffusion at the beginning of the 1980s.

43. See *Impact of Gush Emunim*, ed. Newman.

44. Benvenisti, *West Bank Data Project*, 57–60.

45. Sprinzak, *Ascendance of Israel's Radical Right*, 127–129.

46. Pape, *Dying to Win*, 49.

47. Numbers and maps in Benvenisti, *Intimate Enemies*, 61–62. See also the table in Pape, *Dying to Win*, 49, which is based on official Israeli data; East Jerusalem is not included. And see the settlement report of the Foundation for Middle East Peace, www.fmep.org (accessed May 30, 2010).

48. Quigley, *Case for Palestine*, 30–31; 102–104; 146–148, at 146–147; Saltman, "Use of the Mandatory Emergency Laws by the Israeli Government."

49. These figures are taken from the sources cited in n. 47 above.

50. Efrat, *West Bank and Gaza Strip*, 3.

51. For a map showing the areas which Israel (and the USA) envisage as belonging to the future Palestinian state, see Lybarger, *Identity and Religion in Palestine*, 2.

52. Sprinzak, *Ascendance of Israel's Radical Right*, 153–155, describes one such controversy. Rabbi Yehuda Amital, who had studied at the Kook yeshiva, Markaz HaRav, accused Gush Emunim of exaggerating the importance of the "land" at the expense of the "people" and "Torah" in the process of redemption.

53. Sprinzak, "From Messianic Pioneering to Vigilante Terrorism."

54. Newman, "Gush Emunim," describes the balancing act.

55. Sprinzak, "Gush Emunim."

56. Shahak, "Ideology." This account was given by the suspects under interrogation by the Israeli secret service.

57. See Sprinzak, *Ascendance of Israel's Radical Right*, 251–288. Although entirely uninterested in the well-being of Jews, influential "premillenialist" American Evangelicals supported the plans for rebuilding the Temple in word and deed, Gorenberg, *End of Days*, 50, 86, notes.

58. For numbers, see Mishal and Aharoni. *Speaking Stones*, 21, and Sprinzak, *Ascendance of Israel's Radical Right*, 148.

59. Sprinzak, "From Messianic Pioneering to Vigilante Terrorism," 213.

60. Heilman, "Guides of the Faithful," 345; Sprinzak, *Ascendance of Israel's Radical Right*, 164–165.

61. For details of the events, see Sprinzak, *Brother Against Brother*, 14; 238–243; 258–266.

62. Source: www.fact-index.com/b/ba/baruch_goldstein.html (accessed September 13, 2007).

63. Sprinzak, *Brother Against Brother*, 191.

64. Seeman, "Violence"; Sprinzak, *Brother Against Brother*, 258–266. Here we also find the attempt to justify Goldstein's behavior by asserting that he forestalled an imminent Arab pogrom.

65. I owe this information to Professor Dr. Zwi Werblowsky (Jerusalem).

66. Kiener, "Gushist and Qutbian Approaches to Government," examines the theological justification for this attack and compares it with the attack on Anwar al-Sadat.

67. Sprinzak, *Brother Against Brother*, 274–275 (with verbatim quotation). Zwi Werblowsky has informed me that the formula comes from the standard text of the Great Excommunication in KOLBO, a compendium of rituals made probably in the early fourteenth century (Hebrew with Latin translation in Selden, *De iure naturali & gentium*, bk. 4, chap. 8, pp. 510–511).

68. Sprinzak, *Brother Against Brother*, 244–285.

69. In October 2004, Middle East Web Log reported, in connection with Ariel Sharon's withdrawal plan: "One rabbi offered to conduct a medieval Pulsa Di Nura ceremony on PM Ariel Sharon, to cause his demise by magic means. Security experts, including GSS (Shabak) chiefs, warn that we are only one step away from an actual planned assassination attempt, and perhaps worse, that there are Jewish groups planning to destroy the mosques on the Temple Mount in order to bring about the last messianic war and the establishment of the third temple": www.mideastweb.org/log/archives/00000305.htm (accessed May 30, 2010).

70. Netanyahu, "Introduction," in *Terrorism*, ed. id., 3.

71. Ibid., 9.

72. Trabant, *Europäisches Sprachdenken*, 207.

73. Gorenberg, *End of Days,* 244.
74. Ibid., 195.
75. Ibid., 245.
76. Sprinzak, "Fundamentalism, Terrorism and Democracy."
77. Oz, *In the Land of Israel,* 140.
78. Silberstein, *Postzionism Debates,* 80.

CHAPTER 7

1. "The Palestinian National Charter" (1964, 1968), http://avalon.law.yale.edu/20th_century/plocov.asp (accessed May 31, 2010).
2. Croitoru, *Hamas,* 33.
3. On the Nakba, see www.alnakba.org (accessed May 31, 2010).
4. Paz, "Development of Palestinian Islamic Groups."
5. On these two founders, see Abu-Amr, *Islamic Fundamentalism in the West Bank and Gaza,* 93–94.
6. There are few studies of Islamic Jihad. The fundamental works are Abu-Amr, *Islamic Fundamentalism in the West Bank and Gaza,* and Hatina, *Islam and Salvation in Palestine.*
7. Hatina, *Islam and Salvation in Palestine,* 26.
8. Watt and Welch, *Der Islam,* vol. 1: *Muhammed und die Frühzeit,* 102–104.
9. Oliver and Steinberg, *Road to Martyrs' Square,* 65.
10. On the Mi'raj, see the article by J. Horovitz in the *Shorter Encyclopedia of Islam,* 381–384.
11. Seidensticker, "Jerusalem aus der Sicht des Islams," discusses Islamic scholars' investigations of the historical sources.
12. Friedland and Hecht, "Nebi Musa Pilgrimage and the Origins of Palestinian Nationalism."
13. Deut. 34:6 remarks that no one knows where Moses was buried.
14. Krämer, *Geschichte Palästinas,* 264–268. After the conquest of the Old City in 1967, the Israelis demolished the Moroccan quarter.
15. Weber, *On the Road to Armageddon,* 109–112; 156–160.
16. Mitchell, *Society of the Muslim Brothers.*
17. Ibid., 8.
18. In the concepts of Islamic law: the gate of *ijtihad* (legal argumentation) is open once again (ibid., 239).
19. On this, see Cook, *Forbidding Wrong in Islam.*
20. Mitchell, *Society of the Muslim Brothers,* 13–19.
21. Yasin's father had been a farmer in the Gaza Strip; the 1948 war forced him to flee from his home. Yasin, who was born in 1936, grew up in a mosque of the Islamic Brethren. When he was sixteen, he broke his neck while playing

and was almost totally paralyzed thereafter. Important studies include Abu-Amr, "Shaykh Ahmad Yasin and the Origins of Hamas"; Croitoru, *Hamas*, 37–48; and, with ample new information and the correction of mistaken views, Chehab, *Inside Hamas*, and Baumgarten, *Hamas*, 9–36.

22. Mishal and Sela, *Palestinian Hamas*, 20.

23. Chehab, *Inside Hamas*, 150–157.

24. On this legal form in Palestine, see Sullivan, *Private Voluntary Organizations in Egypt*, 142–147; the numbers are taken from Chehab, *Inside Hamas*, 151.

25. Schiff and Ya'ari, *Intifada*, 220–239. These figures are taken over by Abu-Amr, *Islamic Fundamentalism in the West Bank and Gaza*, 15. With the help of interviews, Dumper, "Forty Years Without Slumbering," has shed light on the history of the *waqf* administration in the Gaza Strip; and see also Mishal and Sela, *Palestinian Hamas*, 22.

26. Pape, *Dying to Win*, 191–192.

27. Mitchell, *Society of the Muslim Brothers*, 32–33 (history of this form of organization); 177 (organization chart); 195–200 (presentation of the tasks of the "families"). In Egypt, Islamic underground cells were called *'usar* ("families"): Ibrahim, "Anatomy of Egypt's Militant Islamic Groups," 436.

28. Engelleder, *Islamistische Bewegung*, 108–111. The Syrian Brotherhood has a similar structure: see Reissner, *Ideologie und Politik der Muslimbrüder Syriens*, 103.

29. Kepel, *Muslim Extremism*, chap. 3; see also Göle, "Snapshots of Islamic Modernities."

30. Kepel, *Muslim Extremism*, 210–215 (on Sadat's murder).

31. On December 14, 1981, the Cairo newspaper *al-Ahrar* announced that it was in possession of a text seeking to justify Sadat's murder entitled *al-farida al-gha'iba (The Neglected Duty)*. A few days before this, the Mufti of Egypt had published a refutation of the perpetrators' arguments in *al-Ahrar*. In 1983, the Waqf Ministry published a collection of fatwas that included the statement by the mufti and the entire text of *The Neglected Duty* (printed in an Appendix). In its eventual publication in Amman, Jordan, the honorific title of "martyr" was bestowed on the author, who had been executed with Sadat's killers on April 15, 1982. The most reliable edition is that of the Waqf Ministry, on which the translation and commentary of Jansen, *Neglected Duty*, are based. The text was later used in the training of jihadists in Afghanistan, see below, 162–163.

32. Hatina, *Islam and Salvation in Palestine*, 30.

33. Abu-Amr, *Islamic Fundamentalism in the West Bank and Gaza*, 103.

34. Hatina, *Islam and Salvation in Palestine*, 40 (calculation of numbers); 26.

35. Mishal and Aharoni, *Speaking Stones*, 21.

36. Sprinzak, *Ascendance of Israel's Radical Right*, 148.

37. In addition to earlier academic studies of Hamas such as Mishal and Sela, *Palestinian Hamas,* and Hroub, *Hamas,* see now also Baumgarten, *Hamas;* Croitoru, *Hamas;* and Chehab, *Inside Hamas.*

38. On UNC communiqués from the first years of the First Intifada, see Mishal and Aharoni, *Speaking Stones,* 53–198. On the growing role of young people in the West Bank as a result of Israeli occupation policy, see ibid., 1–12, 18–21; on Hamas and the UNC leaflets, 25–49. For another collection of these early leaflets in Arabic, with a French translation, see Legrain, *Voix du soulèvement palestinien.*

39. Ovendale, *Origins of the Arab-Israeli Wars,* 322, 335.

40. Mishal and Aharoni, *Speaking Stones,* 55–58; Flores, *Intifada,* 90f.–91.

41. For a selection of communiqués in translation, see Mishal and Aharoni, *Speaking Stones,* 201–285.

42. For a comparison of the two camps with regard to the call for violence, see ibid., 39–42.

43. For an English translation of this communiqué, see Hroub, *Hamas,* 265–266. Hamas's leaflet in January 1988 likewise called the insurgents *murabitun,* according to Mishal and Aharoni, *Speaking Stones,* 201–203. Croitoru, *Hamas,* 75–77, attempts to clarify the issue of the diverging enumeration of leaflets.

44. Statistics from Mishal and Sela, *Palestinian Hamas,* 57, 209n6).

45. Hamas Covenant (1988), http://avalon.law.yale.edu/20th_century/hamas.asp (accessed May 31, 2010)

46. Ibid.; for another English translation, see Hroub, *Hamas,* 267–291.

47. Cohn, *Warrant for Genocide.*

48. Cook, *Contemporary Muslim Apocalyptic Literature,* 184–200.

49. Oliver and Steinberg, *Road to Martyrs' Square,* 72–76.

50. Ibid., fig. 3.

51. Flores, "Judaeophobia in Context."

52. Krämer, *Geschichte Palästinas,* 292–296.

53. Both Hamas and the UNC invoked the memory of Izz al-Din al-Qassam in their leaflets (Mishal and Aharoni, *Speaking Stones,* 33); see, e.g., UNC leaflet 2 and Hamas leaflet 31.

54. Juergensmeyer, *Terror in the Mind of God,* 73–74.

55. Pape, *Dying to Win,* 253–264.

56. Oliver and Steinberg, *Road to Martyrs' Square,* 79.

57. Stork, *Erased in a Moment,* 43–61; www.hrw.org/reports/2002/isrl-pa (accessed May 25, 2010).

58. Pape, *Dying to Win,* 280–282, shows the explosion of violence and the participation of the al-Aqsa Brigades and the PFLP.

59. Pedahzur, *Suicide Terrorism,* 242.

60. Croitoru, *Märtyrer als Waffe,* 80–94, 165–171.

61. Pape, *Dying to Win*, 265–267.
62. Ibid., 49–50.
63. Ibid., 192; testimony from sources about all three points of view, 192–193.
64. Reuter, *Mein Leben ist eine Waffe*, agrees that this phenomenon is not specifically Islamic.
65. Nedelmann, "Selbstmordbomber," 400–401.
66. On this, see Robinson, "Hamas as a Social Movement."
67. Mishal and Sela, *Palestinian Hamas*, 113–146, esp. 126.
68. Ibid., 83–112.
69. Jansen, *Neglected Duty*, 182–185.
70. Reetz, *Sendungsbewusstsein*, 11–12.
71. Mishal and Sela, *Palestinian Hamas*, 63.
72. Ibid., 86.
73. Lohlker, *Islamisches Völkerrecht*, 33–34, 41–43.
74. See Fawzi and Lübben, *Die ägyptische "Jama'a al-islamiya,"* and Krämer, "Aus Erfahrung lernen?"

CHAPTER 8

1. For a comprehensive view, see Marty, *Modern American Religion*.
2. This is the diagnosis of Brocker, *Protest—Anpassung—Etablierung*, 60.
3. For a very useful summary of all the decisions by the Supreme Court since 1947 on matters of religion, classified by case groups, see ibid., 325–344.
4. See ibid., 35–74 (for quantitative data, 73–74), and Lieven, *America Right or Wrong*, 139–140.
5. Halper and Clarke, *America Alone*, 68–73.
6. Brocker, *Protest—Anpassung—Etablierung*, 121–179, with an overview of all the organizations of the Christian Right (122–123). See also Prätorius, *"In God We Trust,"* 112–119.
7. Perle et al., "Clean Break," www.iasps.org/strat1.htm (accessed May 25, 2010).
8. *Desecularization of the World*, ed. Berger, esp. 1–18.
9. Böckenförde, "Rise of the State." The caution with which Böckenförde expresses himself is worthy of note. In European historical reality, the state has never been neutral with respect to religions.
10. Toynbee, preface to Cogley, *Religion in a Secular Age*, xvi.
11. See chap. 2 above.
12. Finke and Stark, *Churching of America*.
13. Finke and Stark argue that the strength of organizations is proportionate to the height of the costs they demand of their members in the form of sacrifices or stigma (ibid., 238). This formulation is couched in the terms of an explanato-

ry hypothesis borrowed from economics, namely, that believers understand religious actions as an investment in a future salvation and that in view of this expectation, they regard it as more sensible to invest in a faith community that makes demands of them than in one that asks little of them. The refusal to grant one's wishes is the best guarantee of future salvation. This is why we can see a tendency throughout Christian history to turn from the church to the sect. This hypothesis was first elaborated in Stark and Bainbridge, *Theory of Religion.*

14. This is called the "rational choice theory of religion." It is intended as an explanation why religion—contrary to many people's expectations—has not disappeared in the modern period. For an overview of the representatives of this approach, see *Rational Choice Theory and Religion,* ed. Young.

15. Bruce, *Choice and Religion,* criticizes rational choice theory's concept of religion as an investment and argues that no general hypothesis can cover all modern instances of religiosity's vitality.

16. Lieven, *America Right or Wrong,* 139–140, points to the connection between "suburbanization" and the increase in the formation of faith communities.

17. The relevant data were gathered in a 1998 "National Congregations Study," www.cpanda.org/data/a00189/a00189.html (accessed May 31, 2010), which was the basis for studies such as Ammerman, *Pillars of Faith;* Chaves, *Congregations in America;* and Wuthnow, *Saving America?*

18. Joas and Knöbl, *Sozialtheorie,* 430–473, discusses modernization theory's rejection and subsequent reinstatement of religion.

19. Brown, *Death of Christian Britain;* id., "Secularisation Decade."

20. Sandeen, *Roots of Fundamentalism,* xiv–xv, 188–207.

21. Ibid., xv.

22. Ibid., 246. Ammermann, "North American Protestant Fundamentalism," 4–8, concurs that millenarianism is a central characteristic of Evangelical fundamentalism, along with belief in missionary work, the infallibility of the Bible, and moral separation from unbelievers.

23. On Evangelical millenarianism, see also Timothy Weber, *Living in the Shadow* and *On the Road to Armageddon.*

24. For what is known of the provenance of the "rapture" notion, see Sandeen, *Roots of Fundamentalism,* 62–70, and Timothy Weber, *On the Road to Armageddon,* 23–26. The great popularity of this belief has kindled a theological debate: see, e.g., Rossing, *Rapture Exposed.* She complains that the biblical Apocalypse has been transformed from hope into fear, and from peace into violence. "Such blessing of violence is the very reason why we cannot afford to give in to the dispensationalist version of the biblical storyline—because real people's lives are at stake" (46). One could confirm this view by adding that theology's responsibility is not only dogmatic but also ethical.

25. *Scofield Study Bible* (1996), 1269.

26. The restoration of Israel at the end of the present period, together with a chronology of the Last Days and the return of Jesus, had already been taught in English prophecy conferences between 1826 and 1829; see Sandeen, *Roots of Fundamentalism,* 18–22.

27. Many other variant constructions of the millennium are possible, and the basic elements can be related to each other in different ways. For example, the rapture may be placed in the midst of the time of tribulation, or only at its end (Timothy Weber, *Living in the Shadow,* 10; Ariel, *On Behalf of Israel,* 20–23). The terms "pretribulation" and "posttribulation" refer to these variants.

28. On this, see the essays in *Apokalyptik und kein Ende?* ed. Plasger and Schipper.

29. O'Leary, *Arguing the Apocalypse.*

30. Text in Ariel, *On Behalf of Israel,* 70–72, quotation at 71.

31. On Blackstone, see ibid., 55–96; Timothy Weber, *Living in the Shadow,* 137–139; id., *On the Road to Armageddon,* 102–106.

32. Ariel, *On Behalf of Israel,* 60–65; Timothy Weber, *On the Road to Armageddon,* 112–113.

33. Timothy Weber, *Living in the Shadow,* 135–136 (statistics); id., *On the Road to Armageddon,* 101–106 (on dispensationalism and Zionism in the United States).

34. Ariel, *On Behalf of Israel,* 92–93. As shown by Lincoln, "Cyrus Cylinder," the biblical portrayal of Cyrus continued to play a role in the religious legitimation of the George W. Bush administration.

35. McGinn, *Antichrist,* 250–280; Fuller, *Naming the Antichrist.*

36. McGinn, *Antichrist,* 260; Boyer, *When Time Shall be No More,* 176–180.

37. Boyer, *When Time Shall be No More,* 78.

38. Boyer, "When U.S. Foreign Policy Meets Biblical Prophecy."

39. Timothy Weber, *On the Road to Armageddon,* 15.

40. On this, see Mearsheimer and Walt, "The Israel Lobby and U.S. Foreign Policy," which gave rise to a controversial discussion and has since been expanded into a book with the same title.

41. Lindsey and Carlson, *Late Great Planet Earth.*

42. On Hal Lindsey, see Timothy Weber, *On the Road to Armageddon,* 188–192; O'Leary, *Arguing the Apocalypse,* 134–171.

43. Lindsey and Carlson, *Late Great Planet Earth,* 53–54 (exposition of the parable of the fig tree).

44. Lindsey, *1980's.*

45. O'Leary, *Arguing the Apocalypse,* 172–193.

46. See Shuck, *Marks of the Beast*; Timothy Weber, *On the Road to Armageddon,* 192–196; *Rapture, Revelation, and the End Times,* ed. Forbes and Kilde, esp. 5–32 (sixty million copies sold, 7–8).

47. Kilde, "How Did Left Behind's Particular Vision of the End Times Develop?," 60.

48. Frykholm, *Rapture Culture*; id., "What Social and Political Messages Appear in the Left Behind Books?"

49. Gorenberg, "Intolerance."

50. Gorenberg, *End of Days,* 50, 85. The fact that the Jews in the series are portrayed as an erring people, but not wicked, consoles Yaakov Ariel ("How Are the Jews and Israel Portrayed in the Left Behind Series?" 132).

51. Jewett and Lawrence, *Captain America.*

52. The concept of a "religious semi-product" comes from Simmel. See Krech, *Georg Simmels Religionstheorie.*

53. Timothy Weber, *On the Road to Armageddon,* 244–248.

54. Quoted in Halsell, *Prophecy and Politics,* 16. On the provenance of these words, see Bruce David Forbes, "How Popular Are the Left Behind Books . . . and Why?" in *Rapture, Revelation, and the End Times,* ed. Forbes and Kilde, 28.

CHAPTER 9

1. English translation of a video of the conversation in *Anti-American Terrorism and the Middle East,* ed. Rubin and Rubin, 246. Islamic underground cells were called "families" (*'usar*) in Egypt too: see chap. 7 above.

2. Bergen, *Osama bin Laden I Know,* 74–107, provides new sources on the early history.

3. Cook, *Contemporary Muslim Apocalyptic Literature,* 173–174.

4. Bergen, *Holy War Inc.,* 56.

5. Statistics in Steinberg, *Der nahe und der ferne Feind,* 36; on the jihad in Afghanistan, see Kepel, *Jihad,* 136–150.

6. Peters, *Jihad in Classical and Modern Islam,* 149–169 (presentation of the various Jihad groups in Egypt under Sadat); on the meeting between bin Laden and az-Zawahiri, see Bergen, *Holy War Inc.,* 62.

7. On the difference between the two points of view and the groups, see Steinberg, *Der nahe und der ferne Feind,* 46–47.

8. For English trans., see Alexander and Swetnam, *Usama bin Laden's al-Qaida,* Appendix 1A, p. 2; and Bin Laden, *Messages to the World,* 23–30 (statement 3).

9. Rifa'i Ahmad Taha was subsequently forced to withdraw his signature, since Jama'a al-Islamiyya changed its position on violence. On this, see Fawzi and Lübben, *Die ägyptische Jama'a al-islamiya und die Revision der Gewaltstrategie.*

10. English translation in *Usama,* ed. Alexander and Swetnam, Appendix 1B; and in *Messages,* ed. Lawrence, 58–62 (statement 6).

11. Cook, *Understanding Jihad,* 136–139; id., *Contemporary Muslim Apocalyptic Literature,* 180–183.

12. *Usama,* ed. Alexander and Swetnam, Appendix 2, p. 2; *Messages,* ed. Lawrence, 61.

13. Bergen, *Holy War Inc.,* 77.

14. Jacquard, *In the Name of Osama Bin Laden,* 60, and Appendix, doc. 12, 200–201.

15. Jansen, *Neglected Duty,* 6–7. On the difference between Faraj's position and competing groups and views, see Peters, *Jihad in Classical and Modern Islam,* 149–169.

16. A right to resistance of this kind was not generally recognized among the Sunnites either in the Middle Ages or in the modern period (Sivan, *Radical Islam,* 94–107). Every ruler, no matter how bad he was, was preferable to a schism (*fitna*) of the Islamic community (ibid., 83–139).

17. Emmanuel Sivan has studied the connections between medieval theology, including the writings of Ibn Taymiyya, and modern political Islam. In the foreword to *Radical Islam,* he describes how he had wanted to put dusty folios behind him after doing research on the jihad in the Middle Ages, only to discover to his astonishment at Arabic bookstores in Cairo and East Jerusalem that the old books had been republished and were being bought by young people in modern clothing (p. ix).

18. Cook, *Understanding Jihad,* 106–110, shows that views about the jihad are partly rooted in apocalyptic scenarios of history, and that this also applies to *Neglected Duty.*

19. Jansen, *Neglected Duty,* 54–60, summarizes the fatwa of the Egyptian mufti and the objections it makes to this interpretation of the situation of Egypt and of Islam.

20. Qutb, *Milestones,* 30–39; Cook, *Understanding Jihad,* 103; Damir-Geilsdorf, *Herrschaft und Gesellschaft,* 181–190.

21. On this traditional balance, see Nasr, *Mawdudi and the Making of Islamic Revivalism,* 53–57.

22. See also Israeli, "A Manual of Islamic Fundamentalist Terrorism"; the manual in question says of the prohibition of suicide: "What matters is not the act, but the intention (*niyya*) of the martyr" (35).

23. On the history of this term, its semantics, and the social entity to which it refers, see Jason Burke, *Al-Qaeda,* 7–12.

24. Bin Laden, *Messages to the World,* e.g., 108 and 115.

25. Jason Burke, *Al-Qaeda,* 13–22.

26. Bergen, *Osama bin Laden I Know,* 74–107; formula of the oath, 81.

27. Ibid., 86; examples: ibid., 102, 117, 138–139, 263.

28. Sageman, *Understanding Terror Networks,* 122 and 123.

29. Ibid., 107–120.

30. Jacquard, *In the Name of Osama bin Laden,* 55–72.

31. Mayntz, "Hierarchie oder Netzwerk?"

32. See chapter 2 above.

33. Ruthven, *A Fury for God,* 51–53. On Ibn Khaldūn's model of the emergence of rulers in tribal Islamic societies, see Gellner, *Muslim Society,* 1–85.

34. See National Commission on Terrorist Attacks upon the United States, *9/11 Commission Report,* 169–183, and the section "Financial Network" in Gunaratna, *Inside al Qaeda,* 80–92, and Jacquard, *In the Name of Osama Bin Laden,* 126–134. For a list of the charitable foundations linked to al-Qaeda, see Burr and Collins, *Alms for Jihad,* 37.

35. National Commission on Terrorist Attacks upon the United States, *9/11 Commission Report,* 171–172, with n. 124; Bergen, *Holy War Inc.,* 106; Gunaratna, *Inside al Qaeda,* 17, 84. On the financial transaction system called *hawala,* see Burr and Collins, *Alms for Jihad,* 71–75.

36. McDermott, *Perfect Soldiers,* 65, 85.

37. National Commission on Terrorist Attacks upon the United States, *9/11 Commission Report,* 438; cf. 164.

38. Ibid., 155–156.

39. *Der Spiegel,* October 27, 2003, 122–123, gave an account of a propaganda video featuring three other perpetrators, who included the presumed author of the *Spiritual Manual,* Abdul Aziz al-Omari.

40. *Anti-American Terrorism and the Middle East,* ed. Rubin and Rubin, 276.

41. Fielding and Fouda, *Masterminds of Terror,* 124–128. Bin al-Shib gave Fouda a computer disk with the names. On the designation "living martyr" for one who has already confessed to a deed on video, but has not yet carried it out, see Pedahzur, *Suicide Terrorism,* 179.

42. www.fbi.gov/pressrel/pressrel01/letter.htm (accessed July 3, 2010). On this text and the issues connected with it, see *9/11 Handbook,* ed. Kippenberg and Seidensticker, quoted parenthetically in the text here according to the division into sections in the English edition.

43. Fielding and Fouda, *Masterminds of Terror,* 161 and 180. According to Jason Burke, *Al-Qaeda,* 221, Atta dictated the text to al-Omari.

44. Atta's father later confirmed in an interview with Fouda that his son had a strange, childish handwriting, but he did not show him anything written by the latter (Fielding and Fouda, *Masterminds of Terror,* 130–131).

45. National Commission on Terrorist Attacks upon the United States, *9/11 Commission Report,* 232–233, with notes.

46. Bin Laden declared in Arabic in a video: "The brothers, who conducted the operation, all they knew was that they have a martyrdom operation and we asked each of them to go to America but they didn't know anything about the operation, not even one letter. But they were trained and we did not reveal the

operation to them until they are there and just before they boarded the planes" (Mneimneh and Makiya, "Manual for a 'Raid,'" 303–304n2). The organizer of the attacks, Khalid Sheikh Muhammad, used similar language (Fielding and Fouda, *Masterminds of Terror*, 155).

47. Mottahedeh, *Loyalty and Leadership in an Early Islamic Society*, 50–54.

48. Jansen, *Neglected Duty*, § 95, 204.

49. Schacht, *Introduction to Islamic Law*, 116.

50. Steinberg, *Der nahe und der ferne Feind*, 41. Damir-Geilsdorf, *Herrschaft und Gesellschaft*, 294–299, compares Muhammad Qutb's teachings with those of his brother.

51. On this, see Holmes, "Al-Qaeda, September 11, 2001," 140.

52. Fouda's interview with bin al-Shib revealed that the Capitol, not the White House, was the target (Fielding and Fouda, *Masterminds of Terror*, 144).

53. This is the interpretation of Cole, "Al-Qaeda's Doomsday Document," 8; see also the al-Qaeda training manual, UK/BM-22 (photographs of the brothers should show them without beards).

54. Cook, "Suicide Attacks or 'Martyrdom Operations' in Contemporary *Jihad* Literature," 22, 27.

55. Ibid., 23.

56. Appealing to the authority of the Sudanese scholar Mahmud Mohammad Taha, Abdullah Ahmed An-Na'im rejects the principle of the abrogation of all the prescriptions from the time in Mecca that do not agree with those from Medina. By means of a historicization of traditions, similar to that carried out in the Jewish and Christian theologies of the modern period, An-Na'im establishes a basis for a legitimate Islamic legal order, which also includes non-Muslims (An-Na'im, *Toward an Islamic Reformation*, 52–60).

57. Jansen, *Neglected Duty*, 55–56.

58. Cole, "Al-Qaeda's Doomsday Document," 5, notes that unlike the Salafis, the Egyptian tradition of the Muslim Brethren did not completely reject Sufi ideas.

59. El Fadl, "9/11 and the Muslim Transformation," 81–86.

60. Cook, *Understanding Jihad*, 136–139; id., *Contemporary Muslim Apocalyptic Literature*, 180–183.

61. On the principle of concealment in the history of ancient religion and in the history of Islam, see *Secrecy and Concealment*, ed. Kippenberg and Stroumsa. The principle of assuming a disguise was already practiced by the Gnostics in antiquity, since they regarded the visible world as a Satanic creation incapable of recognizing those who belonged to the invisible God. The concealment of one's own identity was a part of the Gnostic creed. Later, this principle recurs among Shi'ites: see Kohlberg. "Taqiyya in Shi'i Theology and Religion."

62. On the tension between martyrdom as one's own deed and as God's decree, see Strenski, "Sacrifice, Gift and the Social Logic of Muslim 'Human Bombers,'" 12–13.

63. Ruthven, *Fury for God*, 102.

64. *Shorter Encyclopaedia of Islam* (1974), "Rahbānīya" (Monasticism), 466–467.

65. Noth, *Heiliger Krieg und Heiliger Kampf*, 55–56.

66. On the Qur'anic *ghazwa* and its tribal prehistory, see As'ad Abu Khalil, "Ghazw," in *Oxford Encyclopedia of the Modern Islamic World*, 2: 66–67; Thomas Muir Johnstone, "Ghazw," in *Encyclopedia of Islam* (1991), 1055–1056; Irène Melikoff, "Ghāzāw," ibid., 1043–1045.

67. Noth, *Heiliger Krieg und Heiliger Kampf*, 61.

68. Max Weber, *From Max Weber*, ed. and trans. Gerth and Mills, 278.

69. Max Weber, *Economy and Society*, ed. Roth and Wittich, 544–545.

70. "Post-Islamism means the privatization of re-Islamization" (Roy, *Globalized Islam*, 97).

71. In my view, Roy does not pay sufficient attention to religious ethics as a substitute for the tie to a geographical territory.

72. Gambetta, "Can We Make Sense of Suicide Missions?"

73. McDermott, *Perfect Soldiers*, xvi–xvii.

74. Roy, *Globalized Islam*, 39.

75. Holmes, "Al-Qaeda, September 11, 2001."

76. Seidensticker, "Jihad Hymns."

77. Khosrokhavar, *Suicide Bombers*, looks at how martyrdom was detached from the idea of defending Islamic territory.

CHAPTER 10

1. Woodward, *Bush at War*, 15–17.

2. Brocker, "Zivilreligion—missionarisches Sendungsbewusstsein—christlicher Fundamentalismus?"

3. Shultz, "Challenge to Democracies," 18–19.

4. Hoffman, *Terrorismus—der unerklärte Krieg*, 16.

5. Eisenstadt, *Fundamentalism, Sectarianism, and Revolution*, 68.

6. U.S. Department of State, Counterterrorism Office, "Patterns of Global Terrorism 2000," Introduction, www.state.gov/s/ct/rls/crt/2000/2419.htm (accessed July 4, 2010).

7. On this, see Townshend, *Terrorism*, 1–6.

8. Kapitan, "Terrorism." There are very few studies of the *morality* of terrorism. When these look at past history, they confirm that in fact the perpetrators were often moral rigorists. On this, see *Morality of Terrorism*, ed. Rapoport and Yonah.

9. Shultz, "Challenge to Democracies," 19.

10. Ganor, "Defining Terrorism."

11. Bush, *We Will Prevail*, 214–221.

12. On Michael Gerson, see *USA Today*, April 4, 2001.

13. Bush, *We Will Prevail*, 214.

14. Ibid., 46 (from a speech delivered on October 17, 2001).

15. Ibid., 216.

16. Ibid., 216, 220.

17. See, e.g., Lawrence and Jewett, *Myth of the American Superhero* and Jewett and Lawrence, *Captain America*.

18. Bush, *We Will Prevail*, 216–217.

19. Ibid., 221.

20. See Lincoln, "Symmetric Dualisms"; id., "Cyrus Cylinder."

21. See the following website: http://en.wikisource.org/wiki/The_National_Security_Strategy_%28September_2002%29/III (accessed July 22, 2010).

22. Lustick, *Trapped in the War on Terror*, 23.

23. Bin Laden, *Messages to the World*, 242 (statement 23).

24. Gambetta, "Reason and Terror," http://bostonreview.net/BR29.2/gambetta.html (accessed May 1, 2010) (page references to the online edition).

25. Ibid., 7.

26. Lustick, *Trapped in the War on Terror*, 29.

27. Ibid., 58.

28. U.S. Department of Homeland Security, "Department of Homeland Security Launches Citizen Preparedness Campaign" (ad in the *New York Times*, April 9, 2003, p. A17); www.dhs.gov/xnews/releases/press_release_0089.shtm (accessed May 31, 2010).

29. The U.S. State Department's list of terror organizations in May 2003 can be found in Frum and Perle, *An End to Evil*, 263–264. On the case of the Mujahedin-e Khalq, see Pipes and Clawson. "Terrorist U.S. Ally?" (2003); www.danielpipes.org/1100/mujahedeen-e-khalq-a-terrorist-us-ally (accessed May 31, 2010).

30. Burr and Collins, *Alms for Jihad*, 9–10. All the documents mentioned here have been placed online by the White House, the State Department, and the Department of the Treasury.

31. Department of the Treasury, Office of Public Affairs, "U.S. Designates Five Charities Funding Hamas and Six Senior Hamas Leaders as Terrorist Entities," August 22, 2003, www.treas.gov/press/releases/js672.htm (accessed May 27, 2010).

32. Chehab, *Inside Hamas*, 153–154.

33. White House, memorandum, "Humane Treatment of Taliban and al Qaeda Detainees," February 7, 2002, www.pegc.us/archive/White_House/bush_memo_20020207_ed.pdf (accessed May 27, 2010).

34. Hersh, *Chain of Command,* 1–20.

35. *Harper's Magazine,* "Semper Sensitive," June 2004, www.harpers.org/ SemperSensitive.html (accessed May 27, 2010).

36. Here I follow Danner, *Torture and Truth,* 18–19.

37. *Washington Post,* "A Matter of Honor," September 28, 2005, www.washingtonpost.com/wp-dyn/content/article/2005/09/27/AR2005092701527.html (accessed May 27, 2010).

38. *Terrorism and International Justice,* ed. Sterba.

39. Archibugi and Young, "Envisioning a Global Rule of Law."

CHAPTER II

1. Andreas Gryphius, "Thränen des Vatterlandes" (Tears of the Fatherland), anon. English trans., www.poemhunter.com/poem/tr-nen-des-vaterlandes (accessed May 28, 2010).

2. On the analogy between the new wars and the Thirty Years' War, see Münkler, *Die neuen Kriege,* 75–89.

3. When a secular conflict is interpreted in religious violent language, however, there are still more circumstances that must be taken into account, namely, a growing societal power of religious communities and a new relevance of salvation-historical views of the world. Jessica Stern found a way to treat both aspects by dividing her book *Terror in the Name of God* into two parts: "Grievances That Give Rise to Holy War" and "Holy War Organizations."

4. See, e.g., McDermott, *Perfect Soldiers,* on the Hamburg group around Mohammed Atta. "The men of September 11 were, regrettably, I think, fairly ordinary men," McDermott observes (xvi).

5. Formulated by the American sociologists William I. Thomas (1863–1947) and Dorothy Swaine Thomas; see Thomas and Thomas, *Child in America,* 572.

6. See Kippenberg, "Religiöse Sinn-Deutungen in säkularen Konflikten."

7. Friedrich Nietzsche, *On the Genealogy of Morals* (New York, 1967), II: 13.

8. Joas, *Entstehung der Werte,* 34.

9. Weisbrod, "Religious Languages of Violence."

10. On the rivalry between the secular nation-state and religious communality, see Juergensmeyer, *Global Religion,* 9–38.

11. Burke, *Popular Culture in Early Modern Europe,* 273–274, quoting Reeves, *Influence of Prophecy in the Middle Ages,* 508.

12. Katz and Popkin, *Messianic Revolution,* 253.

13. Sandeen, *Roots of Fundamentalism,* 5–7.

14. Hobsbawn, "The Labour Sects," in id., *Primitive Rebels,* 126–149.

15. Thompson, *Making of the English Working Class,* 411–440.

16. Hölscher, *Weltgericht oder Revolution.*

17. Ibid., 23; 32–34. Hölscher also discusses this in *Entdeckung der Zukunft*.

18. On this, see Gebhardt, "'Politik' und 'Religion,'" and Willems and Minkenberg, "Politik und Religion im Übergang." And see Assmann, *Herrschaft und Heil*, 29–31, on theological concepts in modern constitutional theory and political ideas in early monotheism.

19. Eliade, *Le mythe de l'éternel retour* (1949), trans. as *Kosmos und Geschichte*, 7. On Eliade, see Turcanu, *Mircea Eliade*. On time as a topic in philosophy, see *Klassiker der modernen Zeitphilosophie*, ed. Zimmerli and Sandbothe.

20. *Rätsel der Zeit*, ed. Baumgartner.

21. Bergson, *Creative Evolution*, trans. Mitchell, 11.

22. Bergson, *Les deux sources de la morale et de la religion* (1932), trans. as *Die beiden Quellen der Moral und der Religion*, 124.

23. See Shulman, *Dark Hope*, 220.

Select Bibliography

Abrahamian, Ervand. *Iran: Between Two Revolutions.* Princeton, NJ, 1982.

———. *Radical Islam: The Iranian Mojahedin.* London, 1989.

Abu-Amr, Ziad. *Islamic Fundamentalism in the West Bank and Gaza: Muslim Brotherhood and Islamic Jihad.* Bloomington, IN, 1994.

———. "Shaykh Ahmad Yasin and the Origins of Hamas." In *Spokesmen for the Despised,* ed. R. Scott Appleby, 225–256. Chicago, 1997.

Ajami, Fouad. *The Vanished Imam: Musa al Sadr and the Shia of Lebanon.* London, 1986.

Akhavi, Shahrough. *Religion and Politics in Contemporary Iran: Clergy–State Relations in the Pahlavī Period.* Albany, NY, 1980.

Alagha, Joseph. "Hizbollah and Martyrdom." *Orient* 45 (2004): 47–74.

Alavi, Hamza. "Peasant Classes and Primordial Loyalties." *Journal of Peasant Studies* 1 (1973): 23–60.

Āl-i Ahmad, Jalāl. *Occidentosis: A Plague from the West.* Translated by R. Campbell with annotations and Introduction by Hamid Algar. Berkeley, CA, 1984.

Alexander, Yonah, and Michael S. Swetnam. *Usama bin Laden's "al-Qaida": Profile of a Terrorist Network.* Ardsley, NY, 2001.

Algar, Hamid. *Religion and State in Iran, 1785–1906.* Berkeley, CA, 1969.

Allievi, Stefano, *Conflicts over Mosques in Europe. Policy Trends.* London, 2009. www.nefic.org/docs/projects/NEF%20RelDem%20-%20RELIGION%20&%20MOSQUES%20-%20Final.pdf (accessed July 22, 2010).

Almond, Gabriel A., R. Scott Appleby, and Emmanuel Sivan. *Strong Religion: The Rise of Fundamentalisms Around the World.* Chicago, 2003.

Ammerman, Nancy T. "North American Protestant Fundamentalism." In *Fundamentalisms Observed,* ed. Martin E. Marty and R. Scott Appleby, 1–65. The Fundamentalism Project, vol. 1. Chicago, 1991.

———. "Waco, Federal Law Enforcement, and Scholars of Religion." In *Armageddon in Waco,* ed. Stuart A. Wright, 282–296. Chicago, 1995.

———. *Pillars of Faith: American Congregations and Their Partners.* Berkeley, CA, 2005.

Angenendt, Arnold. *Toleranz und Gewalt. Das Christentum zwischen Bibel und Schwert.* Münster, 2007.

An-Na'im, Abdullah Ahmed. *Toward an Islamic Reformation: Civil Liberties, Human Rights, and International Law.* Syracuse, NY, 1990.

Appleby, R. Scott, ed. *Spokesmen for the Despised: Fundamentalist Leaders of the Middle East.* Chicago, 1997.

———. *The Ambivalence of the Sacred: Religion, Violence, and Reconciliation.* Lanham, MD, 2000.

Aran, Gideon. "The Gospel of the Gush: Redemption as a Catastrophe." In *Religious Radicalism and Politics in the Middle East,* ed. Emmanuel Sivan and Menachem Friedman, 157–175. New York, 1990.

———. "Jewish Zionist Fundamentalism: The Bloc of the Faithful in Israel (Gush Emunim)." In *Fundamentalisms Observed,* ed. Martin E. Marty and R. Scott Appleby, 265–344. Chicago, 1991.

———. "The Father, the Son, and the Holy Land." In *Spokesmen for the Despised,* ed. R. Scott Appleby, 294–327. Chicago, 1997.

Archibugi, Daniele, and Iris Maron Young. "Envisioning a Global Rule of Law." In *Terrorism and International Justice,* ed. James P. Sterba, 158–170. New York, 2003.

Arendt, Hannah. *Macht und Gewalt.* 1970. Munich, 2000. Translated as *On Violence* (New York, 1970).

Ariel, Yaakov. *On Behalf of Israel: American Fundamentalist Attitudes Towards Jews, Judaism, and Zionism, 1865–1945.* New York, 1991.

———. "How Are the Jews and Israel Portrayed in the Left Behind Series?" In *Rapture, Revelation, and the End Times,* ed. Bruce David Forbes and Jeanne Halgren Kilde, 131–166. New York, 2004.

Arjomand, Said Amir. *The Turban for the Crown: The Islamic Revolution in Iran.* Oxford, 1988.

Asad, Talal. "Religion, Nation-State, Secularism." In *Nation and Religion. Perspectives on Europe and Asia,* ed. Peter van der Veer and Hartmut Lehmann, 178–196. Princeton, NJ, 1999.

Assmann, Jan. *Monotheismus und Kosmotheismus. Ägyptische Formen eines "Denkens des Einen" und ihre europäische Rezeptionsgeschichte.* Sitzungsberichte der Heidelberger Akademie der Wissenschaften philos.-histor. Klasse 1993, 2. Heidelberg, 1993.

———. *Moses der Ägypter. Entzifferung einer Gedächtnisspur.* Munich, 1998.

———. *Herrschaft und Heil. Politische Theologie in Altägypten, Israel und Europa.* Munich, 2000.

———. *Die mosaische Unterscheidung, oder, Der Preis des Monotheismus.* Munich,

2003. Translated by Robert Savage as *The Price of Monotheism* (Stanford, CA, 2010).

———. *Monotheismus und die Sprache der Gewalt.* Vienna, 2006.

———, ed. *Die Erfindung des inneren Menschen. Studien zur religiösen Anthropologie.* Gütersloh, 1993.

Aubin, Eugène. "Le Chi'isme et la nationalité persane." *Revue du monde musulman* 4 (1906): 457–490.

Azarine, Sussan. "Frauen in der islamischen Bewegung. Interviews und Erlebnisse." In *Umbruch im Iran,* ed. Ulrich Tilgner, 110–131. Reinbek b. Hamburg, 1979.

Aziz, Talib. "Fadlallah and the Remaking of the Marja'iya." In *The Most Learned of the Shi'a: The Institution of the Marja' Taqlid,* ed. Linda S. Walbridge, 205–215. Oxford, 2001.

Bani, Omol. *Fatima statt Farah. Erfahrungen einer Frau in der iranischen Revolution.* Edited by Karl Heinz Roth. Tübingen, 1980.

Bar, Shmuel. *Warrant for Terror: Fatwās of Radical Islam and the Duty of Jihad.* Lanham, MD, 2006.

Bateson, Mary C. " 'This Figure of Tinsel': A Study of Themes of Hypocrisy and Pessimism in Iranian Culture." *Daedalus* 108 (1979): 125–134.

Baumgarten, Helga. *Hamas. Der politische Islam in Palästina.* Munich, 2006.

Baumgartner, Hans Michael, ed. *Das Rätsel der Zeit. Philosophische Analysen.* Freiburg, 1993.

Beckert, Jens. "Soziologische Netzwerkanalyse." In *Aktuelle Theorien der Soziologie. Von Shmuel N. Eisenstadt bis zur Postmoderne,* ed. Dirk Kaesler, 286–312. Munich, 2005.

Beeman, William O. "Images of the Great Satan: Representations of the United States in the Iranian Revolution." In *Religion and Politics in Iran,* ed. Nikki R. Keddie, 191–217. London, 1966.

———. *The "Great Satan" vs. the "Mad Mullahs." How the United States and Iran Demonize Each Other.* Westport, CT, 2005.

Benthall, Jonathan, and Bellion-Jourdan, Jérôme. *The Charitable Crescent: Politics of Aid in the Muslim World.* London, 2003.

Benvenisti, Meron. *The West Bank Data Project: A Survey of Israel's Policies.* American Enterprise Institute Studies, 398. Washington, DC, 1984.

———. *1986 Report: Demographic, Economic, Legal, Social and Political Developments in the West Bank.* Jerusalem, 1986.

———. *Intimate Enemies: Jews and Arabs in a Shared Land.* Berkeley, CA, 1995.

Bergen, Peter L. *Holy War Inc.: Inside the Secret World of Osama bin Laden.* New York, 2001.

————. *The Osama bin Laden I Know: An Oral History of al Qaeda's Leader.* New York, 2006.

Berger, Peter L. *The Sacred Canopy: Elements of a Sociological Theory of Religion.* Garden City, NY, 1967. Translated as *Zur Dialektik von Religion und Gesellschaft. Elemente einer soziologischen Theorie* (Frankfurt a.M., 1973).

————, ed. *The Desecularization of the World: Resurgent Religion and World Politics.* Grand Rapids, MI, 1999.

Bergson, Henri. *L'évolution créatrice.* 1907. Translated by Arthur Mitchell as *Creative Evolution* (New York, 1911).

————. *Les deux sources de la morale et de la religion.* Paris, 1932. Translated by Eugen Lerch as *Die beiden Quellen der Moral und der Religion* (1933; reprint Frankfurt a.M., 1992).

Bin Laden, Osama. *Messages to the World: The Statements of Osama bin Laden.* Translated by James Howarth. Edited by Bruce Lawrence. New York, 2005.

Blackstone, William E. *Jesus Is Coming.* New York, 1908.

Blumenberg, Hans. *Die Legitimität der Neuzeit.* Frankfurt a.M., 1966.

————. *Lebenszeit und Weltzeit.* Frankfurt a.M., 1986.

Böckenförde, Ernst-Wolfgang. "Die Entstehung des Staates als Vorgang der Säkularisation." In id., *Staat, Gesellschaft, Freiheit,* 42–64. Frankfurt a.M., 1976.

Bonner, Michael. *Jihad in Islamic History: Doctrines and Practice.* Princeton, NJ, 2006.

Bonner, Michael, Mine Ener, and Amy Singer, eds. *Poverty and Charity in Middle Eastern Contexts.* New York, 2003.

Bonney, Richard. *Jihād: From Qur'ān to Bin Laden.* New York, 2004.

Borgolte, Michael. *Europa entdeckt seine Vielfalt, 1050–1250.* Stuttgart, 2002.

————. *Christen, Juden, Muselmanen.* Munich, 2006.

————. "How Europe Became Diverse: On the Medieval Roots of the Plurality of Values." In *The Cultural Values of Europe,* ed. Hans Joas and Klaus Wiegandt, 77–114. Liverpool, UK, 2008.

Boyer, Paul S. *When Time Shall be No More: Prophecy Belief in Modern American Culture.* Cambridge, MA, 1992.

————. "When U.S. Foreign Policy Meets Biblical Prophecy." AlterNet, February 20, 2003, www.alternet.org/story/15221 (accessed July 28, 2007).

Bräunlein, Peter. "Victor Witter Turner (1920–1983)." In *Klassiker der Religionswissenschaft. Von Friedrich Schleiermacher bis Mircea Eliade,* ed. Axel A. Michaels, 324–341. Munich, 1997.

Brocker, Manfred. "Politisierte Religion: Die Herausforderung des Fundamentalismus in vergleichender Perspektive." *Zeitschrift für Politikwissenschaft* 13 (2003): 23–52.

———. "Zivilreligion—missionarisches Sendungsbewusstsein—christlicher Fundamentalismus? Religiöse Motivlagen in der (Außen-)Politik George W. Bushs." *Zeitschrift für Politik* 50 (2003): 119–143.

———. *Protest, Anpassung, Etablierung. Die Christliche Rechte im politischen System der USA.* Frankfurt a.M., 2004.

Bromley, David G. "The Social Construction of Contested Exit Roles: Defectors, Whistleblowers, and Apostates." In *The Politics of Religious Apostasy: The Role of Apostates in the Transformation of Religious Movements,* ed. id., 19–48. Westport, CT, 1998.

———, ed. *The Politics of Religious Apostasy: The Role of Apostates in the Transformation of Religious Movements.* Westport, CT, 1998.

Bromley, David G., and Edward D. Silver. "The Branch Davidians: A Social Profile and Organizational History." In *America's Alternative Religions,* ed. Timothy Miller, 149–158. Albany, NY, 1995.

Brown, Callum G. *The Death of Christian Britain.* London, 2001.

———. "The Secularisation Decade: What the 1960s Have Done to the Study of Religion." In *The Decline of Christendom in Western Europe, 1750–2000,* ed. Hugh McLeod and Werner Ustorf, 29–46. Cambridge, 2003.

Bruce, Steve. *Choice and Religion: A Critique of Rational Choice Theory.* Oxford, 1999.

Bucaille, Laetitia. *Generation Intifada.* Hamburg, 2004.

Bull, Malcom, ed. *Apocalypse Theory and the Ends of the World.* Oxford, 1995.

Burke, Jason. *Al-Qaeda Casting a Shadow of Terror.* London, 2003.

Burke, Peter. *Popular Culture in Early Modern Europe.* New York, 1978.

Burkert, Walter. *Homo necans. Interpretationen altgriechischer Opferriten und Mythen.* Berlin, 1972, 2nd ed. 1997. Translated by Peter Bing as *Homo necans: The Anthropology of Ancient Greek Sacrificial Ritual and Myth* (Berkeley, CA, 1983).

———. *Anthropologie des religiösen Opfers.* 2nd ed. Munich, 1987.

Burr, J. Millard, and Robert O. Collins. *Alms for Jihad.* Cambridge, 2006.

Burton, John. "The Exegesis of Q. 2:106 and the Islamic Theories of Naskh." *Bulletin of the School of Oriental and African Studies* 48 (1985): 452–469.

Buschmann, Nikolaus, and Dieter Langewiesche, eds. *Der Krieg in den Gründungsmythen europäischer Nationen und der USA.* Frankfurt a.M., 2001.

Bush, George W. *"We Will Prevail": President George W. Bush on War, Terrorism, and Freedom.* Selected and edited by *National Review.* New York, 2003.

Caradon, Hugh Foot, Baron. *U.N. Security Council Resolution 242: A Case Study in Diplomatic Ambiguity.* Washington, DC, 1981.

Casanova, José. *Public Religions in the Modern World.* Chicago, 1994.

———. "Chancen und Gefahren öffentlicher Religion. Ost- und Westeuropa im

Vergleich." In *Das Europa der Religionen,* ed. Otto Kallscheuer, 181–210. Frankfurt a.M., 1996.

Cattan, Henry, "The Law of Waqf." In *Law in the Middle East,* vol. 1: *Origin and Development of Islamic Law,* ed. Majid Khadduri and Herbert Liebesny, 203–222. Washington, DC, 1955.

Chaves, Mark. *Congregations in America.* Cambridge, MA, 2004.

Chehab, Zaki. *Inside Hamas: The Untold Story of Militants, Martyrs and Spies.* London, 2007.

Cherki, Alice. *Frantz Fanon. Ein Porträt.* Hamburg, 2002.

Chidester, David. *Salvation and Suicide: An Interpretation of Jim Jones, the People's Temple, and Jonestown.* Bloomington, IN, 1988; 2nd ed., 2003.

Clark, Janine A. *Islam, Charity, and Activism: Class Networks and Social Welfare in Egypt, Jordan, and Yemen.* Bloomington, IN, 2004.

Clifford, James. "Diasporas." *Cultural Anthropology* 9 (1995): 302–338.

Cogley, John. *Religion in a Secular Age.* New York, 1968.

Cohn, Norman. *Warrant for Genocide: The Myth of the Jewish World Conspiracy and the "Protocols of the Elders of Zion."* London, 1966.

Coleman, James S. "Social Capital in the Creation of Human Capital." *American Journal of Sociology* 99 (1988): 95–120.

———. *Foundations of Social Theory.* Cambridge, MA, 1990.

Collings, Deirdre, ed. *Peace for Lebanon? From War to Reconstruction.* Boulder, CO, 1994.

Cook, David. "Suicide Attacks or 'Martyrdom Operations' in Contemporary *Jihad* Literature." *Nova Religio* 6 (2002): 7–44.

———. "Recovery of Radical Islam in the Wake of the Defeat of the Taliban." *Terrorism and Political Violence* 15 (2003): 31–56.

———. *Contemporary Muslim Apocalyptic Literature.* Syracuse, NY, 2005.

———. *Understanding Jihad.* Berkeley, CA, 2005.

Cook, Michael. *Forbidding Wrong in Islam: An Introduction.* Cambridge, 2003.

Cook, Miriam, and Bruce Lawrence, eds. *Muslim Networks from Hajj to Hip Hop.* Chapel Hill, NC, 2005.

Croitoru, Joseph. *Der Märtyrer als Waffe. Die historischen Wurzeln des Selbstmordattentates.* Munich, 2003.

———. *Hamas. Der islamische Kampf um Palästina.* Munich, 2007.

Damir-Geilsdorf, Sabine. *Herrschaft und Gesellschaft. Der islamische Wegbereiter Sayyid Qutb und seine Rezeption.* Würzburg, 2003.

Dan, Joseph. "Rav Kooks Stellung im zeitgenössischen jüdischen Denken." In Abraham Isaak Kook, *Die Lichter der Tora,* 125–133. Berlin, 1995.

Danawi, Dima. *Hizbullah's Pulse: Into the Dilemma of Al-Shahid and Jihad Al-Bina Foundations.* Bonn, 2002.

Danner, Mark. *Torture and Truth: America, Abu Ghraib, and the War on Terror.* New York, 2004.

Davie, Grace. *Religion in Britain Since 1945: Believing Without Belonging.* Oxford, 1994.

———. *Europe: The Exceptional Case. Parameters of Faith in the Modern World.* London, 2002.

Davis, Joyce M. *Martyrs: Innocence, Vengeance, and Despair in the Middle East.* New York, 2003.

Delafon, Gilles. *Beyrouth: Les soldats de l'Islam.* Paris, 1989.

DellaValle, Pietro. *Reisebeschreibung in unterschiedliche Teile der Welt.* Part II. Geneva, 1674.

Douglas, Mary, "Grid and Group, New Developments." Paper presented at the Workshop on Complexity and Cultural Theory in Honour of Michael Thompson, LSE, June 27, 2005. www.psych.lse.ac.uk/complexity/Workshops/MaryDouglas.pdf (accessed May 29, 2010).

Dumont, Louis. *Essais sur l'individualisme: Une perspective anthropologique sur l'idéologie moderne.* Paris: Seuil, 1983. Translated by Una Pfau and Achim Russer as *Individualismus. Zur Ideologie der Moderne* (Frankfurt a.M., 1991).

Dumper, Michael. "Forty Years Without Slumbering: *waqf* Politics and Administration in the Gaza-Strip, 1948–1987." *British Journal of Middle Eastern Studies* 20 (1993): 174–190.

Durkheim, Emile. *Suicide.* 1897. New York, 1951.

Dutton, Yasin. *The Origins of Islamic Law.* London, 1999.

Efrat, Elisha. *The West Bank and Gaza Strip: A Geography of Occupation and Disengagement.* London, 2006.

Egelhaaf-Gaiser, Ulrike, and Alfred Schäfer, eds. *Religiöse Vereine in der römischen Antike. Untersuchungen zu Organisation, Ritual und Raumordnung.* Tübingen, 2002.

Eickelman, Dale F. "Trans-State Islam and Security." In *Transnational Religion and Fading States,* ed. Susanne H. Rudolph and James Piscatori, 27–46. Boulder, CO, 1997.

Eickelman, Dale F., and James Piscator. *Muslim Politics.* Princeton, NJ, 1996.

Eickelman, Dale F., and Jon W. Anderson, eds. *New Media in the Muslim World: The Emerging Public Sphere.* 2nd ed. Bloomington, IN, 2003.

Eisenstadt, Shmuel. *Fundamentalism, Sectarianism, and Revolution: The Jacobin Dimension of Modernity.* Cambridge, 2000.

El Fadl, Khaled Abou. "9/11 and the Muslim Transformation." In *September 11 in History: A Watershed Moment?* ed. Mary L. Dudziak, 70–111. Durham, NC, 2003.

Eliade, Mircea. *Le mythe de l'éternel retour: Archétypes et répétition.* Paris, 1949. Translated as *Cosmos and History: The Myth of the Eternal Return* (Princeton, NJ, 1954); *Kosmos und Geschichte. Der Mythos der ewigen Wiederkehr* (Frankfurt a.M., 1984).

Elwert, Georg. "Charismatische Mobilisierung und Gewaltmärkte. Die Attentäter des 11. September." In *Gewalt und Terror. 11 Vorlesungen,* ed. Wolfgang Bergsdorf, Dietmar Herz, and Hans Hoffmeister, 91–117. Weimar, 2003.

Engelleder, Denis. *Die islamistische Bewegung in Jordanien und Palästina 1945–1989.* Wiesbaden, 2002.

Esser, Hartmut. "Die Definition der Situation." *Kölner Zeitschrift für Soziologie und Sozialpsychologie* 48 (1996): 1–34.

———. *Soziologie. Spezielle Grundlagen.* 6 vols. Frankfurt a.M., 1999–2001. Vol. 1: *Situationslogik und Handeln* (1999); vol. 4: *Opportunitäten und Restriktionen;* vol. 5: *Institutionen* (2000); vol. 6: *Sinn und Kultur* (2001).

———. "Die Rationalität der Werte. Die Typen des Handelns und das Modell der soziologischen Erklärung." In *Das Weber-Paradigma. Studien zur Weiterentwicklung von Max Webers Forschungsprogramm,* ed. Gert Albert, Agathe Bienfait, Steffen Sigmund, and Claus Wendt, 153–187. Tübingen, 2003.

Fallaci, Oriana. *Insciallah: romanzo.* Milan, 1990. Translated by James Marcus as *Inshallah* (New York, 1992). German translation, *Inschallah* (Munich, 1994).

Fanon, Frantz. *Les damnés de la terre.* Paris, 1961. Translated as *The Wretched of the Earth* (New York, 1963); *Die Verdammten dieser Erde* (Reinbek bei Hamburg, 1969).

Fawzi, Issam, and Ivesa Lübben. *Die ägyptische "Jama'a al-islamiya" und die Revision der Gewaltstrategie.* Deutsches Orient-Institut Focus 15. Hamburg, 2004.

Fellmann, Ferdinand. *Lebensphilosophie. Elemente einer Theorie der Selbsterfahrung.* Reinbek bei Hamburg, 1993.

Festinger, Leon, Henry W. Riecken, and Stanley Schachter. *When Prophecy Fails: A Social and Psychological Study of a Modern Group That Predicted the Destruction of the World.* New York, 1956.

Fielding, Nick, and Yosri Fouda. *Masterminds of Terror: The Truth Behind the Most Devastating Terrorist Attack the World Has Ever Seen.* New York, 2003.

Finke, Roger, and Rodney Stark. *The Churching of America, 1776–1990: Winners and Losers of Our Religious Economy.* New Brunswick, NJ. 1992.

Fischer, Michael M. J. *Iran: From Religious Dispute to Revolution.* Cambridge MA, 1980.

Fischer-Lichte, Erika. *Ästhetik des Performativen.* Frankfurt a.M., 2004.

Flores, Alexander. *Intifada. Aufstand der Palästinenser.* Berlin, 1989.

———. "Judaeophobia in Context: Anti-Semitism Among Modern Palestinians." *Die Welt des Islams* 46 (2006): 307–330.

Forbes, Bruce David, and Jeanne Halgren Kilde, eds. *Rapture, Revelation, and the End Times: Exploring the Left Behind Series.* New York, 2004.

Forst, Rainer. *Toleranz im Konflikt: Geschichte, Gehalt und Gegenwart eines umstrittenen Begriffs.* Frankfurt a.M., 2003.

Franke, Patrick. "Rückkehr des Heiligen Krieges? Dschihad-Theorien im modernen Islam." In *Religion und Gewalt. Der Islam nach dem 11. September,* ed. André Stanisavlejevic and Ralf Zwengel, 47–68. Potsdam, 2002.

Freamon, Bernard K. "Martyrdom, Suicide, and the Islamic Law of War: A Short Legal History." *Fordham International Law Journal* 27 (2003): 299–369.

Frevert, Ute, ed. *Vertrauen. Historische Annäherungen.* Göttingen, 2003.

Friedland, Roger, and Richard Hecht. "The Nebi Musa Pilgrimage and the Origins of Palestinian Nationalism." In *Pilgrims & Travelers to the Holy Land,* ed. Bryan F. le Beau and Menachem Mor, 89–118. Omaha, 1996.

Friedman, Yohanan. *Tolerance and Coercion in Islam: Interfaith Relations in the Muslim Tradition.* Cambridge, 2003.

Frum, David, and Richard Perle. *An End to Evil: How to Win the War on Terror.* New York, 2003.

Frykholm, Amy Johnson. *Rapture Culture: Left Behind in Evangelical America.* Oxford, 2004.

———. "What Social and Political Messages Appear in the Left Behind Books? A Literary Discussion of Millenarian Fiction." In *Rapture, Revelation, and the End Times,* ed. Bruce David Forbes and Jeanne Halgren Kilde, 167–195. New York, 2004.

Fuller, Robert C. *Naming the Antichrist: The History of an American Obsession.* Oxford, 1995.

Gabriel, Karl, ed. *Europäische Wohlfahrtsstaatlichkeit. Soziokulturelle Grundlagen und religiöse Wurzeln.* Jahrbuch für Christliche Sozialwissenschaften, 46. Münster, 2005.

Gambetta, Diego. "Reason and Terror: Has 9/11 Made It Hard to Think Straight?" *Boston Review* 29, 2 (2004). http://bostonreview.net/BR29.2/gambetta.html (accessed May 1, 2010).

———. "Can We Make Sense of Suicide Missions?" In *Making Sense of Suicide Missions,* ed. id., 259–299. Oxford, 2005.

Ganor, Boaz. "Defining Terrorism: Is One Man's Terrorist Another Man's Freedom Fighter?" *Police Practice and Research* 3 (2002): 287–304.

Gebhardt, Jürgen. " 'Politik' und 'Religion': Eine historisch-theoretische Problemskizze." In *Religion und Politik. Zu Theorie und Praxis des theologisch-politischen Komplexes,* ed. Manfred Walther, 51–71. Baden-Baden, 2004.

Gellner, Ernest. *Muslim Society.* Cambridge, 1981.

Girard, René. *La violence et le sacré.* Paris, 1972. Translated by Patrick Gregory as *Violence and the Sacred* (Baltimore, 1977).

———. "Generative Scapegoating." In *Violent Origins: Walter Burkert, René Girard and Jonathan Z. Smith on Ritual Killing and Cultural Formation,* ed. Robert G. Hamerton-Kelly, 73–105. Stanford, CA, 1987.

Gladigow, Burkhard. "Gewalt in Gründungsmythen." In *Der Krieg in den Gründungsmythen europäischer Nationen und der USA,* ed. Nikolaus Buschmann and Dieter Langewiesche, 23–38. Frankfurt a.M., 2001.

Gluckman, Max. "Rituale der Rebellion in Süd-Ost-Afrika." In *Gesellschaften ohne Staat,* vol. 1: *Gleichheit und Gegenseitigkeit,* ed. Fritz Krame and Christian Sigrist, 250–280. Frankfurt a.M., 1978.

Gold, Dore. "From 'Occupied Territories' to 'Disputed Territories.'" *Jerusalem Letter* 470 (2002).

Goldziher, Ignaz. "Das Prinzip der takijja im Islam" (1906). In id., *Gesammelte Schriften,* 5: 59–72. Hildesheim, 1970.

Göle, Nilüfer. "Snapshots of Islamic Modernities." In *Multiple Modernities,* ed. Shmuel N. Eisenstadt, 91–117. New Brunswick, NJ, 2002.

Gorenberg, Gershom. *The End of Days: Fundamentalism and the Struggle for the Temple Mount.* Oxford, 2000.

———. "Intolerance: The Bestseller." *American Prospect* 17 (September 23, 2002).

———. *The Accidental Empire: Israel and the Birth of the Settlements, 1967–1977.* New York, 2006.

Graf, Friedrich-Wilhelm. "'In God We Trust.' Über mögliche Zusammenhänge von Sozialkapital und kapitalistischer Wohlfahrtsökonomie." In *Soziales Kapital in der Bürgergesellschaft,* ed. id. et al., 93–130. Stuttgart, 1999.

Graf, Friedrich Wilhelm, Andreas Platthaus, and Stephan Schleissing, eds. *Soziales Kapital in der Bürgergesellschaft.* Stuttgart, 1999.

Granovetter, Mark. "The Strength of Weak Ties." *American Journal of Sociology* 78 (1973): 1360–1380.

Greeley, Andrew. *Religion in Europe at the End of the Second Millennium.* New Brunswick, NJ, 2003.

Gunaratna, Rohan. *Inside al Qaeda: Global Network of Terror.* New York, 2002.

Hall, John R. *Gone from the Promised Land: Jonestown in American Cultural History.* New Brunswick, NJ, 1987.

———. "Peoples Temple." In *America's Alternative Religions,* ed. Timothy Miller, 301–311. Albany, NY, 1995.

———. "Public Narratives and the Apocalyptic Sect: From Jonestown to M. Carmel." In *Armageddon in Waco: Critical Perspectives on the Branch Davidian Conflict,* ed. Stuart A. Wright, 205–235. Chicago, 1995.

———. "Apocalypse 9/11." In *New Religious Movements in the Twenty-First Cen-*

tury: Legal, Political, and Social Challenges in Global Perspective, ed. Phillip Charles Lucas and Thomas Robbins, 265–282. London, 2004.

Hall, John R., and Philip Schuyler. "Apostasy, Apocalypse, and Religious Violence: An Exploratory Comparison of Peoples Temple, the Branch Davidians, and the Solar Temple." In *The Politics of Religious Apostasy,* ed. David G. Bromley, 141–169. Westport, CT, 1998.

Hall, John R., Philip D. Schuyler, and Sylvaine Trinh. *Apocalypse Observed: Religious Movements and Violence in North America, Europe, and Japan.* New York, 2000.

Hallaq, Wael B. *A History of Islamic Legal Theories: An Introduction to Sunnī Uṣūl al-fiqh.* Cambridge, 1997.

Halm, Heinz. *Die Schia.* Darmstadt, 1988.

———. *Shi'a Islam: From Religion to Revolution.* Translated by Allison Brown. Princeton, NJ, 1996.

Halper, Stefan, and Jonathan Clarke. *America Alone: The Neo-Conservatives and the Global Order,* 68–73. Cambridge, 2004.

Halsell, Grace. *Prophecy and Politics: Militant Evangelists on the Road to Nuclear War.* Westport, CT, 1986.

Hamzeh, Ahmad Nizar. *In the Path of Hizbullah.* Syracuse, NY, 2004.

Hanf, Theodor. "Ethnurgy: On the Analytical Use and Normative Abuse of the Concept of 'Ethnic Identity.'" In *Nationalism, Ethnicity and Cultural Identity in Europe,* ed. Keebet van Benda-Beckman and Maykel Verkuyten, 40–51. Utrecht, 1999.

Hanson, Brad. "The 'Westoxication' of Iran: Depictions and Reactions of Behrangi, Al-e Ahmad and Shari'ati." *International Journal of Middle East Studies* 15 (1983): 1–23.

Harik, Judith Palmer. *Hezbollah: The Changing Face of Terrorism.* London, 2004.

Harkabi, Yehoshafat. *Das palästinensische Manifest und seine Bedeutung.* Stuttgart, 1980.

Harris, Duchess, and Adam John Waterman. "To Die for the Peoples Temple." In *Peoples Temple and Black Religion in America,* ed. Rebecca Moore, Anthony B. Pinn, and Mary P. Sawyer, 103–122. Bloomington, IN, 2004.

Hartung, Jan-Peter. "Die fromme Stiftung [*waqf*]. Eine islamische Analogie zur Körperschaft?" In *Die verrechtlichte Religion,* ed. Hans G. Kippenberg and Gunnar Folke Schuppert, 287–314. Tübingen, 2005.

Hase, Thomas. "Waco—die inszenierte Apokalypse." *Zeitschrift für Religionswissenschaft* 3 (1995): 29–48.

Hatina, Meir. *Islam and Salvation in Palestine.* Tel Aviv, 2001.

Hawking, Stephen. *A Brief History of Time.* 10th ed. London, 1998.

Heilman, Samuel C. *Defenders of the Faith: Inside Ultra-Orthodox Jewry.* New York, 1992.

———. "Guides of the Faithful: Contemporary Religious Zionist Rabbis." In *Spokesmen for the Despised,* ed. R. Scott Appleby, 328–362. Chicago, 1997.

Heilman, Samuel C., and Menachem Friedman. "Religious Fundamentalism and Religious Jews: The Case of the Haredim." In *Fundamentalisms Observed,* ed. Martin E. Marty and R. Scott Appleby, 197–264. Chicago, 1991.

Henten, Jan Willem van. *The Maccabean Martyrs as Saviours of the Jewish People: A Study of 2 and 4 Maccabees.* Leiden, 1997.

———, ed. *Die Entstehung der jüdischen Martyrologie.* Leiden 1989.

Hersh, Seymour M. *Chain of Command: The Road from 9/11 to Abu Ghraib.* New York, 2004.

Hertzberg, Arthur. *The Zionist Idea: A Historical Analysis and Reader.* New York, 1966.

Hobbes, Thomas. *Leviathan, or the Matter, Forme, & Power of a Common-Wealth Ecclesiastical and Civill.* 1651. London, 1968.

Hobsbawm, Eric J. *Primitive Rebels: Studies in Archaic Forms of Social Movement in the 19th and 20th Centuries.* New York, 1959.

———. "Die Arbeitersekten." In id., *Sozialrebellen: Archaische Sozialbewegungen im 19. u. 20. Jahrhundert,* 161–190. Neuwied a. Rh., 1971. German translation by Renate Müller-Isenburg and C. Barry Hyams of *Primitive Rebels.*

Hochgeschwender, Michael. "Religion, Nationale Mythologie und Nationale Identität. Zu den methodischen und inhaltlichen Debatten in der amerikanischen 'New Religious History.'" *Historisches Jahrbuch* 124 (2004): 435–520.

Hoexter, Miriam. "The 'Waqf' and the Public Sphere." In *The Public Sphere in Muslim Societies,* ed. id., Shmuel N. Eisenstadt and Nehemia Levtzion, 119–138. Albany, NY, 2002.

Hoexter, Miriam, Shmuel N. Eisenstadt, and Nehemia Levtzion, eds. *The Public Sphere in Muslim Societies.* Albany, NY, 2002.

Hoffman, Bruce. *Inside Terrorism.* Rev. ed. New York, 2006. German translation, *Terrorismus—der unerklärte Krieg. Neue Gefahren politischer Gewalt* (Frankfurt a.M., 1999).

Holmes, Stephen. "Al-Qaeda, September 11, 2001." In *Making Sense of Suicide Missions,* ed. Diego Gambetta, 131–172. Oxford, 2005.

Hölscher, Lucian. *Weltgericht oder Revolution. Protestantische und sozialistische Zukunftsvorstellungen im deutschen Kaiserreich.* Stuttgart, 1989.

———. *Die Entdeckung der Zukunft.* Frankfurt a.M., 1999.

Honegger, Claudia, ed. *Die Hexen der Neuzeit. Studien zur Sozialgeschichte eines kulturellen Deutungsmusters.* Frankfurt a.M., 1988.

Horowitz, Elliott. *Reckless Rites: Purim and the Legacy of Jewish Violence*. Princeton, NJ, 2006.

Hroub, Khaled. *Hamas: Political Thought and Practice*. Washington, DC, 2000.

Ibrahim, Saad Eddin. "Anatomy of Egypt's Militant Islamic Groups: Methodological Note and Preliminary Findings." *Journal of Middle East Studies* 12 (1980): 423–453.

Iriye, Akira. "Culture and International History." In *Explaining the History of American Foreign Relations,* ed. Michael J. Hogan and Thomas G. Paterson, 214–225. Cambridge, 1991.

Isensee, Josef, ed. *Der Terror, der Staat und das Recht*. Berlin, 2004.

Ismael, Jacqueline S., and Tareq Y. Ismael. "Cultural Perspectives on Social Welfare in the Emergence of Modern Arab Social Thought." *Muslim World* 85 (1995): 82–106.

Ismail, Salwa. "Religious 'Orthodoxy' as Public Morality: The State, Islamism, and Cultural Politics in Egypt." *Critique: Journal for Critical Studies of the Middle East* 14 (1999): 25–47.

———. "The Popular Movements Dimension of Contemporary Militant Islamism: Socio-Spatial Determinants in the Cairo Urban Setting." *Comparative Studies in Society and History* 42 (2000): 363–393.

———. *Rethinking Islamist Politics: Culture, the State and Islamism*. London, 2003.

Israeli, Raphael. "A Manual of Islamic Fundamentalist Terrorism." *Terrorism and Political Violence* 14 (2002): 23–40.

Jaber, Halal. *Hezbollah: Born with a Vengeance*. London, 1997.

Jacquard, Roland. *Au nom d'Oussama Ben Laden: Dossier secret sur le terroriste le plus recherché du monde*. Paris, 2001. Translated by George Holoch as *In the Name of Osama Bin Laden: Global Terrorism and the Bin Laden Brotherhood* (Durham, NC, 2002).

Jansen, Johannes J. G. "The Creed of Sadat's Assassins: The Context of 'The Forgotten Duty' Analysed." *Welt des Islams* 25 (1985): 1–30.

———. *The Neglected Duty: The Creed of Sadat's Assassins and Islamic Resurgence in the Middle East*. New York, 1986.

Janssen, Hans-Gerd. "Streitfall Monotheismus. Einführung in das Thema." In *Monotheismus,* ed. Jürgen Manemann, 20–27.

Jaspers, Karl. *Max Weber. Deutsches Wesen im politischen Denken, im Forschen und Philosophieren*. Oldenburg, 1932.

Jenkins, Philip. *Mystics and Messiahs: Cults and New Religions in American History*. New York, 2000.

———. *God's Continent. Christianity, Islam and Europe's Religious Crisis*. Oxford, 2007.

Jewett, Robert, and John Shelton Lawrence. *Captain America and the Crusade*

Against Evil: The Dilemma of Zealous Nationalism. Grand Rapids, MI, 2003.

Joas, Hans. *Die Kreativität des Handelns.* Frankfurt a.M., 1996.

———. *Die Entstehung der Werte.* Frankfurt a.M., 1997.

———. *Kriege und Werte. Studien zur Gewaltgeschichte des 20. Jahrhunderts.* Weilerswist, 2000.

———. *Braucht der Mensch Religion? Über Erfahrungen der Selbsttranszendenz.* Freiburg, 2004.

———. "Die religiöse Lage in den USA." In *Säkularisierung und die Weltreligionen,* ed. Hans Joas and Klaus Wiegandt, 358–375. Frankfurt a.M., 2007.

Joas, Hans, and Wolfgang Knöbl. *Sozialtheorie. Zwanzig einführende Vorlesungen.* Frankfurt a.M., 2004.

Juergensmeyer, Mark. "Nonviolence." *ER* 10 (1986): 463–468.

———. "Antifundamentalism." In *Fundamentalisms Comprehended,* ed. Martin E. Marty and R. Scott Appleby, 353–366. The Fundamentalism Project, vol. 5. Chicago, 1995.

———. *Terror in the Mind of God: The Global Rise of Religious Violence.* Berkeley, CA, 2000.

———. *Global Rebellion: Religious Challenges to the Secular State, from Christian Militias to al Qaeda.* Berkeley, CA, 2008.

Kakar, Sudhir. *The Colors of Violence.* Chicago, 1996.

Ibn Kaldūn. *The Muqaddimah.* Translated by Franz Rosenthal. Princeton, NJ, 1958.

Kapitan, Tomis. "The Terrorism of 'Terrorism.'" In *Terrorism and International Justice,* ed. James P. Sterba, 47–66. New York, 2003.

Karpin, Michael, and Friedman, Ina. *Murder in the Name of God. The Plot to Kill Yitzhak Rabin.* London, 1999.

Katouzian, Homa. "Land Reform in Iran: A Case Study in the Political Economy of Social Engineering." *Journal of Peasant Studies* 1 (1974): 220–239.

Katz, David S., and Richard Popkin. *Messianic Revolution: Radical Religious Politics to the End of the Second Millennium.* New York, 1998.

Kazemi, Farhad. *Poverty and Revolution in Iran: The Migrant Poor, Urban Marginality and Politics.* New York, 1980.

Keddie, Nikki. *Religion and Rebellion in Iran: The Tobacco Protest of 1891–1892.* London, 1966.

———. *Roots of Revolution: An Interpretive History of Modern Iran.* New Haven, CT, 1981.

———, ed. *Religion and Politics in Iran: Shi'ism from Quietism to Revolution.* New Haven, CT, 1983.

Kepel, Gilles. *Muslim Extremism in Egypt.* 1984. 3rd ed. Berkeley, CA, 2003.

————. *Jihad: The Trail of Political Islam*. Translated by Anthony F. Roberts. Cambridge, MA, 2002.

Kepel, Gilles, and Jean-Pierre Milelli, eds. *Al-Qaida. Texte des Terrors*. Munich, 2006.

Kermani, Navid. "Katharsis und Verfremdung im schiitischen Passionsspiel." *Die Welt des Islams* 39 (1999): 31–63.

————. "Märtyrertum als Topos politischer Selbstdarstellung in Iran." In *Figurative Politik. Zur Performanz der Macht in der modernen Gesellschaft*, ed. Hans-Georg Soeffner and Dirk Tänzler, 89–100. Opladen 2001.

————. *Dynamit des Geistes. Martyrium, Islam und Nihilismus*. Göttingen, 2002.

Khalaf, Samir. *Civil and Uncivil Violence in Lebanon: A History of the Internationalization of Communal Conflict*. New York, 2002.

————. "The Radicalization of Communal Loyalties." In *Religion Between Violence and Reconciliation*, ed. Thomas Scheffler, 283–299. Beirut and Würzburg, 2002.

Khosrokhavar, Farhad. *L'islamisme et la mort: Le martyre révolutionnaire en Iran*. Paris, 1995.

————. *Les nouveaux martyrs d'Allah*. Paris, 2002. Translated by David Macey as *Suicide Bombers: Allah's New Martyrs* (London, 2005).

Khoury, Adel Theodor. *Der Koran. Arabisch-Deutsch*. Gütersloh, 2004.

Kiener, Ronald C. "Gushist and Qutbian Approaches to Government: A Comparative Analysis of Religious Assassination." *Numen* 44 (1997): 229–241.

Kilde, Jeanne Halgren. "How Did Left Behind's Particular Vision of the End Times Develop? A Historical Look at Millenarian Thought." In *Rapture, Revelation, and the End Times*, ed. Bruce David Forbes and Jeanne Halgren Kilde, 33–70. New York, 2004.

Kippenberg, Hans G. "Jeder Tag Ashura, jedes Grab Kerbala. Zur Ritualisierung der Straßenkämpfe im Iran." In *Religion und Politik im Iran*, ed. Kurt Greussing, 217–256. Frankfurt a.M., 1981.

————. "Die Entlassung aus Schuldknechtschaft im antiken Judäa. Eine Legitimitätsvorstellung von Verwandtschaftsgruppen." In *"Vor Gott sind alle gleich." Soziale Gleichheit, soziale Ungleichheit und die Religionen*, ed. Günter Kehrer, 74–104. Düsseldorf, 1983.

————. "Religionssoziologie ohne Säkularisierungsthese: E. Durkheim und M. Weber aus der Sicht der Symboltheorie." *Neue Zeitschrift für systematische Theologie und Religionsphilosophie* 27 (1985): 177–193.

————. *Die vorderasiatischen Erlösungsreligionen in ihrem Zusammenhang mit der antiken Stadtherrschaft*. Frankfurt a.M., 1991.

————. "Die Verheimlichung der wahren Identität vor der Außenwelt in der antiken und islamischen Religionsgeschichte." In *Die Erfindung des inneren Menschen. Studien zur religiösen Anthropologie,* ed. Jan Assmann, 183–198. Gütersloh, 1993.

———. "Religionsentwicklung." In *Max Weber's "Religionssystematik,"* ed. Hans G. Kippenberg and Martin Riesebrodt, 77–99. Tübingen, 2001.

———. *Discovering Religious History in the Modern Age.* Translated by Barbara Harshaw. Princeton, NJ, 2002.

———. "Christliche Gemeinden im Römischen Reich: *Collegium licitum* oder *illicitum.*" In *Hairesis. Festschrift für Karl Hoheisel zum 65. Geburtstag,* ed. Manfred Hutter, Wassilios Klein, and Ulrich Vollmer, 172–183. Münster, 2002.

———. "Religiöse Gemeinschaften. Wo die Arbeit am Sinn-Problem der Welt und der Bedarf sozialen Handelns an Gemeinschaftlichkeit zusammentreffen." In *Das Weber-Paradigma. Studien zur Weiterentwicklung von Max Weber's Forschungsprogramm,* ed. Gert Albert et al., 211–233. Tübingen, 2003.

———. "'Nach dem Vorbild eines öffentlichen Gemeinwesens.' Diskurse römischer Juristen über private religiöse Vereinigungen." In *Die verrechtlichte Religion,* ed. id. and Gunnar Folke Schuppert, 11–35. Tübingen, 2005.

———. "Religiöse Sinn-Deutungen in säkularen Konflikten." In *Religionen im Konflikt,* ed. Vasilios N. Makrides and Jörg Rüpke, 18–26. Münster, 2005.

———. "Das Sozialkapital religiöser Gemeinschaften im Zeitalter der Globalisierung." In *Religion und Respekt. Beiträge zu einem spannungsreichen Verhältnis,* ed. Georg Pfleiderer and Ekkehard W. Stegemann, 245–271. Zürich, 2006.

Kippenberg, Hans G., and Guy G. Stroumsa, eds. *Secrecy and Concealment: Studies in the History of Mediterranean and Near Eastern Religions.* Leiden, 1995.

Kippenberg, Hans G., and Gunnar Folke Schuppert, eds. *Die verrechtlichte Religion. Der Öffentlichkeitsstatus von Religionsgemeinschaften.* Tübingen, 2005.

Kippenberg, Hans G., and Kocku von Stuckrad. *Einführung in die Religionswissenschaft. Gegenstände und Begriffe.* Munich, 2003.

Kippenberg, Hans G., and Martin Riesebrodt, eds. *Max Weber's "Religionssystematik."* Tübingen, 2001.

Kippenberg, Hans G., and Tilman Seidensticker, eds. *Terror im Dienste Gottes. Die "Geistliche Anleitung" der Attentäter des 11. September 2001.* Frankfurt a.M., 2004.

———. *The 9/11 Handbook: Annotated Translation and Interpretation of the Attackers' Spiritual Manual.* London, 2006.

Kloppenborg, John S., and Stephen G. Wilson, eds. *Voluntary Associations in the Graeco-Roman World.* London, 1996.

Kohlberg, Etan. "Some Imami-Shi'i Views on Taqiyya." *JAOS* 95 (1975): 395–402.

———. "Taqiyya in Shi'i Theology and Religion." In *Secrecy and Concealment,* ed. Hans G. Kippenberg and Guy G. Stroumsa, 345–380. Leiden, 1995.

Kohlmann, Evan F. *Al-Qaida's Jihad in Europe: The Afghan-Bosnian Network.* Oxford, 2004.

Kook, Abraham Isaak. *Die Lichter der Tora,* ed. Eveline Goodman-Thau and Christoph Schulte. Berlin, 1995.

———. "Die Tora des Auslandes und die Tora des Landes Israel." In id., *Die Lichter der Tora,* 111–123. Berlin, 1995.

Kook, Zvi Yehuda, *Torat Eretz Yisrael: The Teachings of HaRav Tzvi Yehuda Hacohen Kook.* Translated and edited by Tzvi Fishman. Jerusalem, 1991.

Krämer, Gudrun. *Geschichte Palästinas. Von der osmanischen Eroberung bis zur Gründung des Staates Israel.* Munich, 2002.

———. "Aus Erfahrung lernen? Die islamische Bewegung in Ägypten." In *Religiöser Fundamentalismus. Vom Kolonialismus zur Globalisierung,* ed. Clemens Six, Martin Riesebrodt, and Siegfried Haas, 185–200. Innsbruck, 2005.

Kramer, Martin. *Hezbollah's Vision of the West.* Washington Institute for Near East Policy, Policy Papers, 16. Washington, DC, 1989.

———. "The Moral Logic of Hizballah." In *Origins of Terrorism. Psychologies, Ideologies, Theologies, States of Mind,* ed. Walter Reich, 131–157. Cambridge, 1990.

———. "Sacrifice and Fratricide in Shiite Lebanon." *Terrorism and Political Violence* 3 (1991): 30–47.

———. "Hizbullah: The Calculus of Jihad." In *Fundamentalism and the State: Remaking Politics, Economies, and Militancy,* ed. Martin E. Marty and R. Scott Appleby, 539–556. The Fundamentalism Project, vol. 3. Chicago, 1993.

———. "The Oracle of Hizbullah: Sayyid Muhammad Husayn Fadlallah." In *Spokesmen for the Despised: Fundamentalist Leaders of the Middle East,* ed. R. Scott Appleby, 83–181. Chicago, 1997.

Krebs, Valdis E. "Mapping Networks of Terrorist Cells." *Connections* 24 (2002): 43–52.

Krech, Volkhard. *Georg Simmels Religionstheorie.* Tübingen, 1998.

———. "Sacrifice and Holy War: A Study of Religion and Violence." In *International Handbook of Violence Research,* ed. Wilhelm Heitmeyer and John Hagan, 1005–1021. Dordrecht, 2003.

Lambton, Ann K. S. *Landlord and Peasant in Persia.* 2nd ed. Oxford, 1969.

Landes, Richard. "Apocalyptic Islam and Bin Laden." www.mille.org/people/rl-pages/Bin_Laden.html (accessed May 2, 2010).

Lang, Bernhard. "Monotheismus." In *Handbuch religionswissenschaftlicher Grundbegriffe,* 4: 148–165. Stuttgart, 1998.

LaPiere, Richard T. "Attitudes vs. Actions." *Social Forces* 13 (1934–1935): 230–237.

Laqueur, Walter, and Barry Rubin, eds. *The Israel-Arab Reader: A Documentary*

History of the Middle East Conflict. Harmondsworth, U.K., 2001.

Laursen, John Christian, and Cary J. Nederman, eds. *Beyond the Persecuting Society. Religious Toleration Before the Enlightenment.* Philadelphia, 1998.

Lawrence, John Shelton, and Robert Jewett. *The Myth of the American Superhero.* Grand Rapids, MI, 2002.

Legrain, Jean-François. *Les voix du soulèvement palestinien: 1987–1988: Edition critique des communiqués du Commandement national unifié du soulèvement et du Mouvement de la résistance islamique.* Cairo, 1991.

———. "Palestinian Islamisms: Patriotism as a Condition of their Expansion." In *Accounting for Fundamentalisms,* ed. Martin E. Marty and R. Scott Appleby. Chicago, 1994.

Lehmann, Hartmut. *Säkularisierung. Der europäische Sonderweg in Sachen Religion.* Göttingen, 2004.

Lehmkuhl, Ursula. "Diplomatiegeschichte als internationale Kulturgeschichte: Theoretische Ansätze und empirische Forschung zwischen Historischer Kulturwissenschaft und Soziologischem Institutionalismus." *Geschichte und Gegenwart* 27 (2001): 394–423.

Lemann, Nicholas. "Kicking in Groups." *Atlantic Monthly* 277 (1996): 22–26.

Lepsius, M. Rainer. "Parteiensystem und Sozialstruktur: Zum Problem der Demokratisierung der deutschen Gesellschaft." In *Deutsche Parteien vor 1918,* ed. Gerhard A. Ritter, 56–80. Cologne, 1973.

———. "Institutionenanalyse und Institutionenpolitik." In *Politische Institutionen im Wandel,* ed. Birgitta Nedelmann, 392–403. Opladen, 1995.

———. "Institutionalisierung und Deinstitutionalisierung von Rationalitätskriterien." In *Institutionenwandel,* ed. Gerhard Göhler, 57–69. Opladen, 1997.

———. "Die 'Moral' der Institutionen." In *Eigenwilligkeit und Rationalität sozialer Prozesse. Festschrift Friedhelm Neidhardt.* Opladen, 1999.

———. "Eigenart und Potenzial des Weber-Paradigmas." In *Das Weber-Paradigma. Studien zur Weiterentwicklung von Max Webers Forschungsprogramm,* ed. Gert Albert et al., 32–41. Tübingen, 2003.

Levitt, Matthew. *Hamas: Politics, Charity, and Terrorism in the Service of Jihad.* New Haven, CT, 2006.

Lewis, James R. *Legitimating New Religions.* New Brunswick, NJ, 2003.

Lichtblau, Klaus. "'Vergemeinschaftung' und 'Vergesellschaftung' bei Max Weber. Eine Rekonstruktion seines Sprachgebrauchs." *Zeitschrift für Soziologie* 29 (2000): 423–443.

Lieven, Anatol. *America Right or Wrong: An Anatomy of American Nationalism.* Oxford, 2004.

Lifton, Robert J. *Destroying the World to Save It: Aum Shinrikyo, Apocalyptic Violence, and the New Global Terrorism*. New York, 1999.

Lincoln, Bruce. "Symmetric Dualisms: Bush and bin Laden on October 7." In id., *Holy Terrors: Thinking About Religion After September 11*, 19–33. Chicago, 2003.

———. "The Cyrus Cylinder: The Book of Virtues, and the 'Liberation' of Iraq: On Political Theology and Messianic Pretensions." In *Religionen im Konflikt*, ed. Vasilios N. Makrides and Jörg Rüpke, 248–264. Münster 2005.

Lindsey, Hal, and Carole C. Carlson. *The Late Great Planet Earth*. Grand Rapids, MI, 1970.

———. *The 1980's: Countdown to Armageddon*. New York, 1981.

Lohlker, Rüdiger. *Islamisches Völkerrecht. Studien am Beispiel Granada*. Bremen, 2007.

Löwith, Hans. *Weltgeschichte und Heilsgeschehen. Die theologischen Voraussetzungen der Geschichtsphilosophie*. Stuttgart, 1953.

Lustick, Ian S. *Trapped in the War on Terror*. Philadelphia, 2006.

Lutterbach, Hubertus, and Manemann, Jürgen, eds. *Religion und Terror. Stimmen zum 11. September aus Christentum, Islam und Judentum*. Münster, 2002.

Lybarger, Loren D. *Identity and Religion in Palestine: The Struggle Between Islamism and Secularism in the Occupied Territories*. Princeton, NJ, 2007.

Macdonald, Andrew. *The Turner Diaries: A Novel*. 1978. 2nd ed. New York, 1996.

McDermott, Terry. *Perfect Soldiers: The Hijackers: Who They Were, Why They Did It*. New York, 2005.

McGinn, Bernard. *Antichrist: Two Thousand Years of the Human Fascination with Evil*. New York, 1996.

Makdisi, Ussama. "Revisiting Sectarianism." In *Religion Between Violence and Reconciliation*, ed. Thomas Scheffler, 179–191. Beirut and Würzburg, 2002.

Makropoulos, Michael, "Kontingenz. Aspekte einer theoretischen Semantik der Moderne." *Archive européenne de sociologie* 45 (2004): 369–399.

Manemann, Jürgen, ed. *Monotheismus*. Münster, 2003.

Martin, David. *Tongues of Fire: The Explosion of Protestantism in Latin America*. Oxford, 1990.

———. *Pentecostalism: The World Their Parish*. Oxford, 2002.

Marty, Martin E. *Modern American Religion*. Vol. 1: *The Irony of It All, 1893–1919*; vol. 2: *The Noise of Conflict, 1919–1941*; vol. 3: *Under God, Indivisible, 1941–1960*. Chicago, 1986–1996.

Marty, Martin E., and R. Scott Appleby. *The Glory and the Power: The Fundamentalist Challenge to the Modern World*. Boston, 1992.

———, eds. *Fundamentalisms Observed*. The Fundamentalism Project, vol. 1. Chicago, 1991.

Mayntz, Renate. "Hierarchie oder Netzwerk? Zu den Organisationsformen des Terrorismus." *Berliner Journal für Soziologie* 14 (2004): 251–262.

Mead, Sidney E. *The Lively Experiment: The Shaping of Christianity in America.* New York, 1976.

Mearsheimer, John J., and Stephen M. Watt. "The Israel Lobby and U.S Foreign Policy." www.lrb.co.uk/v28/no6/print/mear01_.html (accessed May 22, 2010).

Mehl, A. "*Doriktetos chōra.* Kritische Bemerkungen zum 'Speererwerb' in Politik und Völkerrecht der hellenistischen Epoche." *Ancient Society* 11–12 (1980–1981): 173–212.

Meier, Andreas. *Der politische Auftrag des Islam. Programme und Kritik zwischen Fundamentalismus und Reformen. Originalstimmen aus der islamischen Welt.* Wuppertal, 1995.

Melton, J. Gordon. "Anti-Cultists in the United States: An Historical Perspective." In *New Religious Movements: Challenge and Response,* ed. Bryan Wilson and Jamie Cresswell, 213–233. New York, 1999.

———. "Einleitung: Gehirnwäsche und Sekten—Aufstieg und Fall einer Theorie." In *Gehirnwäsche und Sekten,* ed. id. and Massimo Introvigne, 9–36. Marburg, 2000.

Melton, J. Gordon, and Massimo Introvigne, eds. *Gehirnwäsche und Sekten. Interdisziplinäre Annäherungen.* Marburg, 2000.

Menke, Christoph. "Innere Natur und soziale Normativität. Die Idee der Selbstverwirklichung." In *Die kulturellen Werte Europas,* ed. Hans Joas and Klaus Wiegand, 304–352. Frankfurt 2005.

Merari, Ariel. "The Readiness to Kill and to Die: Suicidal Terrorism in the Middle East." In *Origins of Terrorism,* ed. Walter Reich., 193–207. Cambridge, 1990.

Merton, Robert K. "The Thomas Theorem and the Matthew Effect." *Social Forces* 74 (1995): 379–424.

Meyer, Egbert. "Anlass und Anwendungsbereich der taqiyya." *Der Islam* 57 (1980): 246–280.

Michel, Lou, and Dan Herbeck. *American Terrorist: Timothy McVeigh and the Oklahoma City Bombing.* New York, 2001.

Milani, Mohsen M. *The Making of Iran's Islamic Revolution: From Monarchy to Islamic Republic.* 2nd ed. Boulder, CO, 1994.

Miller, Timothy, ed. *America's Alternative Religions.* Albany, NY, 1995.

Mishal, Shaul, and Reuben Aharoni. *Speaking Stones: Communiqués from the Intifada Underground.* New York, 1994.

Mishal, Shaul, and Avraham Sela. *The Palestinian Hamas: Vision, Violence, and Coexistence.* New York, 2000.

Mitchell, Richard P. *The Society of the Muslim Brothers.* Oxford, 1969. Reprint with foreword by John O. Voll. Oxford, 1993.

Mneimneh, Hassan, and Kanan Makiya. "Manual for a 'Raid.'" In *Striking Terror: America's New War*, ed. Robert B. Silvers and Barbara Epstein, 301–318. New York, 2002.

Möller, Jochen. "'Islamisch und noch einmal islamisch.' Zur *Jama'a al-Islamiyya* als politische Kraft Oberägyptens." In *Sendungsbewusstsein oder Eigennutz. Zu Motivation und Selbstverständnis islamischer Mobilisierung*, ed. Dietrich Reetz, 183–198. Berlin, 2001.

Monchi-Zadeh, Davoud. *Ta'ziya. Das persische Passionsspiel.* Stockholm, 1967.

Moore, Rebecca. "American as Cherry Pie." In *Millennialism, Persecution, and Violence: Historical Cases*, ed. Catherine Wessinger, 121–137. Syracuse, NY.

Moore, Rebecca, and Fielding McGhee III, eds. *New Religious Movements, Mass Suicide, and Peoples Temple: Scholarly Perspectives on a Tragedy.* Lewiston, NY, 1989.

Moore, Robert Ian. *The Formation of a Persecuting Society: Power and Deviance in Western Europe, 950–1250.* Oxford, 1987.

Mottahedeh, Roy P. *Loyalty and Leadership in an Early Islamic Society.* Princeton, NJ, 1980.

Münkler, Herfried. *Die neuen Kriege.* Reinbek bei Hamburg, 2002.

Musharbash, Yassin. *Die neue al-Qaida. Innenansichten eines lernenden Terrornetzwerks.* Cologne, 2006.

Nagel, Alexander-Kenneth. *Charitable Choice. Religiöse Institutionalisierung im politischen Raum. Religion und Sozialpolitik in den USA.* Hamburg, 2006.

Nasr, Salim. "Mobilisation communautaire et symbolique religieuse: L'Imam Sadr et les Chi'ites du Liban (1979–1975)." In *Radicalismes islamiques*, vol. 1: *Iran, Liban, Turquie*, ed. Olivier Carré and Paul Dumont, 119–158. Paris, 1985.

Nasr, Seyyed Vali Reza. *Mawdudi and the Making of Islamic Revivalism.* Oxford, 1996.

National Commission on Terrorist Attacks upon the United States. *The 9/11 Commission Report: Final Report of the National Commission on Terrorist Attacks upon the United States.* New York, 2004.

Nedelmann, Birgitta. "Die Selbstmordbomber. Zur symbolischen Kommunikation extremer politischer Gewalt." In *Eigenwilligkeit und Rationalität sozialer Prozesse. Festschrift Friedhelm Neidhardt*, ed. Jürgen Gerhards and Ronald Hitzler, 379–414. Opladen and Wiesbaden, 1999.

Netanyahu, Benjamin, ed. *Terrorism: How the West Can Win.* New York, 1986.

Newman, David. *The Impact of Gush Emunim: Politics and Settlement in the West Bank.* London, 1985.

———, ed. "Gush Emunim: Between Fundamentalism and Pragmatism." *Jerusalem Quarterly* 39 (1986). http://members.tripod.com/alabasters_archive/gush_pragmatism.html (accessed May 22, 2010).

Newport, Kenneth. "The Heavenly Millennium of Seventh-Day Adventism." In *Christian Millenarianism: From the Early Church to Waco,* ed. Stephen Hunt, 131–148. Bloomington, IN, 2001.

———. *The Branch Davidians of Waco: The History and Belief of an Apocalyptic Sect.* New York, 2006.

Nirenberg, David. *Communities of Violence: Persecution of Minorities in the Middle Ages.* Princeton, NJ, 1998.

Noethlichs, Karl Leo. *Das Judentum und der Römische Staat. Minderheitenpolitik im antiken Rom.* Darmstadt, 1996.

———. *Die Juden im christlichen Imperium Romanum (4.–6. Jahrhundert).* Berlin, 2001.

Norton, Augustus R. "Shi'ism and Social Protest in Lebanon." In *Shi'ism and Social Protest,* ed. Juan R. I. Cole and Nikki R. Keddie, 156–178. New Haven, CT, 1986.

———. *Amal and the Shi'a: Struggle for the Soul of Lebanon.* Austin, 1987.

———. *Hezbollah: A Short History.* Princeton, NJ, 2007.

Noth, Albrecht. *Heiliger Krieg und Heiliger Kampf im Islam und Christentum. Beiträge zur Vorgeschichte und Geschichte der Kreuzzüge.* Bonn, 1966.

———. "Möglichkeiten und Grenzen islamischer Toleranz." *Saeculum* 29 (1978): 190–204.

Oberdorfer, Bernd, and Peter Waldmann, eds. *Die Ambivalenz des Religiösen. Religionen als Friedensstifter und Gewalterzeuger.* Freiburg i. Br., 2008.

Oexle, Otto Gerhard. "Das Mittelalter und das Unbehagen an der Moderne. Mittelalterbeschwörungen in der Weimarer Republik und danach." In *Gedenkschrift für František Graus,* 125–153. Sigmaringen, 1992.

O'Leary, Stephen D. *Arguing the Apocalypse: A Theory of Millennial Rhetoric.* Oxford, 1994.

Oliver, Anne Marie, and Paul F. Steinberg. *The Road to Martyrs' Square: A Journey into the World of the Suicide Bomber.* Oxford, 2005.

The Oxford Encyclopedia of the Modern Islamic World. Edited by John L. Esposito et al. 4 vols. New York, 1995.

Oz, Amos. *In the Land of Israel.* San Diego, 1983.

Pannewick, Friederike. "Passion and Rebellion. Shi'ite Visions of Redemptive Martyrdom." In id., *Martyrdom in Literature: Visions of Death and Meaningful Suffering in Europe and the Middle East from Antiquity to Modernity,* 47–62. Wiesbaden, 2004.

———. "Tödliche Selbstopferung in der palästinensischen Belletristik—eine Frage von Macht und Ehre?" In *Ein Denken, das zum Sterben führt. Selbsttötung—das Tabu und seine Brüche,* ed. Ines Kappert, Benigna Gerisch, and Georg Fiedler, 158–184. Göttingen, 2004.

Pape, Robert A. *Dying to Win: The Strategic Logic of Suicide Terrorism.* New York, 2005.

Paret, Rudi. "Toleranz und Intoleranz im Islam." *Saeculum* 21 (1970): 344–365.

Paz, Reuven. "The Development of Palestinian Islamic Groups." In *Revolutionaries and Reformers: Contemporary Islamist Movements in the Middle East,* ed. Barry Rubin, 23–40. New York, 2003.

Pedahzur, Ami. *Suicide Terrorism.* Cambridge, 2005.

Perle, Richard, et al. "A Clean Break: A New Strategy for Securing the Realm." Institute for Advanced Strategic and Political Studies' Study Group on a New Israeli Strategy Toward 2000 report. June 1996. www.iasps.org/strat1.htm (accessed May 25, 2010).

Perthes, Volker. *Der Libanon nach dem Bürgerkrieg. Von Ta"if zum gesellschaftlichen Konsens?* Baden-Baden, 1994.

Peters, Rudolph. *Jihad in Classical and Modern Islam.* 2nd ed. Princeton, NJ, 2005.

Peterson, Eric. "Der Monotheismus als politisches Problem." 1935. In id., *Theologische Traktate,* 45–147. Munich, 1951.

Picard, Elizabeth. "La violence milicienne et sa légitimation religieuse." In *Religion Between Violence and Reconciliation,* ed. Thomas Scheffler, 319–332. Beirut and Würzburg, 2002.

Pipes, Daniel, and Patrick Clawson. "A Terrorist U.S. Ally?" *New York Post,* May 20, 2003. www.danielpipes.org/1100/mujahedeen-e-khalq-a-terrorist-us-ally (accessed May 31, 2010).

Planck, Ulrich. "Der Teilbau im Iran." *Zeitschrift für ausländische Landwirtschaft* 1 (1962): 47–81.

Plasger, Georg, and Bernd Schipper, eds. *Apokalyptik und kein Ende?* Göttingen, 2007.

Plessner, Helmut. "Grenzen der Gemeinschaft. Eine Kritik des sozialen Radikalismus" (1924). In id., *Gesammelte Schriften,* vol. 5: *Macht und menschliche Natur,* 7–133. Frankfurt a.M., 1981.

Poland, James. "Suicide Bombers: A Global Problem." *Humboldt Journal of Social Relations* 27 (2003): 100–135.

Portes, Alejandro. "Social Capital: Its Origins and Applications in Modern Sociology." *Annual Review of Sociology* 24 (1998): 1–24.

Portes, Alejandro, and Patricia Landolt. "The Downside of Social Capital." *American Prospect* 26 (1996): 18–21.

Prätorius, Rainer. *"In God We Trust." Religion und Politik in den USA.* Munich, 2003.

Preuß, Ulrich K. *Krieg, Verbrechen, Blasphemie. Zum Wandel bewaffneter Gewalt.* Berlin, 2002.

Pufendorf, Samuel. *De officio hominis et civis iuxta legem naturalem libri duo.* 1673.

Translated by Klaus Luig as *Über die Pflicht des Menschen und des Bürgers nach dem Gesetz der Natur* (Frankfurt a.M., 1994) and by Michael Silverthorne as *On the Duty of Man and Citizen According to Natural Law* (New York, 1991).

Putnam, Robert D. *Making Democracy Work: Civic Traditions in Modern Italy.* Princeton, NJ, 1993.

———. "The Prosperous Community: Social Capital and Public Life." *American Prospect* 13 (1993): 35–42.

———. "Bowling Alone: America's Declining Social Capital." *Journal of Democracy* 6 (1995): 65–78.

———. *Bowling Alone: The Collapse and Revival of American Community.* New York, 2000.

———, ed. *Gesellschaft und Gemeinsinn. Sozialkapital im internationalen Vergleich.* Gütersloh, 2001.

Qassem, Naim. *Hizbollah: The Story from Within.* Translated by Dalia Khalil. London, 2005.

Quigley, John. *The Case for Palestine: An International Law Perspective.* Rev. ed. Durham, NC, 2005.

Qureshi, Emran, and Michael A. Sells, eds. *The New Crusades: Constructing the Muslim Enemy.* New York, 2003.

Qutb, Sayyid. *Milestones.* Delhi, 1985.

Rahnema, Ali. *An Islamic Utopian: A Political Biography of Ali Shari'ati.* New York, 1998.

Ram, Haggay. *Myth and Mobilization in Revolutionary Iran: The Use of the Friday Congregational Sermon.* Washington, DC, 1994.

Rajak, Tessa. "Was There a Roman Charter for the Jews?" *Journal of Roman Studies* 74 (1984): 107–123.

———. "Jewish Rights in the Greek Cities Under Roman Rule: A New Approach." In *Approaches to Ancient Judaism,* ed. William S. Green, 19–35. Atlanta, 1985.

Rapoport, David C., and Yonah, Alexander, eds. *The Morality of Terrorism: Religious and Secular Justifications.* New York, 1982.

Ravitzky, Aviezer. *Messianism, Zionism, and Jewish Radicalism.* Translated by M. Swirsky and J. Chipman. Chicago, 1996.

———. "The Messianism of Success in Contemporary Judaism." In *The Continuum History of Apocalypticsm,* ed. Bernard J. McGinn, John J. Collins, and Stephen J. Stein, 563–581. New York, 2003.

Reese-Schäfer, Walter. *Kommunitarismus.* 3rd ed. Frankfurt a.M., 2001.

Reetz, Dietrich, ed. *Sendungsbewusstsein oder Eigennutz. Zu Motivation und Selbstverständnis islamischer Mobilisierung.* Berlin, 2001.

Reeves, Marjorie. *The Influence of Prophecy in the Middle Ages.* Oxford, 1969.

Reissner, Johannes. *Ideologie und Politik der Muslimbrüder Syriens. Von den Wahlen 1947 bis zum Verbot unter Adib Ash-Shishakli 1952.* Freiburg, 1980.

Rekhess, Elie. "The Iranian Impact on the Islamic Jihad Movement in the Gaza Strip." In *The Iranian Revolution and the Muslim World,* ed. David Menasheri, 189–206. Boulder, CO, 1990.

Rengstorf, Karl Heinrich, and Siegfried von Kortzfleisch, eds. *Kirche und Synagoge. Handbuch zur Geschichte von Christen und Juden. Darstellung mit Quellen.* 2 vols. Munich, 1988.

Reuter, Christoph. *Mein Leben ist eine Waffe. Selbstmordattentäter—Psychogramm eines Phänomens.* Munich, 2002. Translated by Helena Ragg-Kirkby as *My Life Is a Weapon: A Modern History of Suicide Bombing* (Princeton, NJ, 2004).

Ricolfi, Luca. "Palestinians, 1981–2003." In *Making Sense of Suicide Missions,* ed. Diego Gambetta, 77–129. Oxford, 2005.

Rieck, Andreas. *Die Schiiten im Kampf um den Libanon. Politische Chronik, 1958–1988.* Hamburg, 1989.

Riesebrodt, Martin. *Fundamentalismus als patriarchalische Protestbewegung. Amerikanische Protestanten (1910–28) und iranische Schiiten (1961–79) im Vergleich.* Tübingen, 1990.

Robbins, Thomas, and Dick Anthony. "Cults, Porn, and Hate. Convergent Discourses on First Amendment Restriction." In *New Religious Movements in the Twenty-First Century. Legal, Political, and Social Challenges in Global Perspective,* ed. Phillip Charles Lucas and Thomas Robbins, 329–341. London, 2004.

Roberts, Adam, and Richard Guelff, eds. *Documents on the Laws of War.* Oxford, 2000.

Robinson, Glenn E. "Hamas as a Social Movement." In *Islamic Activism: A Social Movement Theory Approach,* ed. Quintan Wiktorowicz, 112–139. Bloomington, IN, 2004.

Rosen, Lawrence. "Constructing Institutions in a Political Culture of Personalism." In id., *The Culture of Islam: Changing Aspects of Contemporary Muslim Life,* 56–72. Chicago, 2002.

Rosenfeld, Jean E. "A Brief History of Millennialism and Suggestions for a New Paradigm for Use in Critical Incidents." In *Millennialism, Persecution, and Violence,* ed. C. Wessinger, 347–351. Syracuse, NY, 2000.

———. "The Justus Freemen Standoff: The Importance of the Analysis of Religion in Avoiding Violent Outcomes." In *Millennialism, Persecution, and Violence,* ed. C. Wessinger, 323–344. Syracuse, NY, 2000.

Rosenthal, Franz. "On Suicide in Islam." *Journal of the American Oriental Society* 66 (1946): 239–269.

Rosiny, Stephan. *Islamismus bei den Schiiten im Libanon. Religion im Übergang von Tradition zur Moderne.* Berlin, 1996.

———. "Der *jihad.* Eine Typologie historischer und zeitgenössischer Formen islamisch legitimierter Gewalt." In *Gelebte Religion. Untersuchungen zur sozialen Gestaltungskraft religiöser Vorstellungen und Praktiken in Geschichte und Gegenwart. Festschrift Hartmut Zinser,* ed. Hildegard Piegeler, Inken Prohl, and Stefan Rademacher, 133–149. Würzburg, 2004.

———. "Religiöse Freigabe und Begrenzung der Gewalt bei Hizb Allāh im Libanon." In *Die Ambivalenz des Religiösen. Religionen als Friedensstifter und Gewalterzeuger,* ed. Bernd Oberdorfer and Peter Waldmann, 157–183. Freiburg i. Br., 2008.

Rossing, Barbara R. *The Rapture Exposed: The Message of Hope in the Book of Revelation.* New York, 2004.

Rousseau, Jean-Jacques. *Émile; or, Education.* 1762. Translated by Barbara Foxley. New York, 1914. Translated by Allan Bloom. New York, 1979.

Roy, Olivier. *Globalized Islam.* London, 2004.

Rubin, Barry, and Judith Colp Rubin, eds. *Anti-American Terrorism and the Middle East: A Documentary Reader.* Oxford, 2002.

Rudolph, Susanne H., and James Piscatori, eds. *Transnational Religion and Fading States.* Boulder, CO, 1997.

Ruthven, Malise. *A Fury for God: The Islamist Attack on America.* London, 2002.

Saadeh, Sofia. "Basic Issues Concerning the Personal Status Laws in Lebanon." In *Religion Between Violence and Reconciliation,* ed. Thomas Scheffler, 449–456. Beirut and Würzburg, 2002.

Sachedina, Abdulaziz A. "A Treatise on the Occultation of the Twelfth Imamite Imam." *Studia Islamica* 48 (1978): 109–124.

———. *Islamic Messianism: The Idea of the Mahdi in Twelver Shi'ism.* Albany, NY, 1981.

———. *The Just Ruler (al-sultan al-'adil) in Shi'ite Islam: The Comprehensive Authority of the Jurist in Imamite Jurisprudence.* Oxford, 1988.

Sageman, Marc. *Understanding Terror Networks.* Philadelphia, 2004.

Sahebjam, Freidoune. *"Ich habe keine Tränen mehr." Iran: Die Geschichte des Kindersoldaten Reza Behrouzi.* Reinbek b. Hamburg, 1988.

Saltman, Michael. "The Use of the Mandatory Emergency Laws by the Israeli Government." *International Journal of the Sociology of Law* 10 (1982): 385–394.

Salvatore, Armando, and Dale F. Eickelman, eds. *Public Islam and the Common Good.* Leiden, 2004.

Sandeen, Ernest R. *The Roots of Fundamentalism: British and American Millenarism, 1800–1930.* Chicago, 1970.

Sankari, Jamal. *Fadlallah: The Making of a Radical Shi'ite Leader.* London, 2005.

Schäbler, Birgit, and Leif Stenberg, eds. *Globalization and the Muslim World. Culture, Religion, and Modernity.* Syracuse, NY, 2004.

Schacht, Joseph. *An Introduction to Islamic Law,* Oxford, 1964.

Schäfer, Peter. *Geschichte der Juden in der Antike. Die Juden Palästinas von Alexander dem Großen bis zur arabischen Eroberung.* Stuttgart, 1983.

———. "Geschichte und Gedächtnisgeschichte: Jan Assmanns 'Mosaische Unterscheidung'." In *Memoria—Wege jüdischen Erinnerns. Festschrift für Michael Brocke,* ed. Birgit E. Klein and Christiane E. Müller, 19–39. Berlin, 2005.

Scheffler, Thomas. "Religion, Violence and the Civilizing Process. The Case of Lebanon." In *Guerres civiles: Économies de la violence, dimensions des la civilité,* ed. Jean Hannoyer, 163–185. Paris, 1999.

———. "'Allahu Akbar': Zur Theologie des Widerstandsgeistes im Islam." In *Religion und Gewalt: Der Islam nach dem 11. September,* ed. André Stanisavljevic and Ralf Zwengel, 21-46. Potsdam, 2002.

———. "Islamischer Fundamentalismus und Gewalt." In *Friedensbedrohung Terrorismus: Ursachen, Folgen und Gegenstrategien,* ed. Ulrike Kronfeld-Goharani, 88–111. Berlin, 2005.

———. "Religious Hierarchies and the Dynamics of Violence: Christian and Muslim Clerics and the Lebanese War of 1975–1990." In *Religionen im Konflikt,* ed. Vasilios N. Makrides and Jörg Rüpke, 97–108. Münster, 2005.

———, ed. *Religion Between Violence and Reconciliation.* Beiruter Texte und Studien, 76. Beirut and Würzburg, 2002.

Schiff, Ze'ev, and Ehud Ya'ari. *Intifada: The Palestinian Uprising—Israel's Third Front.* New York, 1990.

Schluchter, Wolfgang. "Gesinnungsethik und Verantwortungsethik: Probleme einer Unterscheidung." In *Religion und Lebensführung,* vol. 1: *Studien zu Max Webers Kultur- und Werttheorie,* 165–200. Frankfurt a.M., 1988.

Schmidinger, Heinrich, ed. *Wege zur Toleranz. Geschichte einer europäischen Idee in Quellen.* Darmstadt, 2003.

Schmidt, Walter. *Option für die Armen? Erkenntnistheoretische, sozialwissenschaftliche und sozialethische Überlegungen zur Armutsbekämpfung.* Mering, 2005.

Schmitt, Carl. *Der Begriff des Politischen.* 1932. Berlin, 1979.

Schmitthenner, W. "Über eine Formveränderung der Monarchie seit Alexander d.Gr." *Saeculum* 19 (1968): 31–46.

Schmucker, Werner. "Iranische Märtyrertestamente." *Welt des Islams* 27 (1987): 185–249.

Schneckener, Ulrich. *Transnationaler Terrorismus. Charakter und Hintergründe des 'neuen' Terrorismus.* Frankfurt a.M., 2006.

Schoeps, Hans Joachim, ed. *Jüdische Geisteswelt.* Hanau, 1986.

Scholem, Gershom. *Die jüdische Mystik in ihren Hauptströmungen.* Frankfurt a.M., 1967.

————. *Über einige Grundbegriffe des Judentums.* Frankfurt a.M., 1970.

Schulze, Reinhard. *Geschichte der Islamischen Welt im 20. Jahrhundert.* Munich, 1994.

Schuppert, Gunnar Folke. "Skala der Rechtsformen für Religion: vom privaten Zirkel zur Körperschaft des öffentlichen Rechts. Überlegungen zur angemessenen Organisationsform für Religionsgemeinschaften." In *Die verrechtlichte Religion,* ed. Hans G. Kippenberg and Gunnar Folke Schuppert, 11–35. Tübingen, 2005.

Schwartz, Regina M. *The Curse of Cain: The Violent Legacy of Monotheism.* Chicago, 1997.

————. "Holy Terror." In *"Holy War" and Gender: Violence in Religious Discourses. "Gotteskrieg" und Geschlecht. Gewaltdiskurse in der Religion,* ed. Christina von Braun, 13–22. Berlin, 2006.

Scofield, C. I. *Scofield Study Bible.* 1909. Oxford, 1996.

Scott, James. "Patronage or Exploitation?" In *Patrons and Clients in Mediterranean Societies,* ed. Ernest Gellner and John Waterbury, 21–39. London 1977.

Seeman, Don. "Violence, Ethics, and Divine Honor in Modern Jewish Thought." *Journal of the American Academy of Religion* 73 (2005): 1016–1048.

Seidensticker, Tilman. "Jerusalem aus der Sicht des Islams." In *Jerusalem die heilige, umstrittene Stadt,* ed. Helmut Hubel and Tilman Seidensticker, 63–75. Jena, 2002.

————. "Die Transformation des christlichen Märtyrerbegriffs im Islam." In *Märtyrer und Märtyrerakten,* ed. Walter Ameling, 137–148. Stuttgart, 2002.

————. "Der religiöse und historische Hintergrund des Selbstmordattentates im Islam." In *Terror im Dienste Gottes. Die "Geistliche Anleitung" der Attentäter des 11. September 2001,* ed. Hans G. Kippenberg and Tilman Seidensticker, 107–116. Frankfurt a.M., 2004.

————. "Jihad Hymns (*Nashīds*) as a Means of Self-Motivation in the Hamburg Group." In *The 9/11 Handbook,* ed. Hans G. Kippenberg and Tilman Seidensticker, 71–78. London, 2006.

Selden, John. *De iure naturali & gentium, iuxta disciplinam Ebræorum, libri septem.* London, 1640.

Sen, Amartya. *Development as Freedom.* Oxford, 2001. Translated by Christiana Goldmann as *Ökonomie für den Menschen. Wege zu Gerechtigkeit und Solidarität in der Marktwirtschaft.* 2nd ed. Munich, 2003.

Shahak, Israel. "The Ideology Behind Hebron Massacre." www.radioislam.org/islam/english/toread/hebron3.htm (accessed May 29, 2010).

Sharot, Stephen. *Messianism, Mysticism, and Magic. A Sociological Analysis of Jewish Religious Movements*. Chapel Hill, NC, 1982.

The Shorter Encyclopedia of Islam. Edited by H. A. R. Gibb and J. H. Kramers. Leiden, 1974.

Shuck, Glenn W. *Marks of the Beast: The "Left Behind" Novels and the Struggle for Evangelical Identity*. New York, 2007.

Shulman, David. *Dark Hope: Working for Peace in Israel and Palestine*. Chicago, 2007.

Shultz, George P. "The Challenge to Democracies." In *Terrorism*, ed. Benjamin Netanyahu, 16–24. New York, 1986.

Shupe, Anson, and David G. Bromley. "The Evolution of Modern American Anticult Ideology: A Case Study in Frame Extension." In *America's Alternative Religions*, ed. Timothy Miller, 411–416. Albany, NY, 1995.

Sick, Gary. *All Fall Down: America's Tragic Encounter with Iran*. New York, 1985.

Silberstein, Laurence J. *The Postzionism Debates: Knowledge and Power in Israeli Culture*. New York, 1999.

Singerman, Diane. "The Networked World of Islamist Social Movements." In *Islamic Activism*, ed. Quintan Wiktorowicz, 143–163. Bloomington, IN, 2004.

Sivan, Emmanuel. *Radical Islam: Medieval Theology and Modern Politics*. Rev. ed. New Haven, CT, 1985.

———. "The Enclave Culture." In *Strong Religion: The Rise of Fundamentalisms Around the World*, ed. Gabriel A. Almond, R. Scott Appleby, and Emmanuel Sivan, 23–89. Chicago, 2003.

Smith, Jonathan Z. *Imagining Religion: From Babylon to Jonestown*. Chicago, 1982.

Smith, Wilfred Cantwell. "Faith as Tasdiq." In *Islamic Philosophical Theology*, ed. Parviz Morwedge. Albany, NY, 1979.

Smith-Christopher, Daniel L., ed. *Subverting the Hatred: The Challenge of Nonviolence in Religious Traditions*. New York, 1998.

Sofsky, Wolfgang. *Traktat über die Gewalt*. Frankfurt a.M., 1996.

———. *Zeiten des Schreckens. Amok, Terror, Krieg*. Frankfurt a.M., 2002.

Sorel, Georges. *Réflexions sur la violence*. Paris, 1908. German translation, *Über die Gewalt* (Frankfurt a.M., 1969); English translation, *Reflections on Violence*, ed. Jeremy Jennings (New York, 1999).

Sprinzak, Ehud. "Gush Emunim: The Tip of the Iceberg." *Jerusalem Quarterly* 21 (1981). http://members.tripod.com/alabasters_archive/gush_iceberg.html (accessed July 22, 2010).

———. "Fundamentalism, Terrorism and Democracy: The Case of the Gush Emunim Underground." 1986.http://members.tripod.com/alabasters_archive/gush_underground.html (accessed July 22, 2010).

———. "From Messianic Pioneering to Vigilante Terrorism." In *Inside Terrorist Organizations,* ed. David C. Rapoport, 194–216. New York, 1988.

———. *The Ascendance of Israel's Radical Right.* New York, 1991.

———. *Brother Against Brother. Violence and Extremism in Israeli Politics from Altalena to the Rabin Assassination.* New York, 1999.

Stachura, Mateusz. "Handlung und Rationalität." In *Aspekte des Weber-Paradigmas. Festschrift für Wolfgang Schluchter,* ed. Gert Albert et al., 100–125. Wiesbaden, 2006.

———. "Logik der Situationsdefinition und Logik der Handlungsselektion. Der Fall des wertrationalen Handelns." *Kölner Zeitschrift für Soziologie und Sozialpsychologie* 58 (2006): 433–452.

Stark, Rodney. *One True God: Historical Consequences of Monotheism.* Princeton, NJ, 2001.

Stark, Rodney, and William S. Bainbridge. *A Theory of Religion.* New York, 1987.

———, eds. *The Future of Religion: Secularization, Revival, and Cult Formation.* Berkeley, CA, 1985.

Steinberg, Guido. *Der nahe und der ferne Feind. Die Netzwerke des islamistischen Terrorismus.* Munich, 2005.

Sterba, James P., ed. *Terrorism and International Justice.* New York, 2003.

Stern, Jessica. *Terror in the Name of God: Why Religious Militants Kill.* New York, 2003.

Stobbe, Heinz-Günther. "Monotheismus und Gewalt. Anmerkungen zu einigen Beispielen neurer Religionskritik." In *Monotheismus,* ed. J. Manemann, 166–180. Münster, 2003.

Stork, Joe. *Erased in a Moment: Suicide Bombing Attacks against Israeli Civilians.* A Human Rights Watch report. New York, 2002. www.hrw.org/reports/2002/isrl-pa (accessed May 25, 2010).

Strenski, Ivan. "Sacrifice, Gift and the Social Logic of Muslim 'Human Bombers'." *Terrorism and Political Violence* 15 (2003): 1–34.

Sullivan, Denis J. *Private Voluntary Organizations in Egypt: Islamic Development, Private Initiative, and State Control.* Gainesville, FL, 1994.

Sullivan, Denis J., and Abed-Kotob, *Islam in Contemporary Egypt: Civil Society vs. The State.* Boulder, CO, 1999.

Sullivan, Lawrence E. "'No Longer the Messiah': US Federal Law Enforcement Views of Religion in Connection with the 1993 Siege of Mount Carmel near Waco, Texas." *Numen* 43 (1996): 213–234.

Tabor, James D., and Eugene V. Gallagher. *Why Waco? Cults and the Battle for Religious Freedom in America.* Berkeley, CA, 1995.

Taeschner, Franz. *Zünfte und Bruderschaften im Islam. Texte zur Geschichte der Futuwwa.* Zurich, 1979.

Taheri, Amir. *The Spirit of Allah: Khomeini and the Islamic Revolution*. London, 1985.

Thomas, Keith. *Religion and the Decline of Magic: Studies in Popular Beliefs in Sixteenth and Seventeenth Century England*. Harmondsworth, UK, 1971.

Thomas, William I., and Thomas, Dorothy Swaine. *The Child in America: Behavior Problems and Programs*. New York, 1928.

Thompson, E. P. *The Making of the English Working Class*. London, 1963.

Tilgner, Ulrich, ed. *Umbruch im Iran. Augenzeugenberichte—Analysen—Dokumente*. Reinbek b. Hamburg, 1979.

Tocqueville, Alexis de. *Democracy in America*. New York, 2007. Originally published as *De la démocratie en Amérique* (2 vols., Paris, 1835–1840).

Townshend, Charles. *Terrorism: A Very Short Introduction*. New York, 2003. German translation, *Terrorismus. Eine kurze Einführung* (Stuttgart, 2005).

Trabant, Jürgen. *Europäisches Sprachdenken, Von Platon bis Wittgenstein*. 2nd ed. Munich, 2006.

Ṭurcanu, Florin. *Mircea Eliade: Le prisonnier de l'histoire*. Paris, 2003. Translated as *Mircea Eliade. Der Philosoph des Heiligen im Gefängnis der Geschichte* (Schnellroda, 2006).

Turner, Victor W. *The Ritual Process: Structure and Anti-Structure*. Chicago, 1969.

Tyrell, Hartmann. "Die christliche Brüderlichkeitsethik. Semantische Kontinuitäten und Diskontinuitäten." In *Modernität und Solidarität. Konsequenzen gesellschaftlicher Modernisierung*, ed. Karl Gabriel, A. Herlth, and K. P. Strohmeier, 189–212. Freiburg, 1997.

———. "Intellektuellenreligiosität, 'Sinn'-Semantik, Brüderlichkeitsethik—Max Weber im Verhältnis zu Tolstoi und Dostojewski." In *Max Weber und Osteuropa*, ed. A. Sterbling and H. Zipprian, 25–58. Hamburg, 1997.

———. "Antagonismus der Werte—ethisch." In *Max Webers "Religionssystematik,"* ed. Hans G. Kippenberg and Martin Riesebrodt, 315–334. Tübingen, 2001.

United States. Department of State. Counterterrorism Office. "Patterns of Global Terrorism 2000." www.state.gov/s/ct/rls/crt/2000/2419.htm (accessed July 4, 2010).

Varshney, Ashutosh. *Ethnic Conflict and Civic Life: Hindus and Muslims in India*. Oxford, 2002.

Veer, Peter van der. "Transnational Religion." Paper presented at conference on Transnational Migration: Comparative Perspectives, Princeton University, June 30 –July 1, 2001. www.transcomm.ox.ac.uk/working%20papers/WPTC-01-18%20Van%20der%20Veer.pdf (accessed 29 May 2010).

Veer, Peter van der, and Hartmut Lehmann, eds. *Nation and Religion: Perspectives on Europe and Asia*. Princeton, NJ, 1999.

Vieille, Paul. *La féodalité et l'état en Iran.* Paris, 1975.

Vitzthum, Wolfgang, Graf, et al., eds. *Völkerrecht.* Berlin, 2004.

Waldmann, Peter. *Terrorismus. Provokation der Macht.* Munich, 1998.

———. "Die zeitliche Dimension des Terrorismus." In *Determinanten des Terrorismus,* ed. id., 139–187 Weilerswist, 2004.

———. "The Radical Community: A Comparative Analysis of the Social Background of ETA, IRA, and Hezbollah." *Sociologus* 55 (2005): 239–257.

———. "Wie religiös ist der 'religiöse Terrorismus'?" In *Religionen und Gewalt. Konflikt- und Friedenspotentiale in den Weltreligionen,* ed. Reinhard Hempelmann and Johannes Kandel, 99–109. Göttingen 2006.

Wasserstein, Bernard. *Jerusalem. Der Kampf um die Heilige Stadt.* Munich, 2002.

Watt, W. Montgomery, and Alford T. Welch. *Der Islam I. Muhammed und die Frühzeit—Islamisches Recht—Religiöses Leben.* Stuttgart, 1980.

Weber, Max. *From Max Weber: Essays in Sociology.* Edited and translated by Hans H. Gerth and C. Wright Mills. New York, 1946.

———. *Economy and Society: An Outline of Interpretative Sociology.* Edited by Gunther Roth and Claus Wittich. Berkeley, 1968.

———. *Gesammelte Aufsätze zur Religionssoziologie.* Vol. 1. Reprint. Tübingen, 1971.

———. *Die Wirtschaftsethik der Weltreligionen. Konfuzianismus und Taoismus.* In *Schriften, 1915–1920,* ed. Helwig Schmidt-Glintzer in collaboration with Petra Kolonko. Max Weber Gesamtausgabe, I/19. Tübingen, 1989.

———. *Wirtschaft und Gesellschaft.* Vol. 1: *Gemeinschaften,* edited by Wolfgang Mommsen in collaboration with Michael Meyer. Max Weber Gesamtausgabe, I/22-1. Tübingen, 2001.

———. *Wirtschaft und Gesellschaft.* Vol. 2: *Religiöse Gemeinschaften,* edited by Hans G. Kippenberg in collaboration with Petra Schilm and Jutta Niemeier. Max Weber Gesamtausgabe, I/22-2. Tübingen, 2001.

Weber, Timothy P. *Living in the Shadow of the Second Coming: American Premillennialism, 1875–1925.* Oxford, 1979.

———. *On the Road to Armageddon: How Evangelicals Became Israel's Best Friends.* Grand Rapids, MI, 2004.

Weinfeld, Moshe. *The Organizational Pattern and the Penal Code of the Qumran Sect: A Comparison with Guilds and Religious Associations of the Hellenistic-Roman Period.* Göttingen, 1986.

Weisbrod, Bernd. "Sozialgeschichte und Gewalterfahrung im 20. Jahrhundert." In *Perspektiven der Gesellschaftsgeschichte,* ed. Paul Nolte et al., 112–123. Munich, 2000.

———. "Religious Languages of Violence: Some Reflections on the Reading of

Extremes." In *No Man's Land of Violence: Extreme Wars in the 20th Century*, ed. Alf Lüdtke and Bernd Weisbrod, 251–276. Göttingen, 2006.

Werblowsky, Zwi R. J. *The Meaning of Jerusalem to Jews, Christians, and Muslims.* 3rd ed. Jerusalem, 1995.

Wessinger, Catherine. *How the Millennium Comes Violently: From Jonestown to Heaven's Gate.* New York, 2000.

———, ed. *Millennialism, Persecution, and Violence: Historical Cases.* Syracuse, NY, 2000.

Wiktorowicz, Quintan. *The Management of Islamic Activism: Salafis, Muslim Brotherhood, and State Power in Jordan.* New York, 2001.

———. *Radical Islam Rising: Muslim Extremism in the West.* Lanham, MD, 2005.

———, ed. *Islamic Activism: A Social Movement Theory Approach.* Bloomington, IN, 2004.

Willems, Ulrich, and Minkenberg, Michael. "Politik und Religion im Über-gang—Tendenzen und Forschungsfragen am Beginn des 21. Jahrhunderts." In *Politik und Religion* (Wiesbaden), special issue, 33 (2002): 13–41.

Wilson, Bryan, and Jamie Cresswell, eds. *New Religious Movements: Challenge and Response.* New York, 1999.

Wippel, Steffen. *Islamische Wirtschafts- und Wohlfahrtseinrichtungen in Ägypten zwischen Markt und Moral.* Münster, 1997.

Wirth, Andrzej. "Ein Perserteppich von Codes." *Theater Heute* 19, 10 (1978): 32–37.

Wirth, Uwe, ed. *Performanz. Zwischen Sprachphilosophie und Kulturwissenschaften.* Frankfurt a.M., 2002.

Woodward, Bob. *Bush at War.* New York, 2002.

Wright, Stuart A. "Construction and Escalation of a Cult Threat." In *Armageddon in Waco,* ed. id., 75–94. Chicago, 1995.

———, ed. *Armageddon in Waco: Critical Perspectives on the Branch Davidian Conflict.* Chicago, 1995.

Wuthnow, Robert. *Saving America? Faith-Based Services and the Future of Civil Society.* Princeton, NJ, 2004.

Yokota, Michihiro, "Mit welcher Eigendynamik entwickeln sich Religionen? Eine Studie über 'Brüderlichkeit' und 'Theodizee' in Max Webers Religionssoziologie." *Bulletin of the University of Electro-Communications* 14 (2002): 211–220.

Young, Lawrence A., ed. *Rational Choice Theory and Religion: Summary and Assessment.* New York, 1997.

Zenger, Erich. "Was ist der Preis des Monotheismus?" In Jan Assmann, *Die mosaische Unterscheidung,* 209–220. Munich, 2003.

Zimmerli, Walther Chr., and Mike Sandbothe, eds. *Klassiker der modernen Zeitphilosophie.* Darmstadt, 1993.

Index

THEMATIC INDEX